History of The Green Family Line:

From De La Zouche, to Grene De Boketon, Greene and Green

By

Iva A. Green

Edited by:

Thomas A. Green

Preface

The idea of writing such a manuscript came to light in the late 1980's and early 1990's due to the stories told to me by my Aunt Elizabeth, whom died in 1993. Her stories on the Green family captivated my imagination at an early age and as a born historian I wanted to know just how factual these stories were. What I learned from this two-decade journey of genealogical investigation is her stories were not too far off from the truth. In fact, several instances were spot on. This alone makes this manuscript even more special to me, as my closest aunt was so informed with our particular Green family, despite the fact that she was not even a Green at all. Rather my Aunt Elizabeth's father was not the late James Samuel Green who raised her as his own, after the untimely death of her own father, William O'Connell.

Digressing back to why it has taken this long to write such a manuscript deals with multiple personal set-backs within my personal life. The first has to do with a divorce in the early 1990's. A divorce that left me no choice, but to move around in order to avoid this estranged ex-husband. Second, I decided to go to college to earn my first college degree (Associates of Applied Science) in Law. This degree broadened my mind and taught me how to locate source material, not only for legal purposes, but for historical purposes as well. Less than two years after earning my degree in law, I elected to return to college and earn my Bachelor's Degree in History, with a minor in Political Science.

Throughout this time fame from 1990-1999, I worked on locating source material for this manuscript, while on occasion working two jobs, going to college, and raising three children. As it points out, it was safe to say that sleep was merely a suggestion. The continuation of writing this manuscript and its set-backs went into the next decade (2000-2009). These set-backs included returning to college for my Master's Degree, two children going to war following the terrorist attack on September 11, 2001, and helping my other child through his college endeavors; and then, returning to college to earn a second and final degree (Masters of Science in History). Now I have arrived to this point in time. Granted it only took twenty-five years and four college degrees later, but the work was definitely worth it and an up-date manuscript has been written on this Green family line, which began with the de la Zouche family and their migration to present day England and eventual arrival to the United States.

Table of Contents

Acknowledgements	*iv*
Geographic Journey of Green Family	*v-vi*
Introduction	*vii-viii*
Chapter I: The French Connection	1-7
Chapter II: The Early Grene's of Boketon	8-13
Chapter III: Rise to Prominence	14-18
Chapter IV: Switch of Arms from Boketon to Gillingham	19-22
Chapter V: Fall of Grene Family Name	23-28
Chapter VI: Notable Woman: Catherine Parr	29-31
Chapter VII: The Grene Family Returns from Hiding	32-35
Chapter VIII: Migration to the American Colonies	36-41
Chapter IX: Settling the Colonies	42-47
Chapter X: The Greene Family and the American Revolution	48-51
Chapter XI: The Greene's Settle a Newly Independent Nation	52-55
Chapter XII: Settling the Frontier	56-60
Chapter XIII: Spotlight of A Modern American Hero	61-68
Chapter XIV: Spotlight of A Modern American Woman	69-71
Chapter XV: The Far Western Frontier	72-78
Chapter XVI: The Author	79-82
Chapter XVII: The Present Lines	83-92
Chapter XVIII: The Conclusion	93
Appendix A: Charlemagne to Geoffrey de la Zouche	94-96
Appendix B: De Vere and the de la Zouche Connection	97-98
Appendix C: Powell and its multiple Green Family Connection	99-101
Appendix D: Glenn and the Green Connection	102-103
Appendix E: Crockett and the Green Connection	104-107

Appendix F: The Charlemagne Connection	108-109
Appendix G: Select Green Family Letters and Records	110-128
Appendix H: Other Select Person Records	129-138
Appendix I: Maps	139-142
Appendix J: Select Green Family Photos	143-185
Full Bibliography	186-194
Notes	195-196

Acknowledgements

I would like to take this moment to express my thanks and send out my dedication to the people that provided me support and inspiration to write this manuscript. Thomas A. Green, thank you for your service to our country and assistance by being my editor; as well as, providing geographic contributions in the form of map graphics. Christopher A. Green, thank you for your illustration of the Greene Coat of Arms, your military information and service to our country. Zachary A. Green, thank you for your military information and service to our country.

Dedication goes out not only to the future generations of this Green line, but to my Aunt Elizabeth "Beth" Ingram, who was always there for the little girl who walked the city streets and somehow always found her way to your house. For your kindness and tolerance to that annoying little girl playing your piano on hot summer days; as well as, sharing through the years all of the information and words of advice, with a bored little girl. Thank you, for making a difference in my life. I feel the love you and Uncle Sherman shared with me and my children which still lives on today. You are both forever in our hearts. As my love always says, "I do not love you with my heart, because someday I will die and my heart will cease to beat for you, but I love you with all my soul, because my soul will live on for all eternity."

Finally, to my grandchildren, I hope you will always know and never forget just how much your grandmother loves you; and to the generation of descendants that I may or may not ever meet, please know that I will live on forever in this manuscript. A manuscript that I hope at least one of you will carry on and add to in the centuries to come. It will be this unknown descendant that will ensure everyone will know the story of our family.

Geographic Journey of the Green Family Line

The Green family line that first arrived to the American Colonies in 1635 on the ship "the Mathew" from the West Indies, are the same Green's that went through a series of last name changes, present nation-state changes; as well as, changes in their coat of Arms as knights of England. This is a line that came from and transitioned through the ranks of upper nobility, to royalty and back to upper nobility for more than one thousand years extending from Charlemagne whom was born about 742 that became ruler of the Franks (present-day France), to becoming English due to William the Conquer of England; and finally, becoming wealthy trapper and traders within present-day Rhode Island, United States soon after their arrival to the colonies.

Geographically speaking, many ancestral lines have not made as much movement as this particular Green Family line; nor have most lines experienced as much last name changes going from Martel (last name of Charlemagne), to de la Zouche, to de Grene de la Boketon, to Grene, Greene; and finally, Green. In addition to this, the level of resiliency this particular Green family line displays throughout history, along with their dedication and loyalty to their country and family is evident and resonates from their nobility and life of royalty within present-day France, to their royal titles of Great Baron's and members of parliament as they migrated and embraced their new life in England, to their final geographic destination of the American colonies leaving all they knew behind to take a shot in the new world. Through all of this migration from France, England, to the West Indies; and finally, the United States; this Green family line has shown nothing less than courage, pride of country and ownership to their possessions and titles they have received over the years.

Having said all of this about such a courageous line, the next page will present graphic representation of where the Green family came from during the time of Charlemagne, to their lives in England, and their migration to and throughout what was known as the British American colonies. Additional map graphics are included and embedded in the document to highlight some of the significant events the Green Family name experienced as British knights and American colonist frontiersmen.

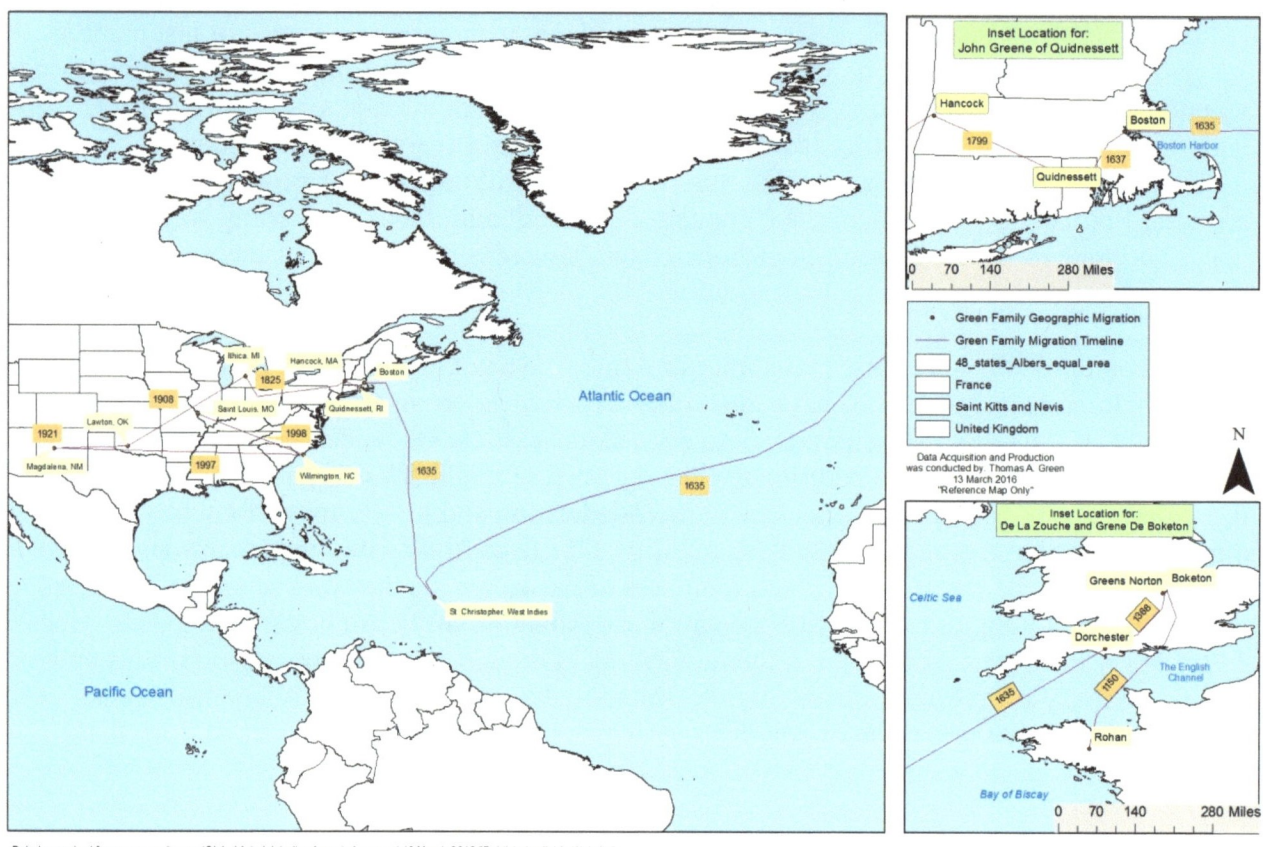

Figure 1: Green, Thomas A. 2016. Data collection acquired from www.gadm.org; accessed 13 March 2016

Introduction

In the decades of researching this Green family line, genealogical evidence has shown that the generations consistently and diligently held great pride in their homeland. Although forced to flee their homeland, on multiple occasions, due to religious beliefs and political tension of the time, documentation will show this Green families lines journey. From the beginning in present-day Bretagne, France with the ancestral l the Green family last name of de la Zouch, to their migration to present-day England, where they adopted the last name Grene and became a treat to the king with their extensive land ownership which eventually lead to their final migration to present-day United States.[1]

At John Greene of Quidnessett's arrival to present-day Salem, Massachusetts on the ship the "Mathew" in 1635 and later moving to Providence, Rhode Island in 1637, where the Greene family continued that same pride and duty here in their new homeland. In addition, I have found the Greene family continued to alter their last name from its original spelling Grene, to Greene and finally in some lines as this particular line to Green.[2]

Through the generations, the Greens fought for land, freedom and religious beliefs. One notable American cousin to this branch was General Nathaniel Greene, who fought in the Revolutionary War. Others may not have received the notoriety and rank as Nathaniel, but their representation in history is worth noting. For example: La Mance stated, Samuel Greene of Rhode Island sent eight sons into the Revolutionary War, while "Joseph Greene's twelve-year-old son from New York was the youngest volunteer." The linage of the Green's is loaded with patriotism. They fought for America from the Revolutionary War to the War in Iraq.[3]

This Green line actually descends from royals presenting a legacy of rich history. My mother's side is equally as grand of a line on her Powell side. A line in which crosses into this Green line through the de la Zouches, which is clearly worthy of a separate manuscript.

The primary aspect that excites me as an Historian is the documentation of the Green family line and its connection with royalty. This Green branch begins with the younger de la Zouche son, Alexander de Grene de la Boketon, the first Lord Grene, who received his titles and estates in 1202. This migration begins again with Sir Simon

---

[1] Beck, William III, A Family Genealogy, 2; La Mance, Lora S., The Greene Family and Its Branches; From A.D. 861 to A.D. 1904. Mayflower Publishing Company, Floral Park, New York 1904.
[2] La Mance 47
[3] La Mance 2

Greene of Ireland (a cousin and youngest son of the ninth Lord Grene), and John of Quidnessett, Rhode Island whom leads this branch to America.[4]

Note: In regards to dates before January 25, 1752, there is a twelve-day difference in "Old Style" verses "New Style" so to convert to "New Style" just add twelve days. In addition, a number has been given to each family member, beginning with the grandfather of Alexander, the first Lord Grene. This line of numbering begins again with John of Quidnessett the first Greene in the colonies.[5]

A Brief History of the Green Family

The Green family originates from the de la Zouche family, one of the most royal bloodlines of Europe. The Green family once was one of the largest land owners in England and descends over fifty times from such royals as Charlemagne, twelve times from Alfred the Great and fifty times from Wittekind, leader of the Saxons, who fought against Charlemagne. The Greens have English, Irish, Scotch, Saxon blood and descend from Bohemian Kings, Constantine the Great, Basil the Great, French Kings, Russian Rulers, and Ancient Parthian Emperors before our lord Jesus Christ' and commoners. The Green family, or as it was spelled, Grene family from Northamptonshire, England, had a reputation for honor and service to the crown. Alexander de Grene de Boketon was applauded for recovering the advowson for the St. John the Baptist church located in Boketon from Simon de Hector and Simon de Boketon twelve years prior to the Magna Charta, granted during King John's fourth year or reign (1203).[6]

---

[4] La Mance 5-6, 47
[5] La Mance 1
[6] La Mance 5, 7, 14a & 14b

Chapter I:
The French Connection

Generation I: Alan de la Zouche

Alan de la Zouche was born about 1093 with his full royal bloodline name being: Alan La Zouche Viscount de Rohan, as he was the son of Joscelin I of Porhoet (born about 1046) and unknown mother. Very little information can be found on Alan de la Zouche, as well as, his parents. The reason for the limitation of source information has to do with Alan's father not being the first born child to his parents; and therefore, his older brother Odo that was given the title of Vicomte is more heavily recorded in historical documents for his title and rule over the House of Rohan, Bretagne, France.[7]

As royal bloodlines and family order tradition goes, it was not uncommon for the younger siblings to take on other titles due to the royal heritage they were born into. While the girls were often married off to prince's, king's or soon to be kings, the sons however; were often put into the role of knights and priests. As the second son Alan de la Zouche was placed in the role of knight, the purpose for this is to provide protection to the immediate homeland, and pay tribute to his father Joscelin I of Porhoet. The battle's Alan fought as a knight are not clear. Based on the time frame, and the instability going on within surrounding areas of the Bretagne, conflict was constant.[8]

During this time period, the province had to endure the constant switch of monarchy control as Britain and France would take turns of being in control over Bretagne and surrounding provinces, such as, Normandy. With Normandy, being under control of William the Conqueror for several decades in the 1100's and into the 1200's, made this region of present-day France very unstable with numerous conflicts. It was during this time Alan de la Zouche would marry Constance La Gros, Princess of Bretagne who was born about 1110. This marriage will allow Alan de la Zouche's children to maintain a royal bloodline, something of extreme importance during the uncertain middle ages, where pedigree was of most importance.[9]

---

[7] Casteland.com, http://www.castleland.com/puk/castle/bretagne/morbihan/josselin.htm, Last Modified: 02 July 2013, Accessed 16 April 2016 & Josselin Society of England, http//web.archive.org/web/2007814061819/http:www.peterjoslin.btinternet.co.uk/chateau_josselin.htm, Land Modified 14 October 2006, Accessed 16 April 2016.

[8] Casteland.com, http://www.castleland.com/puk/castle/bretagne/morbihan/josselin.htm, Last Modified: 02 July 2013, Accessed 16 April 2016 & Josselin Society of England, http//web.archive.org/web/2007814061819/http:www.peterjoslin.btinternet.co.uk/chateau_josselin.htm, Last Modified 14 October 2006, Accessed 16 April 2016.

[9] Castleland.com, http://www.castleland.com/puk/castle/bretagne/morbihan/josselin.htm, Last Modified 02 July 2013, Accessed 16April 2016 & Josselin Society of England,

Despite marrying the Princess of Bretagne, Alan maintained his knight duties and loyalty to his king. Once he married Constance La Gros, Princess of Bretagne, it is important to note the king he began showing loyalty to as a knight, was her father Conan III Le Gros, the Earl of Richmond, and whose wife was Maud Beauclerc. As it will be explained in the section of Alan de la Zouche and Constance La Gros only child, this marriage will be the turning point to their loyalty to the British Crown over the French Crown. It is here that the linguistics of the line, while primarily French speaking became bilingual, as Alan must have had the ability to speak to both his wife and king.[10]

The date of Alan and his wife's marriage is not entirely known, but it is believed they married sometime in 1126. This would make Princess Constance La Gros about sixteen years old, an age that was typical for a young woman during this time period. In fact, princesses and female commoners alike often married their daughters off between the ages of fifteen and eighteen; and often to older men. These older men were usually ten to fifteen years their senior. Together it is recorded Sir Alan de la Zouche and Princess Constance had one child. This child is listed below and is highlighted in bold:

1. **Geoffrey de la Zouche born about 1126**

The year both Sir Alan de la Zouche and his wife Princess Constance died is under debate. One piece of information that remains consistent with sources is the two of them died sometime after 1155; and at some point they migrated from present-day France to present-day England. The reason this is known, is based on numerous records that state both Sir Alan and his wife Princess Constance were laid to rest in Harringworth, Northamptonshire, England. As for the date of their migration from Bretagne, France to Northamptonshire, England is not known. It is possible, however; this migration took place at the hands of his son. At which time, he brought his parents along with him as Bretagne, France fell out of the hands of England and back into French monarchy rule in the 1150's. Thus the reason for the map graphic shown in the section of Green family geographic extent indicates an estimated migration year of 1155.[11]

---

http//web.archive.org/wcb/2007814061819/http:www.peterjoslin.btinternet.co.uk/chateau_josselin.htm, Modified 14 October 2006, Accessed 16 April 2016.
[10] Casteland.com, http://www.castleland.com/puk/castle/bretagne/morbihan/josselin.htm, Last Modified: 02 July 2013, Accessed 16 April 2016 & Josselin Society of England,
http//web.archive.org/web/2007814061819/http:www.peterjoslin.btinternet.co.uk/chateau_josselin.htm, Last Modified: 14 October 2006, Accessed 16 April 2016
[11] Castleland.com, http://www.castleland.com/puk/castle/bretagne/morbihan/josselin.htm, Last Modified; 02 July 2013, Accessed 16 April 2016 & Josselin Society of England,
http//web.archive.org/web/2007814061819/http:www.peterjoslin.btinternet.co.uk/chateau_josselin.htm, Last Modified 14 October 2006, Accessed 16 April 2016

Generation II: Geoffrey de la Zouche

Sir Geoffrey de la Zouche was born 1126, in Rohan, Bretagne, France, and was a Knight in the Kings court (Appendix A). He is the son of Sir Alan de la Zouche, whom was also a knight who married Princess of Bretagne, Constance Le Gros. Geoffrey's mother was born about (1110) in Bretagne, Indre, France, and is the daughter of Conan III Le Gros, Earl of Richmond and Maud Beauclerc. Maud, the mother of Princess Constance, and grandmother to Geoffrey de la Zouche, so happens to also be the daughter of William the Conqueror, a man that would become king of England. This pedigree makes the "Green" family ancestry to be royal descendants of both present-day nation states of England and France.[12]

This duel pedigree results in the de la Zouche family to make the conscience decision to eventually choose which side to make patronage. A patronage that will determine the future of the family line, and the direction future generations will take in carrying the de la Zouche lineage and royal bloodline. Their decision to remain loyal to the British crown or become loyal to the French monarch came to head with Sir Geoffrey de la Zouche, and the reign of Philip II, King of France and Henry II, King of England. The migration from Bretagne Province, in present-day France to Harringworth, Northamptonshire, England is not entirely certain, but is believed to have occurred sometime around the 1150's, which explains the difference in birth place of his children.[13]

The reason for Sir Geoffrey de la Zouche decision to move from Bretagne, France to Harringworth, Northamptonshire, England is because at the time of his birth and upbringing he was born under the British crown. Also, he was the grandchild to Maud Beauclerc, the daughter of William the Conqueror as mentioned earlier. By the time of his birth, this region of France was taken by William the Conqueror, "William I, King of England" around 1076, although re-claimed by Philip I, King of France two years later, this land swap between English and French monarch's continued throughout the next 100 years. During this timeframe, it is recorded that Sir Geoffrey and his parents Sir Alan de la Zouche and his mother Princess Constance Le Gros, although French speaking, were already under the English crown, despite being situated in the Bretagne Province of present-day France. A province that is geographically located north of the Bay of Biscay and south of the English Channel, jutting out as a peninsula westward into the Celtic Sea and Atlantic Ocean. A location of strategic importance during the early middle ages

---

[12] Beck, William Henry., A Family Genealogy: Harkness, Carmichael, Lester, Greene, Andrews, Brown, White, Polhill, Beck families. Lettercraft Shop, Inc., East Point, Georgia, 221-223, Universal Standard Encyclopedia, Vol. 12, 1958; La Mance 7 (Halstead Genealogy A.D. 1585)

[13] Casteland.com, http://www.castleland.com/puk/castle/bretagne/morbihan/josselin.htm, Last Modified: 02 July 2013, Accessed 16 April 2016 & Josselin Society of England, http//web.archive.org/web/2007814061819/http:www.peterjoslin.btinternet.co.uk/chateau_josselin.htm, Last Modified: 14 October 2006, Accessed 16 April 2016

that led to British dominance and fueled a rivalry with France that will last of centuries to come.[14]

Being the son of a knight, it was tradition during this timeframe to train your son to be a knight as well. This training begins at a young age, where the child is given the title of "squire." Under this title, they are taught in weaponry, armor, horse riding and fighting, and hand to hand combat. Knighting ceremonies were not as elaborate in the early middle ages, as they will eventually become in the latter middle ages. During this time, which is historically referenced as the early middle ages, Geoffrey de la Zouche was knighted sometime during the 1140's. Knighthood was commonly granted, when the young man was in his late teens or early twenties and often occurred on the battlefield. At the time of Geoffrey's knighthood, it was common that men would be knighted on the battlefield. In the late middle ages, the practice of knighthood on the battlefield will become less common as grand ceremonies would become more of the norm. Knighthood ceremonies would become so grand that overtime the only people of England that could conduct a knighting ceremony was the king or queen of England.[15]

The exact year that Sir Geoffrey was knighted, and where in present-day France is uncertain; however, there is documentation he was knighted and carried on the legacy of his father and royal duties. Geoffrey is listed as marrying Hawise de Fergant (born about 1130), around 1156 and had three children. It is cited in some sources, the two of them only had two children where they confuse Alan and Alexander as the same child of Sir Geoffrey and Hawise de la Zouche, but these sources that state this are in-correct. The three children of Sir Geoffrey and Hawise de la Zouche are:

1. Eudo de la Zouche born abt. 1156, Harringworth, Northamptonshire, England
2. Alan de la Zouche born abt. 1157, Harringworth, Northamptonshire, England
3. **Alexander de la Zouche born abt. 1181, Northampton, Northamptonshire, England**

---

[14] Castleland.com, http://www.castleland.com/puk/castle/bretagne/morbihan/josselin.htm, Last Modified: 02 July 2013, Accessed 16 April 2016 & Josselin Society of England
http//web.archive.org/web/2007814061819/http:www.peterjoslin.btinternet.co.uk/chateau_josselin.htm, Last Modified: 14 October 2006, Accessed 16 April 2016

[15] Boulyon, D'Arcy Johnson Dacre. The Knights of the Crown: The Monarchial Orders of Knighthood in Later Medieval Europe, 1325-1520. 2nd revised ed. Woodbridges, UK: Boydell Press, 2000; Church, Steven (1995) Papers from the sixth Strewberry Hill Conference 1994. Woodbridge, England: Boydell & Brewer, 1995, pgs. 41-100. Clark, Hugh. A concise History of Knighthood: Containing the Religious and Military Order Which Have Been Instituted in Europe. London, 1784, 1; Lixey L.C., Kevin. Sport and Christianity: A Sign of the Times in the Light of Faith. The Catholic University of America Press, 2012, 6.

It is believed that Sir Geoffrey de la Zouche died in 1187 in Harringworth, Northamptonshire, England, when Alexander, is youngest child was only about five or six years old. The death of Sir Geoffrey de la Zouche, with his youngest son being so young, the knight that was entrusted by the family to train Alexander to be a knight is uncertain.[16]

Generation III: Alexander De La Zouche

Alexander de la Zouche was born about 1181 to the parents of Sir Geoffrey de la Zouche and Hawise de la Zouche in Northampton, Northamptonshire, England. His place of birth being approximately 30 miles south southeast of Harringworth, Northamptonshire, England; which is the location Alexander's parents initially re-located to, sometime around 1150 from Rohan, Bretagne, France. The question as to why the parents of Alexander decided to leave their homeland province within present-day France, as mentioned earlier, is mostly likely contributed to the marriage his grandfather Alan de la Zouche had with the Princess of Bretagne, Constance de Gros who is the grand-daughter of William the Conqueror, "William I, King of England. This marriage automatically made any and all offspring from Alan and Constance of British royal descent. This is due to Alan's wife having a more immediate royal bloodline to a current or former king. Even though, Alan's bloodline was already a direct link to Charlemagne (Charles I of France), his wife had a closer direct link to William the Conqueror than Alan did to his ancestor. Alexander was born under the "Hohenstaufen Dynasty" under Frederick I, who reigned from birth c1152-1190, and was crowned 1155, then under Henry VI 1190-1197, crowned 1191.[17]

Now under British rule, this particular de la Zouche line is the line that becomes de la Grene de Boketon, initially keeping the "de la" as tribute and reference to their French heritage, a heritage they would soon lose with each preceding generation. This change in this lines last name would come soon after Alexander is called to duty by the present king of England. Around 1200 John I, King of England calls upon Sir Alexander de la Zouche to put down the Uprising of Count de la March in 1201 in present-day Normandy, France. As a knight, and being taught to always obey the orders of their king or lordship, Alexander agreed to the kings' request to end

---

[16] Castleland.com, http://www.castleland.com/puk/castle/bretagne/morbihan/josselin/josselin.htm, Last Modified: 02 July 2013, Accessed 16 April 2016 & Josselin Society of England, http://web.archive.org/web/20070823124010/http://www.peterjoslin.btinternet.co.uk/chateau_josselin.htm, Last Modified: 14 October 2006, Accessed 16 April 2016.

[17] Beck, 221-223; Universal Standard Encyclopedia, Vol. 12, 1958 Volume 12, 4370-4373; Greene, George Sears, Louise Brownell and F.V. Greene. *The Greene's of Rhode Island: with Historical Records of English Ancestry, 1534-1902*. Albany, NY: Knickerbocker Press, 1903 1-4; Casteland.com, http://www.castleland.com/puk/castle/bretagne/morbihan/josselin.htm, Last Modified: 02 July 2013, Accessed 16 April 2016 & Josselin Society of England, http//web.archive.org/web/2007814061819/http:www.peterjoslin.btinternet.co.uk/chateau_josselin.htm, Last Modified: 14 October 2006, Accessed 16 April 2016; Beck 221-223

the uprising and bring order back into the province of Normandy, which at the time was under British monarchy rule.[18]

The success in Alexander and his men in putting down the uprising of Count de la March led to being granted fifty hides of land, equivalent to six thousand acres; as well as, the title of Great Baron, a gift from John I, King of England for his loyalty and victory in bringing order back to the province of Normandy. This gift from the king and the title of Great Baron is important to note, as this title and landownership will become crucial in the success of the generations that follow Alexander de la Zouche.[19]

Under British monarchy structure of the time period, the nobility under the king were granted one of two titles: Earl's or Baron's. If the title of Baron was granted to you and your family to carry on, Barons were additionally sub-divided into two groups: Greater and Lesser Barons. In order to obtain and keep the title of Great Baron, the king must have either provided or allowed the knight to keep the land won in battle equal at least fifty hides of land (six thousand acres).[20]

This new title and enormous estate provided to Alexander by the king, put him in the position of being a vassal for his region of England of Northamptonshire; which additionally, improved the House of Arundel, the house Alexander de la Zouche was in at birth. As a vassal who came from generations of knights and royalty, it was his responsibility to conduct military duties, provide supplies to the king in the form of manpower, weaponry, horses, food and room and board for the manpower, king and royal subjects. In addition to this, Alexander was responsible in supplying portions of dowries for princesses, and entertainment to the king and royal subjects as his estate was furnished with one-hundred sixty-six people, with most being maids and servants. An amount of people that Alexander was required to maintain, in order to carry out his duties as a Great Baron and ensure the average amount of fifty guests were always taken care of while present on his estate.[21]

Within ten years of having ownership of Grene's Norton, Alexander de la Zouche changed his last name. The reason for this name change is believed to because of the people of the area began referring to Alexander and the people that lived within his estate as Grene Norton of Boketon or simply Grene Norton. The new last name on royal records began referring to Alexander de la Zouche as Alexander de la Grene de Boketon, Great Baron of Green's Norton of Boketon. "Alexander de la Grene de Boketon, his servants, and courtship were easily recognizable by their required royal attire wardrobe that was distinguishable by its expensive fabric of green and blue colors. Alexander dressed in this expensive fabric and colors, held in place by a belt made possibly of gold or silver. At his waist, he wore his sheathed dagger and a kept his purse attached which contained his personal items, such as keys, his pen, and inkhorn.

---

[18] Beck 221-223; La Mance 6, 15
[19] Beck 221-225; La Mance 6-7
[20] Duiker, William J. & Jackson J. Spielvogel. *World History*. Fourth Edition Ed. Vol. Volume 1. Belmont: Wadsworth, A Division of Thomson Learning Incorporated, 2004, 192; La Mance 7
[21] La Mance 7-8 (Halstead's Genealogy, A.D. 1585); Sterns, Peter. The Encyclopedia of World History. Houghton: Houghton Mufflin Publishing Company, 2001, 195; Turner, Ralph V. *King John: England's Evil King?* Stroud, Gloucestershire, GL5 2QG: The History Press, 1994, 173-174

When riding he had magnificent armor and spurs made of gold. When in attendance at Parliament, they were dressed in robes and while attending court they wore hats and plumes. At the king's coronation they wore royal red velvet caps with a gold band." All of which showed their rank in the Kings court.[22]

Aside from Alexander's duties and title, the land Alexander acquired would become widely known throughout England during the middle ages because of its immense size, its enclosures and abundance of deer that resulted in the land being called by the locals as Boketon; as well as, Alexander being called Lord of the Park of the Deer Enclosure. It is important to recognize the difference of English speaking from this time frame, in relation to the present. In this time fame, a green was a park; Boketon is an old word, which means buck's ton, or paled-in-enclosure. Ton, in its original sense meant town. Boketon, used in the original sense, shows Lord Alexander's estate was named for its extensive parks and abundance of deer. As time passed, Boketon became Bucks, Buckston, followed by its current name Boughton, which is located in Northamptonshire, England.[23]

Alexander de la Grene de Boketon, maintained his estate and carried out his duties with great responsibility, and although still being Norman French speaking, as his family had not officially changed to the English language, he managed to effectively communicate with his king. When not conducting his required military duties, the Grene family as they became known, were avid sportsmen and athletes. They were huntsmen, attended tournaments, played tennis, cricket, and bowled. The Greene's, for generations were noted not only for their bowling skills, but also for the greatest bowling alleys in England. Sir Alexander had a passion for horticulture that dominated his entire line of descendants. His estates were surrounded by some of the most spectacular grounds, flowers, fruit trees and immaculate farms.[24]

Around 1204, Alexander married Lady Isabelle de Cantilupe and together had one child. The name of this child is listed below and is highlighted in bold:

1. **Walter de la Grene de Boketon born about 1206**

It is believed that Alexander and his wife did not have any other children together, but it is documented that his mother re-married to Richard Penebruge; Stephen Devereux and had one child together William Devereux; thus giving Sir Walter de la Grene de Boketon with a younger step-brother born around 1219. Based on these dates, it is clear Alexander and his wife Lady Isabelle divorced for reasons that are most likely to remain unknown, as Alexander is not recorded to have died until 1236. At the time of his death, Alexander's son Walter was approximately thirty years old and was given full and total possession of his father's estate.[25]

---

[22] Beck 222-225; La Mance 5
[23] Beck 221-222; La Mance 8-9
[24] Beck 221-225; Greene 5-11; La Mance 8-9
[25] Beck 221-225; Green 5-11; La Mance 14a

Chapter II:
The Early Grene's of Boketon

Generation IV: Walter de la Boketon

Sir Walter de la Grene de Boketon, was born about 1206 in the Grene Boketon estate, Green's Norton, Northamptonshire, England. He is the son of Alexander de la Grene de Boketon and Lady Isabelle de Cantilupe who wed about 1205, however, it Alexander to did not marry Walter's mother until after he returned from putting down the Uprising of Count de la March in 1201.[26]

As previously stated, Walter's father Alexander de la Grene de Boketon, died around 1236 at the approximate age of 55 years old. At this time, Alexander's son Walter was about 30 years old. Upon his father's death, Walter took over all titles and took control of all estates, which includes Lord of Boketon and Great Baron of Boketon, Northamptonshire, England. Until the passing of his father occurred, however; Walter was in the position of making sure he earned the titles and estates that were within his fathers' possession. This required being trained as a knight by his father, going into battle, being knighted, and when not in battle participating in knight tournaments to practice training to ensure he was always ready for battle.[27]

During Walter de la Grene de Boketon's early years; there is very little information on him because there were surprisingly very few conflicts that required heavy military action and fortification of strategic points within England in his life time. The only major conflict was the First Baron Wars I 1215-1217. At that time, Sir Alexander de la Grene de Boketon was granted exemption for participating, the likely reason for this successful exemption granted by John I, King of England was threefold: First, his son Walter was only nine years old at the time and was in the process of being trained as a knight by his father who needed to be present for his son; a second likely reason comes from his success of putting down the Uprising of Count de la March in 1201 that earned Alexander all of his titles and landownership; and finally, the entire premise for this war was based on Baron's standing up against John I, King of England for not abiding by his very own 15 June 1215 signed Magna Charta.[28]

It is likely the third reason is what allowed Alexander de la Grene de Boketon to be exempt from fighting as this war would put him in a position against the very king that presented him with the Boketon estate as a gift for his success in putting down the Uprising of Count de la March. This war was led by other Baron's, most specifically by, Robert Fitzwalter, whom received support by future king of France, Louis VIII and Louis supplied French Army, to ensure

---

[26] Beck 221; Greene 5-11; La Mance 14A
[27] Beck 221-225; Greene 5-11; La Mance 14A
[28] Beck 221-225; Greene 5-11; La Mance 28

King John of England will abide by his signed Magna Charta. For this reason, Alexander was allowed to stay out of the conflict through continuation of supporting his king, training his son to be knight, and maintaining his estate.[29]

With assistance from Walter, the Boketon estate quickly became widely known throughout all of England for possessing the most beautiful gardens throughout the land. These magnificent gardens were a verity of flowers that lined the walking paths, the main building and perimeter. Despite the absence of graphic evidence of these magnificent gardens on the Boketon Estate, the colorful descriptions illustrated by LaMance, whom got her descriptions of the gardens from family bible's and journals, provides enough proof that all of England was impressed by their horticultural practices and constant care they continuously carried out on the estate.[30]

The years of care to the Boketon estate, and due to the absence of any serious military battle, makes it unclear in the manner of Walter being knighted. It is possible; his knighthood came in a grand ceremony that resulted in the king's presences, along with his royal subjects, fellow Baron's and commoners. The year of his knighthood is not known, however, it is likely this ceremony occurred when Walter was between the ages of 16-20. An age group that is very common to receive the distinction of knight. Based on the age range, it is safe to suggest the year of his knighthood happened sometime around the years of 1220-1224.[31]

Around 1230, it is recorded he married and soon after in 1232 had a child with his wife. Although the name of Walter's wife is not provided and listed as unknown by some sources, other sources believe she was Lady Isabel Alice d'Aubigny born sometime between 1204 and 1214. Together they had quite a few children, but only one son. His name is listed below and highlighted in bold:

1. **John de la Grene de Boketon born abt. 1232 in Boketon, Northamptonshire, England**

In 1236, the same year of the death of Walter's father, Walter was listed in the rolls of Henry III, King of England as knight and Lord of Boketon estate, in Northamptonshire, England. This was the first year Walter was acknowledged as a landowner and Great Baron. Twelve years later, Walter would be called upon to take part in the seventh crusade that was led by Louis IX, king of France from 1248 to 1254. This battle required Walter making a trip by sea to France, and from there it is documented the remainder of the journey to present-day Jerusalem, Israel was by land.

In a route led by King Louis IX of France, it is believed the pilgrimage took about two years to make on horses, while carrying their weaponry, and other previsions. By the time of their arrival it is estimated it was in the year of 1251. As records indicate, the seventh crusade

---

[29] Beck 221-225; Greene 13-14; La Mance 29
[30] Beck 221-225; Greene 13-14; La Mance 2, 7-9
[31] Beck 221-225; Greene 13-14; La Mance 14 A, 19

was very poorly organized by Louis IX, King of France. This poorly led crusade resulted in the king's capture. A capture that resulted in France having no alternative, but to pay a ransom equivalent to 50,000 gold bezants to the Egyptian military before Louis IX would be freed. Needless to say, the seventh crusade was not only a failure, but proved to be extremely costly for the French monarch.[32]

Following the unsuccessful military campaign Walter de la Grene de Boketon participated in, he would return home to a son of about sixteen years of age, and ready for Knighthood. Walter will leave his estate to his son, John, at the time of his passing. In the meantime, and after returning from the crusades, Walter would be mentioned in the rolls of Henry III, King of England in his forty-fifth year as king of England (1236); as well as, in the seventh year of Edward I in 1273. Two years after making his appearance on the king's rolls, Edward I in 1273, Walter de la Grene de Boketon died sometime around 1275. It is recorded that Walter had about seven children and at least one son, whom receives all of his father's titles at the time of his father Walter's death.[33]

Generation V: John de Grene de Boketon

Sir John de Grene de Boketon was born about 1232 in Boughton, Northamptonshire, England to Sir Walter de la Grene de Boketon and Isabel Alice D'Aubigny. John is the first Lord and Great Baron of the Boketon estate to officially add on to his last name "de Grene." His father, Walter, and grand-father, Alexander, unofficially went by the last name of de Grene de Boketon as it was the title of commoners within their region referred to them as, instead of their actual last name of de la Zouche. A last name they had when this particular Green family line migrated to present-day England from present-day France sometime between 1145-1155.

The reason for this official name change, was John de Grene de Boketon, while on the eighth crusade with King Edward I, was given the name "Grene" by Edward I. John de Grene de Boketon, married around 1270 to Millicent de Cantilupe, and she was with child soon after their marriage and his departure to participate in the eighth crusade that was being led by Edward I, King of England. A crusade that is recognized as the final crusade that would deal with religion that was aimed at the Holy Land.[34]

This child John and Millicent had together is listed below and highlighted in bold:

1. **Thomas de la Grene de Boketon born abt. 1270 in Boketon, Northamptonshire, England**

---

[32] Beck 221-225; Greene 13-14; La Mance, 14A-19
[33] Beck 221-225; Greene 13-14; La Mance 9
[34] Beck 221-225; Greene 12-14; La Mance 14A

John de Grene de Boketon, left with King Edward I of England in 1270, not long after marrying his wife Millicent. Unfortunately, Sir John de Grene de Boketon would never see his wife or his unborn child Thomas de Grene de Boketon as he would die in battle, soon after arriving with King Edward of England in Palestine around 1271. The map graphic at the top of the following page: details the journey, provides a timeline, and a back story to the event. This same map graphic can be viewed in a larger layout within Appendix J, in order to better read the included narrative to the right side of the image.[35]

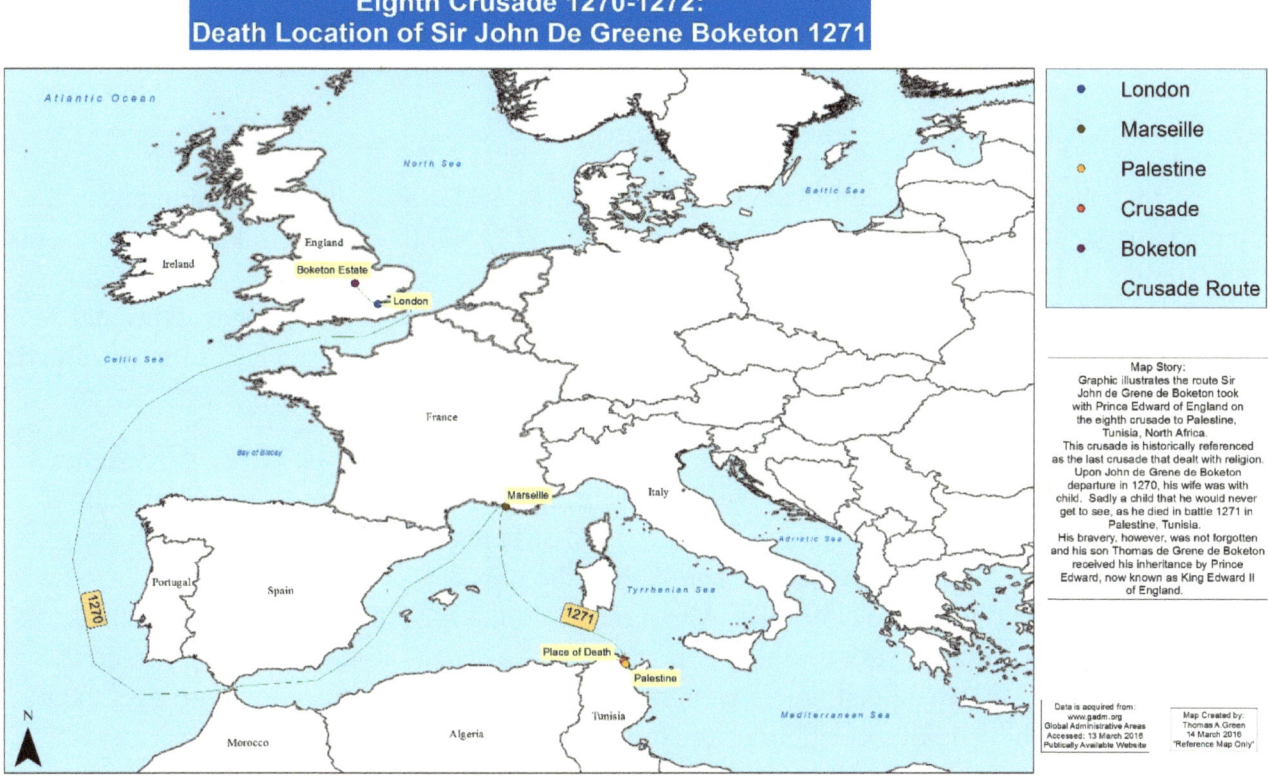

Figure 2: Green, Thomas A. 2016. Data collection acquired from www.gadm.org; accessed 13 March 2016

The unfortunate death of Sir John de Grene de Boketon, and the failure of the eighth crusade, symbolizes the end of the crusades. Yet despite Sir John de Grene de Boketon death, the legacy he left behind is important to note for this particular Green Family line. The change in the last name by officially adding "de Grene," and permanently no longer going by their actual last name of de la Zouche, would be a last name change that would last until the late 1500's. This spelling of Green as being "Grene," would be seen in the generations to come for the next three hundred years, and although Sir John de Grene de Boketon died in 1271 Palestine in the

---

[35] Beck 221-225; Greene 13-14; La Mance 16-19

eighth crusade, he remained listed on the king's rolls until his son was of age to inherit all of his father's land and titles.[36]

The reason for Sir John de Grene de Boketon's name being listed on the rolls, even after death, deals with English law. This is why some confusion in the past has come to light with his name being present on the rolls in the seventh year of King Edward I of England in 1313. Nonetheless, as soon as his son Thomas was of age, John de Grene de Boketon will no longer be mentioned on the rolls. In the meantime, John's son Thomas was left in the trust of William de Nutricilla, Abbot of St. Wondergisle, to oversee the estate of Boketon, and ensure Thomas is trained as a knight and prepared to take the titles that were left to him by his father of Great Baron and Lord of Boketon.[37]

Generation VI: Thomas de Grene de Boketon

Sir Thomas de Grene de Boketon was born about 1270 in Boketon, Northamptonshire, England to Sir John de Grene de Boketon, whom died in the eighth crusade in Palestine, present-day Tunisia in 1271; and his mother Millicent de Cantilupe. After Johns death, Millicent de Cantilupe is documented as re-marrying two more times and having ten to twelve additional children from these two husband's; which does not account for the child she had with Sir John de Grene de Boketon.[38]

It is additionally not known who was left responsible of Thomas de Grene de Boketon's training as a knight. It is possible however; this training might have come from one or both of Thomas's mother's additional husbands that are listed as being knights themselves with their own Coat of Arms. What is known, as mentioned in the previous section of Sir John de Grene de Boketon, is that William de Nutricilla, Abbot of St. Wondergisle was entrusted with the families' estate and money. The reason for the families' selection, in regards to the person that was left to oversee the estate that would be passed down to Thomas at his coming of age, to an Abbot, indicates the religious practices of the family line during this time period.[39]

In this time frame, which is referenced as the middle ages, religious leaders were often considered to be of great importance and the most trustworthy gentleman that someone of royal and nobility standards can entrust to watch over their estate and finances. In addition to this, the title Abbot of St. Wondergisle, indicates the Green Family line during this time frame were Catholic. This can be referenced by the online source www.catholic.org, which states: 'the title

---

[36] Beck 221-225; Greene 13-14; La Mance 14A
[37] Beck 221-225; Greene 13-14; La Mance (Halstead's Genealogy), 9-10 (Abbott William de Nutricilla trust); Sterns 236
[38] Beck 221-225; Greene 13-14; La Mance 5-9, 14A
[39] Beck 221-225; Greene 13-14; La Mance 14A

of Abbot is given to someone that is considered a superior of their respective community that oversees a minimum of twelve monks.'[40]

Sometime around 1288, Thomas de Grene de Boketon came of age and married Alice Boltesham who was born about 1264. His wife, was the daughter of Sir Thomas Boltesham of Braunston, who is a cousin to Thomas de Grene de Boketon. This marriage was clearly arranged by both families in order to keep the royal blood and pedigree within the family lines. During Thomas de Grene de Boketon and his wife Alice's marriage together, it is recorded they had at least one child, a boy.

This child is listed below and is highlighted in bold:

1. **Thomas de Grene de Boketon born abt. 1288 in Boketon, Northamptonshire, England**

Within six years of his marriage and the birth of his son, Thomas, Sir Thomas de Grene de Boketon accompanied Edward I, King of England in the first expedition against the Scots in 1294. This can be proven through "Halstead's Genealogies," who states in his manuscript, on the Green family line, that Sir Thomas appears in an ancient catalogue of knights who went with King Edward I to put down the rebellion in present-day Scotland.[41]

Following his return from Scotland with King Edward I of England, Thomas de Grene de Boketon returned to his estate, and in the process picked up additional titles of leadership. Records indicate, Thomas de Grene de Boketon is listed as being the Sheriff of County Northampton for several years, and was listed on the rolls of King Edward II of England thirteenth year in 1319. Within that same year of his appearance on the king's rolls in 1319, Sir Thomas de Grene de Boketon died. There is proof that Sir Thomas de Grene de Boketon is buried at Boughton with his Tomb is still on display to this day.[42]

---

[40] Catholic Online. 2016. http://www.catholic.org/encyclopedia/view.php?id=22. Date Accessed: 26 March 2016.
[41] Beck 221-225; Greene 15-21; La Mance 16
[42] Beck 221-225; Greene 15-21; La Mance 16-17

Chapter III:

Rise to Prominence: Purchase of Boughton Fair and Green's Norton Estate

Generation VII: Thomas de Grene de Boketon

Sir Thomas de Grene de Boketon was born about 1288 in Boketon, Northamptonshire, England. He is the son of Sir Thomas de Grene de Boketon and Alice Boltesham. The significance of this ancestor is after six generations, he weds his cousin Lady Lucy de la Zouche of Harringworth, Northamptonshire, England. It is important to note, these are the same cousins this particular Green family line originated from with Alan de la Zouche who marrying Constance La Gros, Princess of Bretagne, the grand-daughter of William the Conqueror, William I, King of England. A marriage that ultimately brought them from Alan and his wife Constance birthplace in present-day France to present-day England, where it is recorded they are both laid to rest.

It is from here, everything was passed to Geoffrey de la Zouche, who at some point re-located to present-day Northampton, Northamptonshire, England, the location not far from the Boketon estate, Alexander, the son of Geoffrey de la Zouche would receive as a gift from John I, King of England for his success of ending the Uprising of Count de la March. This marriage, like many other marriages of royalty and nobles was a marriage to maintain their pedigree. It is important to note her pedigree as well. Lady Lucy de la Zouche whom married Sir Thomas de Grene de Boketon is the daughter of Eudo Lord de la Zouche and Millicent Cantilupe. Lucy's mother is the sister of George Cantilupe, who is the Baron of Abergavenny in Wales; as well as, Christian Irwardby. (Appendix A)

Following in his father's footsteps, Sir Thomas de Grene de Boketon became known as the 5th Lord of Boketon, as well as, being appointed High Sheriff of Northampton from 1330-1332. The latter title of sheriff is recorded during the early reign of Edward III, King of England. Thomas is additionally recorded in 1334 of being one of the "Men of Liberty of the Cinque Ports." By being on this list, it meant that he was granted tax exemption by the crown. During his political career, Sir Thomas and Lucy had two daughters and two sons.[43] There children are as follows:

---

[43] Beck 221-225; Greene 1-4, 22-29; La Mance 5-9

1. Nicolas de Grene de Boketon born about 1315, but likely born in 1313 or 1314
2. **Henry de Grene de Boketon born about 1310, but likely born between 1315**
3. Joan who married Sir Thomas Culpepper birth year is unknown
4. Elizabeth who married Sir John Holland.[44] Birth year is unknown

Although Sir Thomas de Grene de Boketon is the main focus in this section, his wife Lucy de la Zouche is the grand-daughter of Lord Alan de la Zouche of Ashby, the Governor of Northampton-shire Castle, and his wife was the granddaughter of Saier de Quincy, Earl of Winchester, recorded as one of twenty-five Magna Charta Barons and a Knight of the Fifth Crusade in the Holy Land in 1220. The reason why this is important is because Lucy's grand-father is the son of Geoffrey de la Zouche, who is additionally the father of Alexander de la Zouche. Alexander being one of the few Baron's that did not rise up against King John of England in the Baron War's 1215-1217, as it is presumed that Alexander did not want to be un-loyal to a king that provided him with his extensive estate of about six thousand acres.[45]

This is possibly the reason behind Alexander de la Zouche, often referred to as Alexander de Grene de Boketon's name not appearing as one of the twenty-five Baron names that rose up against King John of England in 1215 for not abiding by his Magna Charta. The names of the Baron's that are on this list are provided below, with the names of those that are cousins or have married into this particular Green Family line highlighted in bold:

Eustace de Vesci, Robert de Ros, Richard de Percy, William de Mowbray, Roger de Montbegon, John FitzRobert, William de Forz, John de Lacy, **Saer de Quincy, Earl of Winchester**, Richard de Montfichet, William de Huntingfield, Roger Bigod and Hugh Bigod, **Robert de Vere,** Geoffrey de Mandeville, Henry de Bohun, Richard de Clare and Gilbert de Clare, William D'Albini, **Robert Fitzwalter,** William Hardel, William de Lanvallei, William Malet, William Marshall II, Geoffrey de Say.

Sir Thomas de Grene de Boketon it is interesting to note, made his second son Henry heir of the Boketon Estate, with no indication that Thomas's oldest son and child was un-fit. Instead, over the years the de Grene de Boketon family found themselves the inheritors of many estates. It is possible he felt with the amount of land and duties it was becoming too much for only one person to handle. By this division he could have a better chance of keeping all the lands within the family. This action has also been assumed by many researchers that he preferred his second son Henry over his first son.[46]

---

[44] Beck 221-225; Greene 13-14; La Mance 16-17; (Sir Thomas Grene of Buckton is recorded as High Sheriff for the County of Northampton-shire in the 5th year of Edward III's reign. His marriage to Lucie the daughter of Eudo de la Zouche-Halstead) as stated in La Mance.
[45] Beck 221-225; Greene 22-29; La Mance 16-17
[46] Beck 221-225; Greene 22-29; La Mance 19

Generation VIII: Henry de Grene de Boketon

Sir Henry Grene de Boketon was born within the time frame of 1310-1315 in Boketon, Northamptonshire, England. As mentioned previously he is the second child and son of Sir Thomas de Grene de Boketon and Lady Lucy de la Zouche. Sometime around 1340, Henry would marry Catherine Drayton who was born about 1319. Catherine is the daughter of Sir John Drayton of the prestigious de Vere family (Appendix D). This marriage is believed to have occurred within the Northamptonshire, England area.

The significance of Sir Henry de Grene de Boketon is important to this family line, as Henry I, the son of Sir Thomas de Grene de Boketon is responsible for making this Green family line one of the most powerful Barons of all of England. A power that became so great due to all of Henry's titles, estates and land holdings that it would rival and ultimately threaten the king of England. As a result, from this threat, Henry and the immediate descendants would become ostracized and nearly killed off. Prior to this happening though, Sir Henry de Grene de Boketon went on to have a strong political career being recorded as a Sergeant-at-Law.

This position, known as Sergeant-at-Law, or Sergeant-Counter, has been around for centuries and is documented as dating back to the 1300's in France, prior to the Norman conquest. As for its existence in England, it is believed to be brought in to the English social order by Henry II, who so happens to be the father of two future king's, Richard I, The Lionheart, and John I, the latter being the king that gave Henry de Grene de Boketon's great-great-great-grandfather the Boketon estate for squelching the Uprising in 1201 Normandy, France. The title of Sergeant-at-Law is considered to be one of the oldest formally created order in England, and although this order is documented of rising into significant power in the 16th century long after Sir Henry de Grene de Boketon was already dead, what this title basically meant was he was a lawyer and a judge within the king's justice system, often referred as Justice of the King's Bench in later years.

The few men that were granted this title were the legal system within the English monarchy. They were appointed to this position to make sure the king or queen would not over exercise their power, and cause a rebellion. By the end of Sir Henry de Grene de Boketon career, his level of achievement within England's monarchy is well noted. He is recorded as being the second-highest judge of the Courts of England and Wales, a position that is behind the Lord Chancellor himself. It is recorded that Henry de Grene de Boketon received the title of Chief Justice of the King's Bench on 24 May 1361.[47]

Possibly the most notable legal cases he worked on during his career as Chief Justice of the King's Bench was the case against Pope Urban VI and the Bishop of Ely in 1385, where the Bishop was being cited for harboring one of his men who had burnt the Mansion House of Lady Wake and killed one of her servants. In this case, due to the Pope's failure to appear in court, in regards to this case; Henry de Grene de Boketon had him excommunicated. This justice system maintained its prominence as the second highest common law court within the English legal system until 1875. In addition to his Chief Justice career, which he is listed as being dismissed

---

[47] Beck 221-225; Greene 13-14; La Mance 19

with honor, Sir Henry is also recorded for opening up Parliament in 1362 and 1363, and being in attendance in 1364-1365.[48]

Aside from his political and legal career, Sir Henry de Grene de Boketon is credited as the creator of the Boughton Fair. According to records, Sir Henry received the grant of "Boketon Fair" in 1351 and within two years purchased the Manor of Norton. The significance of this fair is well noted as it quickly rose in popularity, becoming the largest fair right behind the London Fair. Noblemen came from miles around to show off their livestock, horses and goods for a grand exhibition on land that contained the ruins of a long abandoned church. This fair would last for the next five and a half centuries in Norton Manor. A manor that is surrounded by the present-day village of Green's Norton.[49]

Below is a visual representation of England that highlights the provinces and location of Boketon, Green's Norton; as well as, the location of the other places and provinces this branch of the Green family line resided. This graphic can additionally be seen in the back of the manuscript in Appendix I, in order to better read the provided narrative that is featured on the side.

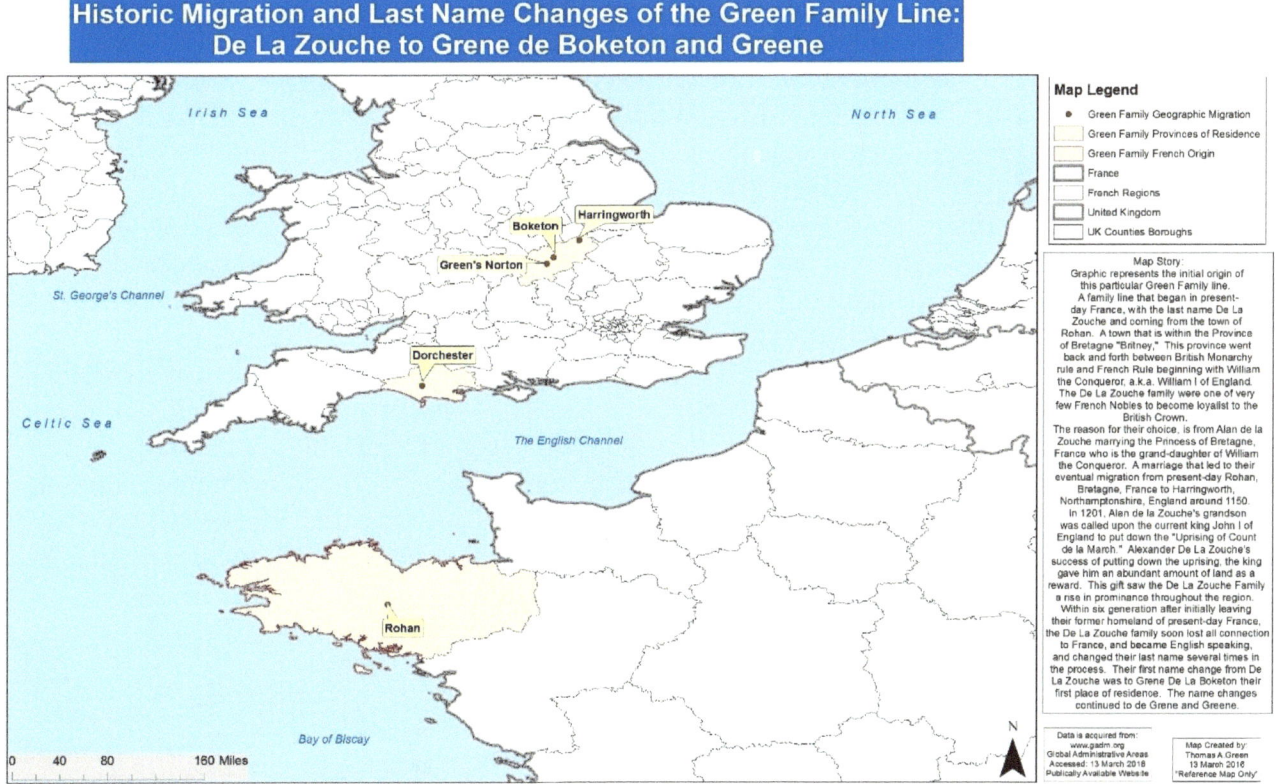

Figure 3: Green, Thomas A. 2016. Data collection acquired from www.gadm.org; accessed 13 March 2016

---

[48] Beck 221-225; Greene 13-14; La Mance 19
[49] La Mance 20

With his wife, Catherine Drayton, the two of them had six children. These children are listed below, with this particular Green family line direct ancestor highlighted in bold:

1. Sir Thomas de Grene, heir of Grene's Norton and Boughton, Knt.,
    m. Lady Margery Isabella Marblethorne, the daughter of Sir John Mablethorpe.
2. **Sir Henry de Grene of Drayton**
    m. Matilda Mauduit, daughter and sole heir of sir Thomas Mauduit of Warminster, County Wilts.
3. Richard de Grene died s. p.
4. Nicholas de Grene died s. p.
5. Amabilia de Grene
    m. 1. Sir Ralph Reyes, Knt. of Clifton Reyes, County Buckingham 2. John Chetwoode
6. Agnes Margaret de Grene
    m. William, Lord Zouche of Harringworth, County Devon.

Sir Henry de Grene de Boketon died in 1393 and was buried in Boketon. At the time of his death, Sir Henry de Grene left the Manors of Boughton, Grene's Norton, the advowson of Heymondecote, Huntington, Sewardsley Priory and others in the counties of Hertford, Leicester, York, etc…In addition to these, the advowson of Boughton, Great Haughton, and lands in Batsaddle in Orlingbury, Cottinham, Isham, Little Harrowden Middleton, Pavelisbury Pightesley, Pittsford , Silveston, Towcester, Wittlebury, and Northampton; as well as, a mansion in Silver Street, Cripplegate, and London to his oldest son, Sir Thomas de Grene.[50]

Whereas, Sir Henry de Grene, the second son of Sir Henry de Grene de Boketon, who married Matilda Mauduit, and this family lines direct descendant, the following properties; Luffwick, Islip, Shipton, one third of Great Haughton as well as, other holdings in the counties of Buckingham and Bedford, along with the advowson of Luffwick, lands in Harringworth, Carleton, Raundes, Kingstead, Cotes and Titchmart. Sir Henry de Grene de Boketon's second son Henry de Grene, additionally inherited Drayton Manor. A manor left to him by his mother Catherine Drayton. Furthermore, Henry who is the second son of Sir Henry de Grene de Boketon and Catherine Drayton received inheritance from his cousin, Sir John Drayton, the son of his mother's brother Sir Simon Drayton. It was with this inheritance that Sir Henry was required to assume the arms of Drayton instead of his paternal arms. Yet, while his descendants do not appear to use the Drayton arms, there are some recorded in Essex.[51]

---

[50] Beck 221-225; Greene 12; La Mance 20-21
[51] Beck 221-225; Greene 12; La Mance 20-21; For descendants of Sir Thomas Grene, see "Pedigree of Greene of Green's Norton."; Stow's Survey of London p 112; H. G. Somerby's extracts of Wills in England in the 15th, 16th and 17th centuries; " 1577, Richard Greene of St. Giles without Cripplegate, London, Gentlemen, Will, dated May 11, 1377 finalized June 15, 1377.

Chapter IV:
The Switch of Arms from Boketon to Gillingham

Generation IX: Sir Henry de Grene

Sir Henry de Grene was born about 1349 at Green's Norton, Northamptonshire, England. His parents were Sir Henry de Grene de Boketon, 6th Lord of the Boketon Estate and Chief Justice of the King's Bench and Lady Catherine Drayton. Henry de Grene is the first in this family line to remove "de Boketon" from his last name and solely going by "de Grene." The reason for this is because, this particular line no longer has the Boketon Estate in their possession. Instead, the Boketon estate was given to Sir Henry de Grene de Boketon's oldest son Thomas Grene de Boketon, whom went on to become the 7th Lord of Boketon and not a part of this particular Green family line.

Despite Sir Henry de Grene not getting ownership of Boketon, as mentioned in the previous chapter, he was given numerous estates by his father; as well as, several others from his mother's side, the Drayton's. In fact, it is noted that Sir Henry de Grene de Boketon gave his son Henry de Grene all, but two of his estates, by successfully setting aside English law; and conducting an action that was considered unheard of at the time. It is possible the reason for Sir Henry de Grene's father's success in overriding tradition and granting his second child and second oldest son more land than his oldest, is most likely due to his fluency in English law as being one of the Chief Justices of the King's Bench. Therefore, his power, second only to the Lord Chancellor gave him a power under English law that no one in the family line possessed.[52]

The land and titles given to Sir Henry de Grene from his father and mother; as well as, his father's rank of Chief Justice of the King's Bench, gave Henry immense power. An amount of power and landownership that only grew overtime, as Henry found himself as one of Richard II's most trusted allies. These additional land possessions given to Sir Henry de Grene began with his marriage about 1368 to Lady Matilda Manduit, in County Wiltshire, England. His wife is the daughter and sole heir of Lord Thomas Manduit and Lady Joan Bassingbourne, and since women cannot officially inherit land and possessions, all of this inheritance went to her husband Sir Henry de Grene. This inheritance Henry received from his wife's father additionally gave him the titles of lordships of Dyechurch, Grateley, Lye, Werminister, Westburg, and others. The only catch to his inheritance from his uncle by marriage, Sir Simon, Lord of Drayton, in order to inherit the land given to him by his wife's family, Sir Henry de Grene had to agree to assume the Coat-of-Arms and take the title of Lord of Drayton. A title he agreed to take, as his uncle through marriage Sir Simon Drayton did not have any children.[53]

---

[52] Beck 221-223; La Mance 20-21
[53] Beck 221-223; La Mance 20-21

Aside from the inheritance he additionally received from his wife, together the two of them had seven children. The names of Sir Henry and Matilda's children are listed below with the direct link to this line highlighted in bold:

1. Ralph de Grene born about 1368
2. **Thomas de Grene born about 1369**
3. Henry de Grene born about 1375
4. Eleanor de Grene born about 1377
5. Elizabeth de Grene born about 1379
6. Mary de Grene born about 1381
7. John de Green born about 1387

The amount of children Sir Henry de Grene and Lady Matilda Manduit would prove to be very beneficial, as Sir Henry's fortune would soon change. Before this change in fortune would happen, Henry would be sent to the House of Commons soon after being knighted by Edward III, King of England. From there, Henry was appointed as one of the kings' counselors, and a members of the Parliament Commissioners. The latter being a group of people that are assigned to help govern the country. Following the sudden death of Edward III, King of England, the crown would be passed down to Edward III's grandson Richard II. A kingship that would be filled with conspiracies that would ultimately led to disaster for Sir Henry de Grene.

This process began when he was called upon by King Richard II. The reason being obvious, as Sir Henry de Grene had just as much as a public life as his father. A combination of his public life, along with the legacy Sir Henry de Grene's father Sir Henry de Grene de Boketon left behind, made Sir Henry de Grene an asset to the new king. Overtime, Richard II would provide Sir Henry de Grene with several confiscated estates, to go along with all of the land and estates he already received from inheritance; and because of the power he had from being the largest landowner in all of England that rivaled the king himself, King Richard II appointed Sir Henry de Grene as Lord Chancellor. A title that was recognized as the highest position any Englishmen during the middle ages could earn, aside from being declared the King of England.[54]

It is important to note, by receiving the title of Lord Chancellor, and already possessing the political titles of kings' counselors and one of the Parliament Commissioners, this made Sir Henry the most powerful man of all of England, aside from King Richard II. By outlining all of the assignments given to him by King Richard II, it can be fair to say, the king was utilizing Sir Henry for additional gain. At least this is what other Baron's will accuse King Richard II of England of doing. Of these assignments Sir Henry was requested to carry out by the king, included the following: restoring the Bristol Castle and stand behind the king with his decision to banish and confiscate the landholdings of one of the conspirators that wanted to take the thrown

---

[54] Beck 221-223; La Mance 20-21

away from King Richard II, a man by the name of Henry Bolingbroke, Duke of Hereford and Lancaster. A title Mr. Bolingbroke held for ten years.[55]

In the request Henry received from the king to conduct obtainment of Bolingbroke's titles and estates, and prior to Bolingbroke's banishment, Mr. Bolingbroke would petition this action as being illegal. This was ultimately met with heavy controversy that the king was over stepping his bounds. In fact, Sir Henry de Grene, being Lord Chancellor, is the person to point out to the Board of Commission that King Richard II's demand for Bolingbroke's estates was legal. As Sir Henry, stated that in accordance to English law of this time period all fiefs of England were directly or indirectly held through the king of England; and therefore, can be confiscated at any time. This addressment to the Board of Commission, by Sir Henry, resulted in the Board to agree and sanctioned the king's claim.[56]

Unfortunately, around the same time of the Board of Commission approving the king's confiscation of Bolingbroke's titles and estates, a rebellion in Ireland broke out that required Richard II, to set out and squelch it. Before King Richard II could return, Henry Bolingbroke set out to seize the thrown and accused Sir Henry de Grene and two others of being the master minds behind the loss of all of his titles and estates. The significance of the capture of Sir Henry de Grene, Sir John Bushy and William le Scrope, Earl of Wiltshire is that all three men would be immortalized by William Shakespeare in his play Richard II. In this play, Shakespeare will devote much of the first two Acts to Sir Henry Grene and his beheading that occurred on 2 September 1399 at Bristol.[57] Below is a portion of William Shakespeare's play and the words that are said to come out of Henry Bolingbroke, as these members of the Commission were brought before him:

"Bring forth these men. —
Bushy and Greene, I will not vex your souls
(Since presently your souls must part your bodies)
With too much urging your pernicious lives,
For 'twere no charity; yet, to wash your blood
From off my hands, here in view of men,
I will unfold some causes of your deaths.
"You have misled a prince, a royal king,
A happy gentleman in blood and lineaments,
By you unhappied and disfigur'd clean.
Myself a prince, by fortune of my birth;
Near to the king in blood: and near in love,
Till you did make him misinterpret me.
Have stooped my neck under your injuries.
And sigh'd my English breath in foreign clouds.
Eating the bitter bread of banishment;

---

[55] La Mance 29-31
[56] La Mance 29-32
[57] La Mance 31-32

While you have fed upon my seignories,
Disparked my parks, and felled my forest woods;
From mine own window torn my household coat,
Raz'd out my impress, leaving me no sign—
Save men's opinions, and my living blood—
To show the world I am a gentleman.
This, and much more, much more than twice all this,
Condemn you to the death. See them delivered over
To execution and the hand of death."[58]

      Following the beheading of Sir Henry II, his son Thomas becomes the next heir and is granted the title, Sir Thomas de Grene.[59]

---

[58] Shakespeare, William. Richard II, Acts I & II, the Quarto Edition, 1597.
[59] La Mance 32

Chapter V:
Fall of the Grene Name

Generation X: Thomas de Grene

Sir Thomas de Grene was born about 1369 in Green's Norton, Northamptonshire, England. He is record as being the second child and son of Sir Henry de Grene whom was beheaded by Henry Bolingbroke, whom was the vindictive former Baron and land owners whose estates and titles were confiscated by King Richard II, as mentioned in the previous chapter; as well as, being the son of Matilda Manduit.

During his younger years, Sir Thomas de Grene was being taught to be a knight to carry on the family tradition of loyalty to the crown, family and land, before the Lord of Jesus Christ. This training required incredible discipline, along with required tournaments to practice their learnt military skills, in the event of being requested for battle by the king. Thus being trained in the same manner as stated in Chapter II of Sir Geoffrey de la Zouche, Sir Thomas de Grene's sixth great grandfather. It is throughout this training; Sir Thomas de Grene's father was an extremely political powerful man, thanks in part to the parents and woman he (Sir Henry de Grene) married.

Unfortunately, little is known of this Thomas de Grene, along with the next few generations to follow. The reason for this will be explained fully; however, the information that is known about Sir Thomas de Grene is that he is the son of Sir Henry de Grene, Lord Chancellor of England, whom is recorded to have married Ela (Mallory) Malorie around 1397. It is possible Sir Thomas de Grene's wife Ela was likely short for Eleanor; but simply went by Ela who is recorded as being born 1382 and laid to rest 13 April 1433. Together Sir Thomas and Ela have on record of having two children, both of them being boys. Their two children are listed below and the one of this direct line is highlighted in bold:

1. Thomas de Grene born about 1398
2. **John de Grene born about 1408**

The estimated date of their marriage is worth noting, as the two of them wed, possibly no more than two years before conspirators that were against the current king of England, Richard II, led by Mr. Bolingbroke, rose up against the king and succeeded in having Sir Thomas de Grene's father, Sir Henry de Grene, Lord Chancellor of England, beheaded at the castle of Bristol.[60]

---
[60] Beck 221-223; La Mance 32-34

As this uprising against Richard II, King of England was beginning to take shape, Henry's son Sir Thomas de Grene and his wife Ela would have their first child, as listed above, a son whom was also named Thomas born about 1398. Around this same time, records that have been found on Sir Thomas de Grene indicate that he was the owner of the most magnificent and beautiful castle in all of England, a castle that is recorded as being destroyed sometime around the early 1400's. In addition to this, it is likely Sir Thomas de Grene accompanied Richard II, King of England to present-day Ireland sometime around 1398 to put down the rebellion. The reason for this assumption is because of the amount of trust and alignment Richard II King of England had with this particular Green family line. An alliance that Richard II clearly felt was a wise choice, as this Green line had become much more than knights; but prominent lawyers and politician of the time period.[61]

Sir Thomas de Grene is recorded to have been knighted on the battlefield, but for which battle is not entirely known; and it is therefore possible, he was knighted following the successful military victory against the people of present-day Ireland around 1398-1399. Nonetheless, whatever victory King Richard II received in Ireland would not be celebrated in England proper. It is mentioned in history and literature on King Richard II that he was met up by Henry IV, during his return from Ireland to England 19 August 1399 at Flint Caste. At Flint Caste, King Richard II, agreed to surrender to Henry IV and abdicated his thrown, in order to spare his own life. His willingness to abdicate is likely due to his realization of the beheading of three of his top advisors and allies that included Sir Henry de Grene of Drayton and Lord Chancellor of England. From Flint Caste, Richard II was escorted by Henry IV to the tower of London were the former king would die 14 February 1400 at Pontefract Caste, Yorkshire, England.[62]

In digression back to Sir Thomas de Grene, he and his wife additionally had one other child, as listed in the previous page, which was also a male and was given the name John. This second child and son is believed to have been born about 1408, and possibly in Gillingham, Devon, England; however, it is likely, he may have been born in Green's Norton, Northamptonshire, England prior to its destruction that is presumed to have been ordered by King Henry IV. Nonetheless, Sir Thomas de Grene did not meet the same fate as is father and is recorded as dying on 14 December 1427 in Gillingham, Devon, England. Gillingham, Devon, England being located 113 miles west/southwest from London, England.[63]

---

[61] Beck 221-223 La Mance 32-33
[62] La Mance 32-33; Saul, Nigel. Richard II. New Haven: Yale University Press, 1997, 406-417; Harris, Gerald. Shaping the Nation: England, 1360–1461. Oxford: Oxford University Press, 2005, 486-487
[63] La Mance 32-33

Generation XI: John de Grene

Sir John de Grene was born about 1408 at either Green's Norton, Northamptonshire, England; which is the same birthplace of his father Sir Thomas de Grene, or was born in Gillingham, Devon, England, along with his older brother Thomas de Grene. Both John and his older brother are believed to have been knighted on the battlefield, same as their father, however; whether they were knighted in the same year and in the same battle is not known. It is likely, based on the near ten-year age difference Sir John de Grene has with his brother, his knighthood came later. Based on the time frame, it would be a safe assumption to speculate that Sir John de Grene, received knighthood during one of the many battles of the hundred years' war between England and France.[64]

As for John de Grene's older brother, Thomas, it is mentioned he received knighthood about ten years after his father. Whether this is true or not, is left to historical records that may have been destroyed as Henry IV felt the need to take vindication on this particular line. It is because of this, the dates of knighthood for all three men, Sir John de Grene (direct descendant of this line), his older brother Thomas, and their father Thomas date of being knighted on the battle is not known. Thankfully the age difference between Sir John de Grene and his older brother Sir Thomas de Grene II, the king of England, Henry IV was more concerned of Sir Thomas II and was therefore; believed to have been locked up under the orders of King Henry IV in the tower of London around the time his younger brother was born.[65]

In order to understand the motive for King Henry IV's actions and for despising this Green family line, it is necessary to investigate the place of birth of King Henry IV. According to records, King Henry IV was born in Bolingbroke Castle, Lincolnshire, England on 15 April 1367. The name of the castle alone should shed light on King Henry IV's dislike towards this Green family line, as Henry Bolingbroke would be a direct relative to the current king. Lord Henry Bolingbroke being the same man that had Sir Henry de Grene and two other men beheaded at the Bristol Castle in 1399, with his conspiracy against the current king at the time Richard II. As mentioned previously, Henry Bolingbroke accused Sir Henry de Grene as being the principle mastermind behind King Richard II of England's success in confiscating all of his lands and titles. Therefore, King Henry IV saw this Green family line as a personal threat; and therefore, is believed Sir Thomas de Grene II was not allowed to have a seat in parliament and possibly banned from most political duties.[66]

Based on this investigation alone towards Henry IV's motives and dispose of Sir Thomas de Grene, the son of Sir Henry de Grene, was to prevent any further supposed damage this family line is believed to have caused to the Bolingbroke legacy. This additionally explains, contradiction in records of whether or not Sir Thomas de Grene, older brother of Sir John de Grene had children or not; where speculation is made of an Unknown Grene, yet this speculation

---

[64] Beck 221-223; La Mance 34
[65] La Mance 34
[66] La Mance 29-34

cannot be entirely proven. The reason for this speculation to be likely false is because based on Sir John de Grene's older brother year of birth of being around 1498, the only way he could have possibly had a child would have been before the age of thirteen. At that young age, and being locked up around the age of fifteen or sixteen makes the likelihood of Sir Thomas de Grene of having an off-spring seriously remote.

As for John de Grene, the direct descendant of this line, the reason for him being safe from King Henry IV's wrath, is simply on the basis of being only five years old at the time of King Henry IV's death in 1413. It is for this reason, for the likelihood that Sir John de Grene's like was spared as he was not seen as a threat. On the other hand, records speculate that relatives of Sir John de Grene, placed the young man in hiding protect him from King Henry IV. A speculation that could be very likely to have occurred as is older brother was deliberately locked away to prevent him from taking on his titles, possibly not long after receiving knighthood.

Of Sir John de Grene's personal life, it is recorded that he may have married a lady by the name of Margaret. Unfortunately, her last name is not known; however, some sources indicate that she was a distant cousin to this family line and her name was Margaret Grene or Mary Margaret Grene. This is not for certain, however, and will thereby simply be referred to as Margaret, wife of direct descendant Sir John de Grene. As for what is known of Sir John de Grene's wife and children is that Margaret is recorded as being born in Shropshire, Bridgenorth, England about 1408, and were wed about 1425. This wedding date, if accurate would have made them both sixteen to seventeen years old, depending on when their birthday's fell, and is likely plausible based on the time period. The reason for this likelihood is based on the information that was mentioned in the second chapter that knighthood typically occurred between the ages of 16-20 years old. Therefore, it is likely that during a battle in the Hundred Years' War that Sir John de Grene was knighted and thereby was considered a man.[67]

As for children, records indicate Sir John de Grene and Margaret had four children. Although it is important to point out, the recorded date of two of their children may be in-correct or may not be their children at all. Nonetheless, these children are listed below and in order based on their estimated year of birth, with the descendant to this direct line highlighted in bold:

1. Ralph Grene b. 1421, but might be 1431
2. Henry Grene b. 1422, but might be 1432
3. Robert Grene Sr. born about 1442
4. **John Grene Sr. born about 1448**

The information provided above makes it likely the last two children of Sir John de Grene and Margaret Grene's are their only children. As for any children being born after this lines descendant John Grene b. 1448, at this time no records indicate additional children of Sir John de Grene. In fact, sources list Sir John de Grene and Margaret died twenty-five years apart from one another. According to genealogical records, consistent time frames indicate that Margaret

---

[67] Beck 221-223; La Mance 32-36

died around 1450 or 1451. This would make her youngest child, John de Grene, the direct descendant to this line; and at the mere age of two or three years old at the time of his mothers' passing. Sir John de Grene, on the other hand, is not listed as being died until 1486. This twenty-five-year gap between Sir John de Grene's list date of death and his wife's, suggests the possibility that John de Grene could have re-married and had additional children, however; at this time sources show no indication of this being fact.

It is interesting that at the time of their death's both were laid to rest in entirely different places in present-day England. This geographic spread in burial sites suggest that Margaret was indeed a cousin to Sir John de Grene as she was laid to rest at Green's Norton, Northamptonshire, England, presumably in a family plot; whereas, he was laid to rest in Gillingham, Dorset, England. The latter likely being families plot as well.

Generation XII: John Grene

John Grene was born about 1448 at Bowbridge Hall, Dorset, England. He is the son of Sir John Grene and Margaret Grene. It is important to note, this estate of Bowbridge Hall is often spoken of as Porridge Hill; which is, the local pronunciation of its name. The information of this John Grene is extremely minimal and according to some records is often confused as being John the Fugitive. This however, is highly unlikely. The reason for this unlikelihood is because the names of his parents and wife are inconsistent, such as; being married three times to an Elizabeth Greene, Matilda Greene and Edith Greene.[68]

By investigating these names further, it can quickly be discovered that Matilda Greene for example, is actually Lady Matilda Grene whose original last name was Manduit, and is this John in question great-grandmother. In addition to this, the entire idea of there ever being a John the Fugitive is up to speculation by genealogists and historians. Where the latter suggest that John the Fugitive could likely be folklore loosely based on the conflict of Thomas More against the king of England, Richard III during the War of Roses (1452-1485).[69]

At the time of this conflict, the descendant of this line, John Grene would have only been four years old. Nonetheless, it is interesting how this descendant for this particular Green family line is suggested to be John the Fugitive.[70]

---

[68] Beck 221-223; La Mance 32-36
[69] Beck 221-223; La Mance 32-36
[70] Cunningham, Sean. 2003. Richard III: A Royal Enigma. The Documents: Number 7, Evidence of the Princes' fate? Chapter I: Richard and the War of the Roses. Published by The National Archives, Kew, Richmond, Surrey TW9 4DU, UK; Evidence of the Princes' fate? Charter recording the grant of the title of Duke of Norfolk to John, Lord Howard, 28 June 1483 (Latin), (the National Archives, E 179/117/77, m.4) pages 46-47; La Mance 33-34; More, Thomas & Webb, Simon. 2015. The History of King Richard III. Published by Langley Press, Durham; Weir, Allison. 1992. The Princes in the Tower. Publication: The Bodley Head, a division of Random House, Inc. Chapter

Returning back to John Grene of this family line, records that are known of the man state he married Elizabeth Warner who was born 1475 in Gillingham, Dorset, England, not far from the birth place of her husband John Grene at Bowbridge Hall in Dorset, England. Records do not indicate, this John Grene, descendant of Sir John Grene and Margaret Greene, with the grandparents of Sir Thomas de Grene and Ela Mallory, of ever being knighted on the battlefield for bravery or in an elaborate ceremony. Instead, it is believed he was a simple horticulturalist on an estate that was passed down to him by his father that was knighted.

John Grene and his wife Elizabeth are recorded of having only one child as shown below in bold:

1. **Robert Grene born about 1490**

There are no records suggesting the two had any additional children. At the time of their passing, John Grene is recorded as being laid to rest in Arlesey, Bedford, England in 1520. As for his wife, she is recorded as being laid to rest in Cumberland, England in 1560. The reason for them not being buried together is unknown, however; the forty-year difference of their passing could indicate that John Grene's wife Elizabeth either re-married or re-sided with her son until her own passing.[71]

Something that is important to highlight is in reference to the map graphic featured in Chapter III, points out the location of this area within Dorset, England that is on the shores of the English Channel. This would be the last location within England for this branch of the Green family line, prior to their departure to the American colonies.[72]

11: Richard III pages, 128-138; Chapter 12: Conspiracies pages, 139-146; Chapter 13: The Princes in the Tower pages, 147-162 and Chapter 14: The Wicked Uncle pages, 163-178.
[71] Beck 221-223; La Mance 36-38
[72] Beck 221-223; La Mance 36-38

Chapter VI:
Notable Women of Grene Family Line Lady Catherine Parr

Lady and Queen of England Catherine Parr

Lady Catherine Parr, although is a cousin to this particular Green family line, the strength, courage and being a woman well ahead of her time makes her worthy of attention. She was born in Blackfriars, London, England, about 1512, to the parents of Thomas Parr and Maud Green. Catherine was the oldest of three children and definitely showed it. The link Catherine Parr has to this Green family line is through the mom, who was Sir Thomas de Grene, the brother to our direct relative Sir Henry de Grene, Chief Justice of the Court's Bench. Historical records show, aside from their own personal endeavors, both brothers were extremely close as they together are listed as the purchasers of Green's Norton for about 20 shillings.[73]

The connection of Catherine Parr to this family line highlights that she too came from a long line of royalty and nobility. A pedigree that was passed down to her from her mother. As personal information of her life unfolds, it is clear she had the most upmost respect towards her mother and applied; as well as, passed down this information to her step-children. Before we get to her adult years, it is interesting to learn just how educated Catherine Parr's mother was; and how it is her mother that opened her daughter's eyes to the world. It might be safe to say Maud Grene saw something extraordinary with her daughter Catherine and embraced it.[74]

When Catherine Parr was young her father died in 1517. This resulted in her mother being a widow and taking on the responsibility of raising her three children on her own. As it was rare in this time period for a woman to remain un-married following the death of her husband, Maud Grene did just that. Instead of getting married and having the possibility of putting the children's inheritance in jeopardy, she made the choice to not re-marry and manage the inheritance and went to great extents to ensure all three of her children were well educated. It is because of this, determination and will of her mother to be both the father and mother that shaped Catherine Parr to become the woman she became to be as an adult. An independent thinker and fluent in three languages before her eighteenth birthday.[75]

All of the efforts Maud Grene did for her children was definitely not a cake walk, as highlighted in Linda Porter 2010 manuscript, Katherine, the Queen: The Remarkable Life of Katherine Parr, the Last Wife of Henry VIII, her mother married Thomas Parr at the age of sixteen and found herself a widow around her twenty-fifth birthday. During their marriage, she

---

[73] Frazer, Antonia. The Wives of Henry VIII. Vintage Publishing, 30 November 1993. Chapter: Catherine Parr; Whellan, Francis (1874). "History, Topography and Dictionary of Northamptonshire." Archaeologia Cantiana (2nd ed.) London: Whittaker and Co. Retrieved 26 March 2016; Whellan 1874, pp. 516-517
[74] La Mance 25-28
[75] Porter, Linda. Katherine, the Queen: The Remarkable Life of Katherine Parr, the Last Wife of Henry VIII. Macmillan. 2010, 117-274

and her husband actually had five children. The first child was a boy, yet as the author Linda Porter explains, Thomas Parr and Maud Grene's joy of the birth of their first child was short as he died not long after being born. Their next three children would be born without any issues with each one living well into adulthood. The fifth child, on the other hand, is documented as being stillborn. It's death being likely due to her devastation over the loss of her husband in 1517.[76]

These hardships clearly shaped Catherine Parr's mother; and in return, shaped Catherine Parr as well. This ambitious nature that Catherine possessed as a child, also proved to be very challenging for her mother. The reason for this being a challenge for her own mother, is through Catherine's ambitious nature, she could not and often would refuse to do womanliest house chores and duties, such as, sewing and embroidery. In fact, Catherine Parr is quoted as saying that "her hands were not made to use the distaff or needle," but rather, "my head was made to wear a crown, and my hands to hold a scepter." Indeed, she was born to be a queen, and indeed she would become one.[77]

Catherine married her first of four husbands at the age of seventeen. Edward Borough, a baron in 1529 and was left a widow by early 1533. A year later she married John Neville in 1534, also a Baron. The Baron Latimer, of Snape Castle. In this marriage, Lady Catherine found herself the step-mother of Baron Latimer's two children, a role she took on gladly. She went on to share the education, affluent heritage and independent thinking she learned from her mother Maud Greene, with her step-children. This marriage lasted for over a decade, ending upon her husbands' death in 1543.[78]

Although a widowed again, Lady Catherine being 31 years old and now maintaining the continual care of her two step-children, she found herself surrounded by many suitors. Despite some sources suggesting on her wanting to marry Thomas Seymour, Catherine instead took the hand of King Henry VIII. An opportunity that is suggested by many scholars' as an offer she could not refuse as fear being one of her motives. Such a motive is potentially not too farfetched as King Henry VIII was known for his brutality and it is estimated that 2,000 people per year were executed during his reign. This included the beheading of most his wives, such as Anne Boleyn and Catherine Howard, the latter being accused of infidelity. It is further suggested some of his wives, including Catherine Parr who would be his final wife, and Anne of Cleves are a few of the fortunate wives of King Henry VIII that did not lose their head. The latter wife simply being divorced by King Henry VIII. Where the reason for the divorce was cited by Henry VIII that she was "fat and stupid;" whatever the reason may be for Catherine Parr to marry King Henry VIII, the two married in a small ceremony on 12 July 1543.

Throughout her marriage to King Henry VIII, her educational pursuits, strong independent thinking would continue to get her into trouble, and conversely, get her out of it. It

---

[76] Porter, Linda. Katherine, the Queen: The Remarkable Life of Katherine Parr, the Last Wife of Henry VIII. Macmillan. 2010, 117-274

[77] "Burke's Genealogical and Heraldic History of the Peerage Bononetage, and Knightage, Privy Council, Order of Preference" (hardback) (96th, Coronation Honours ed.). London: Shaw Publishing, in conjunction with Burke's Peerage. 1938 2416; La Mance 25-28

[78] Burke's 2416; La Mance 25-28

was a during this marriage she became fluent in a fourth language, Spanish, and was often scolded by her husband for being too outspoken and not holding to the standards of what a woman should be with her man. This is because Henry VIII believed women were inferior to man, and God created man in his likeness, but created women to submit and serve man. Due to her outspoken nature, it is believed the king placed spies within the castle to spy and report conversations his wife Catherine Parr had with other nobility and royal guests. The reports from these spies nearly cost Catherine Parr's life as the King was prepared to charge her and have her executed for heresy. An execution that did not get carried out as Catherine knew of her husbands' weakness to flattery and being compared to a grand ruler such as Solomon, that when the Bishop and others came to collect her to be tried and beheaded, King Henry VIII drove them away.

Catherine Parr's intellect and wit saved her from being killed by her husband, King Henry VIII, whom she saw pass away January 1547. Under heavy scrutiny and controversy, she married for her fourth and final time. The fourth marriage was to Thomas Seymour, although he is believed to be the man Catherine initially had intensions to marry and did not in order to, accept the Kings, offer is believed to have been a savage brute himself. Their marriage did not last long as sources suggest Catherine Parr was poisoned by her husband, not long after she gave birth to her one and only child on 30 August 1548, and dying on 5 September 1548.[79]

---

[79] Burke's 2416; La Mance 25-28

Chapter VII:

The Grene Family Returns from Hiding: the final switch of Coat of Arms

Generation XIII: Robert Grene of Gillingham

Sir Robert Grene was born about 1490 in Bowridge Hill, Gillingham, Dorset, England. He is the son of John Grene and Elizabeth Warner. It is evident by this time, the influence of this particular branch of the Grene family line had diminished. This is because with exception of being granted the title Sir, which indicates he was knighted, nothing else is really known. What is known about Sir Robert Grene are the people that are within his personal life, rather than his military or political influence that was clearly seen in the generations that had come a century before.

According to records, it is listed Sir Robert Grene married Elizabeth Worgg 1518, whom was born about 1503. Together they had seven children, which are listed below and the one that is in this direct line is bolded:

1. Mary Greene born 24 November 1519
2. **John Greene born about 1520 died 1560**
3. Peter Greene born, c1525 married Joan? Died without heirs
4. Alice Greene born, c1526 married Mr. Small
5. Richard Greene "of Stanfford Ryvera" born, c1527 died in 1608, married Joan Converse Inherited the estates comes John of Warwick/John the surgeon… five sons and four daughters
6. Joan Greene born about 1533 married Roger Capps
7. Henry Greene born about 1536

It is determined, in accordance to records, both Sir Robert Grene and his wife Elizabeth Worgg lived out the rest of their lives at Bowridge Hill, Gillingham, Dorset, England. An estate that was re-purchased by Robert, which will go on to become the family seat for the next three preceding generations.[80]

Throughout their life on the Bowridge Hill estate, documentation mentions Sir Robert Grene's wife had extraordinary mathematical ability. It is believed that her natural ability for numbers was passed down to future generations that have made the majority of her descendants "quick in figures." The reason for this belief is because ever since her marriage into this Green family line, every so often a Green is born with the

---

[80] La Mance 36-38

capacity to understand and compute numbers, giving the appearance of being instantaneous calculators.[81]

In Sir Robert Grene's later years, he makes an appearance of the subsidy rolls of 1543 as an elderly man with grandchildren. One of his daughter's he and wife named Joan, some records indicate this daughter being named Anne, but these two women are actually the same person. The likely reason for this confusion is because at this particular time period in England, Anne was a very popular name. It was additionally popular within the Gillingham Greene's as well. This diminutive name for which, Welthian, was used in the family for several generations; even after the family had migrated to America. As for Robert's four sons, it is important to note, two of them are the forebears of the two dominant Green families who would settle in America.

This can be best broken down as saying that Sir Robert Grene's fourth child Richard is the father of John Greene, who would be known as Dr. John (the Surgeon) Greene of Warwick, Rhode Island, United States; a cousin to this family line. Thus becoming known as the founder of the Warwick Green's. Whereas, Robert Green's oldest son, John Greene, he will go on to have a son named Henry, who will have a son named Robert; and it is this Robert, son of Henry, whose son that is named John will become known as John Greene of Quidnessett (John the Younger of Rhode Island). As for Robert Greene and his wife Elizabeth Worgg, both are presumed to be buried in the family cemetery of Saint Mary the Virgin Parish Church Cemetery, Gillingham, Dorset, England.

Generation XIV: John Greene

John Greene was born about 1520 in Gillingham, Dorset, England. He is the second child and oldest son of Robert Grene and Elizabeth Worgg. It is believed that around this time, this Green family line officially changed the spelling of their last name from Grene to Greene. With this change in spelling, it is important to point out the journey of their last name changes up to this point. This line began as de la Zouche, in present-day Bretagne (Brittney), France, to de la Grene de Boketon around 1202, to de Grene de Boketon around 1300, to de Grene around 1350, Grene around 1400, and Greene around 1550. This will be the last time the spelling of Green will change, until the mid 1800's by Samuel Green of Michigan in order to separate himself and his family from the slave owners in the American south by the same last name.[82]

As for John Greene, it is recorded that he married a woman by the name of Anne Arthington, who was born about 1520. She is listed as being the daughter of Henry Arthington of Arthington, West Yorkshire, England, and Maude Goldesborough. Anne Arthington is listed as being born in Gillingham, Dorset, England the same place as her husband. The two of them are believed to have married sometime in 1550.[83] Together, John Greene and Anne Arthington had four children. All four children are listed below with the one being the descendent of this line highlighted in bold:

---

[81] Beck 221-223; La Mance 36-38
[82] Beck 221-223; La Mance 36-38
[83] Beck 221-223; La Mance 36-38

1. Gabriel Greene born about 1550 (some sources list this child as being named Robert)
2. Jeremy Greene born about 1551
3. **Henry Greene born about 1552**
4. Michael Greene born about 1555

Aside from the information above, the only other information on record is that John Greene died sometime in 1561 and is laid to rest in Gillingham, Dorset, England. John's wife, on the other hand, is recorded to have either died in 1555 or her death date is listed as unknown. If the former is correct, her death could have likely been contributed to child birth complications from the last child named Michael. It is important to note, both parents are listed as being deceased when all four children were under the age of sixteen. If the dates of death for both parents are in fact correct, it is likely the children went into the care of one of John Greene's siblings.[84]

Generation XV: Henry Greene

Henry Greene was born about 1552 in Gillingham, Medway, England to the parents of John Greene and Anne Arthington. He is recorded as getting married to Lady Catherine De Drayton sometime around 1569, who was born about 1553 (may have been born as late as 1556). Given that Henry Greene's wife is recorded as being Lady Catherine Greene (De Drayton), it is likely Henry was knighted. By this time, during the late Middle Ages, men that were honored with knighthood did not necessarily earn in battle. It is possible that Henry Greene was knighted as he aspired to a certain code of ideals i.e., 'code of conduct,' which earned him the right to be knighted.[85]

Records indicate they had five children. These children are listed below with the child of direct descent to this family line highlighted in bold:

1. Thomas Greene born about 1570
2. Joanna Greene born about 1571
3. Ann Greene born about 1572
4. Maria Greene born about 1573
5. **Robert Greene born about 1776**

The death date of Henry Greene is recorded as 22 August 1578 and being laid to rest in Gillingham, Dorset, England. Whereas is wife, is recorded to have died sometime around 1580, and is laid to rest in Gillingham, Dorset, England; and is likely they are buried in the same place. Like John Greene, Henry Greene and his wife are recorded to have died when all five of their children were young. If the death records are correct, it is likely Henry Greene and Lady Catherine De Drayton's children were taken in by one of Henry's siblings. The reason for this speculation is because their oldest son, Thomas Greene, would have only been eight years old at the time of his father's death and about ten years old at the time of his mother's.

---

[84] Beck 221-223; Greene 38; La Mance 36-38
[85] Beck 221-223; La Mance 36-38

Generation XVI: Robert Greene

Robert Greene was born about 1576 in Gillingham, Dorset, England. He is the youngest child of Robert Greene and Lady Catherine De Drayton. Information on this Greene is extremely limited. All that is known is he married a woman by the name of Joan Tattershall, who was born in Lancashire, England, sometime in the year 1575 or 1576. They may have gotten married around 1605, however; based on recorded birth records; it is possible they married earlier.[86] Together, Robert Greene and his wife Joan are recorded of having two children. Both children are listed below and name of the one that belongs to this family line is highlighted in bold:

1. **John Greene born about 1606 (John of Quidnessett)**
2. Thomas Greene born about 1608

Other than the information provided above, there is no other real reliable information, with exception to the death date of Robert Greene; which is recorded as being sometime in the year 1650. Where he is laid to rest in Cucklington, Suffolk, England. Robert's wife, on the other hand, is listed as dying much earlier than her husband. The records show the year she died is 1643, and is believed to have been laid to rest in Newport, Newport County, Rhode Island, United States. If this information is correct, it is interesting to learn why John of Quidnessett's mother would be buried in present-day Rhode Island, United States; whereas, her husband is supposedly buried in England. It is possible, location of where she is buried is confused with another woman of the same name, and more than likely she is actually buried in England with her husband.[87]

---

[86] Beck 221-223; La Mance 36-38
[87] Beck 221-223; La Mance 47, 65

Chapter VIII:
Migration to the American Colonies

Generation I: John Greene of Quidnessett

John Robert Greene was born in Gillingham, Dorset, England about 1606 to the parents of Robert Greene and Joan Tattersall. It is believed that in 1626, at the approximate age of 20, he immigrated to the New World, by taking passage on the ship, "Matthew", to the West Indies. It is said, that once at the port of St. Christopher, West Indies; which is believed to be present-day, Basseterre, St. Kitts Island of the nation-state of St. Kitts and Nevis, he left within three months to Boston, Massachusetts to the Puritan colony as he felt the people in the West Indies were Godless.

Now in Boston, Massachusetts, John Greene found himself at differences with the people. It is believed these differences were on religious belief and conflict with Puritan community leaders. It is suggested that after a mere six months in Boston, he decide to leave with the company of another gentleman by the name of Richard Smith. Sources indicate they set up their own homestead that was dominated with indigenous people in Narragansett Bay of present-day Rhode Island, as the man John accompanied, Richard Smith is stated to have had a trading post in Quidnessett, sometimes referred to Aquidneset.[88]

It is important to note here, there is debate on how Quidnessett, Rhode Island is spelled. Some people spell it as spelled in the previous sentence, Quidnessett or it is spelled, Quidnesset. It is likely the correct spelling is the former, as this is how it is spelled according to Rand McNally Road Atlas, 2014; and is located southeast of East Greenwich, Rhode Island, United States. Regardless of the spelling of Quidnessett, the two of them are documented of establishing a trading post that became a very lucrative business that relied on the indigenous people for success. The for their dependence on the indigenous people for business at their jointly owned trading post, is for passed down story accounts and documents that state for several years John Greene and Richard Smith were the only two white settlers at Quidnessett.[89]

Sometime around 1643 or 1644, after John Greene and Richard Smith has likely been living in Quidnessett near their trading post for about 10-15 years, two men by the names of Roger Williams and Mr. Wilcox bought land in the area. In less than ten years after these two men are documented to have purchased land, Roger Williams sold his land to Richard Smith sometime in 1651. Eight years after Richard Smith's land purchase from Roger Williams, the indigenous Sachem, Coquinaquant chief of the Narragansett tribe, sold all of Quidnessett to a white spectator land company. This sale of the Quidnessett area is listed of occurring on 11 June 1659 to a man by the name of Major Humphrey Atherton. A purchase that is on recorded for being known as the Atherton Land Company.

---

[88] La Mance 53-59
[89] La Mance 53-59; Rand McNally Road Atlas, 2014, location of East Greenwich, Rhode Island, United States

Within the land company responsible for the purchase, headed by Major Humphrey Atherton, very few people were Rhode Islanders; but are interesting that Richard Smith was one of the few with no mention of a John Greene. The speculation for the reason as to why John Greene was not one of the few Rhode Islanders within the company will be discussed later. In the meantime, documents indicate the majority within the land company were from present-day Connecticut or the city of Boston, Massachusetts.

Returning back to the possible reason as to why John Greene is not listed as one of the original shareholders of the land company, deals with him getting married and recorded as having one of his children in Newport, Newport, Rhode Island. This suggests that he may have left the Quidnessett region for a while, only to return to the area later. On the other hand, it has already been determined by several genealogical research studies that three different men with the last name Greene, and strangely all three having the first name John settled in different areas of Rhode Island, and therefore; one of John Greene of Quidnessett's children may actually be confused with a different John Greene that was in Newport, Newport, Rhode Island the entire time.

John Greene of Quidnessett is recorded as getting married to Joan Beggarly about 1642. His wife is listed as being born about 1620 in Boston, Suffolk, Massachusetts. Not long after John Greene of Quidnessett and Joan Beggarly were married, records indicate they may have had about eight children.[90] These children are listed below with the child that is a direct descendant to this family line is highlighted in bold:

1. Edward Greene born about 1643 (known as Captain Edward Greene)
2. Daniel Greene born about 1647
3. Sarah Greene born about 1648
4. Henry Greene born about 1650
5. John Robert Greene born about 1651 (known as Lieutenant John Robert Greene)
6. **James Greene born about 1655 (known as Lieutenant James Greene)**
7. Benjamin Greene born about 1665

John Greene went on to be one of the early shareholders of land within the Quidnessett region, however; his name does not appear on the original list of shareholders. Soon after being a shareholder, he quickly found himself being the leader and largest land owner of anyone that participated in the Atherton Land Purchase. Yet everyone that participated in the purchase would find themselves either having to lose their land or re-purchase their holdings. This is because the Atherton Land Purchase that was headed by Major Humphrey Atherton was found to have been conducted illegally. It is believed it was brought to the settler's attention, which includes John Greene and Richard Smith, in accordance to colonial Rhode Island laws; colonist could not buy land holdings from the indigenous people. At least not within the boundaries of Rhode Island.

Matters were made worse for the settlers that were entangled in the Atherton Land Purchase and dispute, when Connecticut and Massachusetts were both fighting over present-day Rhode Island of which colonial boundaries it belonged in. This second dispute led to John Greene,

---

[90] La Mance 53-59

Richard Smith and with other settlers to draft a petition in 1663 with a request of wanting to be within the jurisdiction of Connecticut. This petition that was led by John Greene outraged the officials within the colony of Rhode Island, which resulted in the order of Greene's arrest.

Upon John Greene's arrest, it is said that he went peacefully, to which he was taken to Newport, Rhode Island to stand trial. At trial, John Greene remained adamant with his petition of wanting to be a part of Connecticut; and as a result, the courts made a compromise. The compromise was that John Greene made with the courts is to be a "loyal freeman of Rhode Island." A promise he kept, at least until he made it back to his land and quickly reneged on his agreement. This resulted in a seven-year battle between the colony of Rhode Island and John Greene himself. On 20 May 1671, the officials of Rhode Island gave in, but not without arranging a special court hearing within Quidnessett. At this special court hearing, both John Greene and Daniel Greene, his son, had to agree to acknowledge they were within the colony of Rhode Island. The agreement, this time was made and both John Greene and Daniel Greene were official "freemen of the Colony of Rhode Island."

With the dispute over, John Greene's name is found several more times throughout the years within the region of Quidnessett. Most of these appearances of his name had to do with being a witness to the transfer of land; as well as, other official Rhode Island documents. About a decade before his death, John Greene preceded to divide up all of his land to the remaining sons, whom still resided in Rhode Island. An event that is recorded as taking place on 23 March 1682, with his wife still living at the time of these deeds' being signed by his sons. The reason as to why not all of his sons were recipients of land is because of their re-location to present-day state of New Jersey. As to why some of his sons left the Rhode Island Colony to the New Jersey Colony are believed to be due to disagreements between the children that resulted in some of them making the decision to go elsewhere.[91]

As of the time of publication of LaMance genealogy manuscript of the Greene family line of John of Quidnessett in 1912, LaMance mentions that very old graves that are extremely ran-down are still on the site of where John Greene once owned land. These graves have the initials of D.G., which is believed to be the final resting place for Daniel Greene; and the other grave next to it has the initials R.G., which is believed to stand for the name of Daniel's wife Rebecca. As for the other gravestone, LaMance mentions as being on the site, has the initials I.G. According to LaMance, the letter "I" during the colonial period was used interchangeably with the letter "J", it is therefore; that reason the third graves stone that has the initials I.G. is of that of Joan Greene. Joan being the wife of John Greene of Quidnessett and father to Daniel.

The reason as to why John Greene is believed to not be buried next to his own wife, Joan, is because according to findings by LaMance, John went and lived the remainder of his years with his son John and his wife. At which time, he passed away sometime in the year of 1695. It is important to note, this son that is named after him is believed to be his fifth or sixth child and is the direct descendant to this family line. This grave of John Greene of Quidnessett is listed as being within the Old Field Graveyard, a graveyard that is estimated to be about one-mile West of

---

[91] La Mance 53-65, 80

Maple Root Church in Rhode Island, United States. A side note to all of this is the interesting coincidence that both John Greene of Quidnessett and John Greene of Warwick married a woman by the name of Joan. John Greene of Quidnessett would marry Joan Beggarly. A woman that despite being about eighteen-years-old, was supposedly already a widow; and is suggested that John met his wife Joan during a trip he made up to Boston for business in 1642. The confusing part of this is that Joan is listed on some genealogical records as being born in Quidnessett, Washington, Rhode Island, however; it is not unlikely for her to have been born in Boston, Massachusetts. As for John Greene of Warwick, a cousin to John Greene of Quidnessett married Joan Tatarsole. John Greene of Quidnessett's wife Joan Beggarly died in 1682, the same year her husband drafted the deeds for his sons to sign and take ownership of land parcels of their vast land holdings. Whereas John Greene of Quidnessett died thirteen years later on 06 December 1695. The family homestead was left to Daniel, who was residing there with his wife and children.

Generation II: Lieutenant James Greene

James Greene was born about 1655 in Quidnessett, Washington, Rhode Island to the parents of John Greene of Quidnessett and Joan Beggarly. The information known on James Greene is limited, as most of the information known of him is typically in reference of his older brother Lieutenant John Robert Greene. This has become a problem as some genealogists have gotten them confused by stating that John Greene of Quidnessett and his wife Joan Beggarly had only five sons, Edward, Daniel, James, Robert and Benjamin; and James is Lieutenant James Greene and there is no John Greene. In fact, there is no Robert Greene; but there is a John Robert Greene. This brother is the older brother of James Greene. Together, these two migrated between at least four colonies; and both earned the Rhode Island militia title of Lieutenant. It is from their similarities that results in the likely confusion by fellow genealogists that they are the same person.[92]

Although this confusion exists, these two brothers are in all actuality two entirely different people. With their similar journey, it is best to understand the direct descendent of this line James Greene, by including his older brother John Robert Greene. The reason to why this is being done is because during their early years their father John Greene of Quidnessett would send the two of them to look over and occasionally oversee his land holdings and other possible assets in New York. This constant travel together clearly created a bound between these two brothers, were they went on and joined the Rhode Island militia and fought in minor battles, most likely being with indigenous people over land claims. It is these entanglements that earned both brothers their military rank of Lieutenant. Whereas, their oldest brother went on to earn the title of Captain for his efforts of militia battles and duties.

---

[92] La Mance 53-65, 80

Lieutenant James Greene is recorded with his brother John as to living in multiple places within the Northern British Colonies. These locations include Massachusetts and possibly New Jersey. Unlike James Greene's brother, John Robert Green, who met and married his wife, while residing in Massachusetts; it is not clear where James met his. It can be assumed though that around the 1680's, both brothers decided to settle down, and at that time, the two of them may of went their separate ways. If this assumption is correct, this will explain how James Greene finished out his life in Bristol, Rhode Island; whereas his older brother John went on to Coventry, Rhode Island, thus becoming historically known as John of Coventry.

It is at this time frame, where Lieutenant James Greene appears to drop out of site, while his older brother John becomes more widely known. A possible reason for this might be due to John and his wife purchasing major swaths of land, and having eleven children. James Greene, on the other hand, is listed as getting married to Elizabeth Holmes, who was born in 1689. The names of her parents are not known, however; records indicate she was born in Kingston, Washington, Rhode Island. It is likely, she was first generation born colonist and that both parents arrived to Rhode Island after coming from England.

In relation to James Greene's brother John Robert Greene, and in reference to the information stated in the above paragraph, this provides a better understanding of the two brothers moving in different directions in their older years. This is because James's older brother John Robert married his wife in Massachusetts, sometime around 1684. At that time, John Robert was about thirty-three-years-old, his wife Abigail was about nineteen-years-old, and this would mean that John's younger brother was about thirty or thirty-one-years-old. It is from this likely scenario that James decided to return to Rhode Island, and establish himself in Bristol, Rhode Island; which is across the bay from East Greenwich and Coventry, the site where James's older brother would settle with his wife.[93]

Once on the Bristol, Rhode Island side, James Greene would marry Elizabeth Holmes, as mentioned earlier, sometime around 1704.[94] The two of them would have seven children. These children are listed below and the child that is descended from this family line is highlighted in bold:

1. Sarah Greene born about 1704
2. Elizabeth Greene born about 1705
3. Mary Greene born about 1708
4. Daniel Greene born about 1710
5. Thomas Greene born about 1711
6. Enfield Greene born about 1712
7. **James Greene born about 1716-1758**

Elizabeth Holmes is listed as dying in 1763, and was laid to rest in Bristol, Bristol, Rhode Island. As for James Greene, he is listed as dying in 1728, and like his wife, he was laid to rest

---

[93] La Mance 53-65, 80
[94] La Mance 80

in Bristol, Bristol, Rhode Island. There are no other records found for Elizabeth Holmes, so it is not likely she re-married. If she did re-marry, there is no evidence of any additional children. It is possible that because of the six other siblings James Greene had, one of his brothers' possibly John Robert Greene assisted in looking out for her. These final remarks however, cannot be confirmed.[95]

---

[95] La Mance 80, 118

Chapter IX:
Settling the Colonies

Generation III: James Greene

James Greene was born 1716 in Bristol, Bristol, Rhode Island to James Greene and Elizabeth Holmes. All that is known of James Greene is he married Elizabeth Straight sometime around 1726. His wife Elizabeth is recorded as being born in 1707 to John Straight and Rosanna Westcott. The place of her birth is not known with exception of stating it was within the colony of Rhode Island. The two of them had at least six children. These children are listed below with the one that is a direct descendant of this line highlighted in bold:

1. Sarah Greene born about 1728
2. Ann Grene born about 1731
3. Benjamin Greene born about 1734
4. **Jeremiah Greene 01 June 1736**
5. Dinah Greene born about 1739
6. Deborah Greene born about 1744

Aside from the children and wife, the only occupation listed for James Greene is that of a farmer. There is a strong likelihood however, that he was a part of the Rhode Island colony militia. The reason for this assumption is because during this time period, every abled man was expected to fight and usually did in the event of a conflict. James is recorded of passing away about 1758 and his wife Elizabeth one year later in 1759. They are recorded as being laid to rest in East Greenwich, Washington, Rhode Island; which is the reason for the likelihood that John Robert Greene assisted his sister-in-law with the raising of her children following the death of James Greene. James being the younger brother of John and father of this James Greene, who was the youngest child of seven.[96]

Generation IV: Jeremiah Greene

Jeremiah Greene was born 01 June 1736, presumably in West Greenwich, Rhode Island to James Greene and Elizabeth Straight. Sometime around 1760, Jeremiah married Freelove Hopkins. Freelove is recorded as being born in 1739. The names of her parents are not entirely known, however; according to some genealogists, it is believed Freelove's parents are Gardner Hopkins and Freelove Perkins. The last name Hopkins is believed to be one of several last names of white English settlers that migrated to the Rhode Island area, and at some point some of these white settlers possibly married in with the indigenous tribes of the area. Something that

---

[96] La Mance 118-119

could likely explain the first name Freelove. On the other hand, this first name may be pure coincidence and comes directly from English white settlers as well.[97]

As for the marriage of Jeremiah Greene and Freelove Hopkins, the only other information on these two people is they are believed to have had seven children, and Jeremiah was a farmer.[98] There children are listed below with the child being a descendant of this line highlighted in bold:

1. **Russell Greene born about 1760**
2. Barbara Greene born about 1762
3. Gardiner Greene born about 1763
4. Waite Greene born about 1766
5. Jeremiah Greene born about 1768
6. Abial Greene born about 1771
7. Ann Greene born about 1773

The year Jeremiah Greene and his wife Freelove Hopkins died is not entirely known. Some genealogists suggest, however; that Jeremiah died 1805 in Hancock, Berkshire, Massachusetts. If this place of death is accurate, then it can only be presumed that at some point he sold his land and re-located with one or all of his children to Hancock. The likely reason for this assumption is due to the limitation of available land with a growing population that required colonists to move further and further inland, in order to ensure their children will have land titles of their own.[99]

As for his wife Freelove, it is presumed she passed away in the same location, but the year is still not known. The reason for this uncertainly is likely due to poor preservation, complete destruction or misplacement of the grave sites of these two individuals. On the other hand, there is possibility that she passed away in Rhode Island, prior to her husband's death. The

---

[97] Church of Jesus Christ of Latter Day Saints, FamilySearch.org, Rhode Island, Births and Christenings, 1600-1914, index, https://familysearch.org/pal:/MM9.1.1/F83X-WR5, Accessed 28 March 2013, Jeremiah Greene in the entry for Russel Greene, 24 December 1760; Church of Jesus Christ of Latter Day Saints, Rhode Island Births and Christenings, 1600-1914," database, *FamilySearch* (https://familysearch.org/ark:/61903/1:1:F83X-SXP: accessed 24 April 2016), Jeremiah Greene, 01 Jun 1736; citing Rhode Island, USA, reference v 1 p 17; FHL microfilm 925,978; La Mance 118-119; Wiltsee, Jerome. *A Genealogical and Psychological Memoir of Philippe Maton Wiltsee and Descendants*. Atchison: G.W. Myers, 1908 143-144

[98] Church of Jesus Christ of Latter Day Saints, "Rhode Island Marriages, 1724-1916," database, *FamilySearch* (https://familysearch.org/ark:/61903/1:1:F8K1-PTB: accessed 24 April 2016), Jeremiah Greene and Freelove Hopkins, 20 Feb 1803; citing West Greenwich, Kent, Rhode Island, reference; FHL microfilm 908,269; Church of Jesus Christ of Latter Day Saints, "Rhode Island Marriages, 1724-1916," database, *FamilySearch* (https://familysearch.org/ark:/61903/1:1:VK1V-93X: accessed 24 April 2016), Jeremiah Greene and Freelove Hopkins, Oct 1760; citing West Greenwich, Kent, Rhode Island, reference; FHL microfilm 908,269; La Mance 118-119; Wiltsee 143-144

[99] Church of Jesus Christ of Latter Day Saints, "Rhode Island Deaths and Burials, 1802-1950," database, *FamilySearch* (https://familysearch.org/ark:/61903/1:1:F8X9-TX8: accessed 24 April 2016), Jeremiah Greene in entry for Sally Warner, 29 Jun 1880; citing Cranston, Providence, Rhode Island, reference p 16; FHL microfilm 2,384,565; Dempsey, Jack. *Michigan and the Civil War: A Great and Bloody Sacrifice*: The History Press, 2011; La Mance 118-119; Wiltsee 143-144

likeliness of this is due to a speculation of genealogists that mention her as dying in 1798. This would be seven years before her husband if correct. If this is correct, then the speculative scenario that Jeremiah Greene left with one of his children to Hancock, Berkshire, Massachusetts to live out the remaining years of his life as the likely scenario.[100]

Generation V: Russell Greene

Russell Greene was born 24 December 1761 in West Greenwich, Rhode Island to Jeremiah Greene, 01 June 1736 in RI and Freelove Hopkins, born in 1739, which were both born in West Greenwich, Kent, Rhode Island. It is recorded that Russell married Patience Straight Moon about 1782. She was born 01 March 1764, possibly in Rhode Island. The birthplace of Patience not being entirely known or for certain.[101] Together the two of them are recorded as having eight children. These children are listed below with the child that is the descendant of this direct line highlighted in bold:

Abel Greene born 28 July 1784- d. 1869
Francis Greene born 29 Oct 1786-d. 1855
Russell Greene born 13 Nov 1789-d. 1809 died young age of 22-23
Sarah Greene born 14 Dec 1791-d. 1878
Job Greene born 7 Oct 1795-d young
Willet "Gardner" Greene born 23 Oct 1799-1880
Polly Greene born 15 Apr 1802-1865
Lydia Greene born 1806-1864

---

[100] Church of Jesus Christ of Latter Day Saints, "Rhode Island Births and Christenings, 1600-1914," database, *FamilySearch* (https://familysearch.org/ark:/61903/1:1:F83X-4MJ: accessed 24 April 2016), Jeremiah Greene in entry for Anne Greene, 04 Oct 1773; citing Rhode Island, USA, reference v 1 p 141; FHL microfilm 925,978; Church of Jesus Christ of Latter Day Saints, "Rhode Island Births and Christenings, 1600-1914," database, *FamilySearch* (https://familysearch.org/ark:/61903/1:1:F83X-4MS: accessed 24 April 2016), Jeremiah Greene in entry for Barbery Greene, 08 Jul 1762; citing Rhode Island, USA, reference v 1 p 141; FHL microfilm 925,978; Church of Jesus Christ of Latter Day Saints, "Rhode Island Births and Christenings, 1600-1914," database, *FamilySearch* (https://familysearch.org/ark:/61903/1:1:F83X-4MH: accessed 24 April 2016), Jeremiah Greene in entry for Waite Greene, 25 May 1766; citing Rhode Island, USA, reference v 1 p 141; FHL microfilm 925,978; Church of Jesus Christ of Latter Day Saints, "Rhode Island Births and Christenings, 1600-1914," database, *FamilySearch* (https://familysearch.org/ark:/61903/1:1:F83X-4M8: accessed 24 April 2016), Jeremiah Greene in entry for Jeremiah Greene, 14 Dec 1768; citing Rhode Island, USA, reference v 1 p 141; FHL microfilm 925,978; Church of Jesus Christ of Latter Day Saints, "Rhode Island Births and Christenings, 1600-1914," database, *FamilySearch* (https://familysearch.org/ark:/61903/1:1:F83X-4MX: accessed 24 April 2016), Jeremiah Greene in entry for Abiale Greene, 09 Jun 1771; citing Rhode Island, USA, reference v 1 p 141; FHL microfilm 925,978; Church of Jesus Christ of Latter Day Saints, "United States Census, 1830," database with images, *FamilySearch* (https://familysearch.org/ark:/61903/1:1:XH5V-RPS: accessed 24 April 2016), Jeremiah Green, South Reading, Middlesex, Massachusetts, United States; citing 144, NARA microfilm publication M19, (Washington D.C.: National Archives and Records Administration, n.d.), roll 66; FHL microfilm 337,924; La Mance 118-119; Wiltsee 143-144

[101] La Mance 119

Revolutionary War and military records state that Russell Greene participated in the American Revolution. This information can be found in the manuscript entitled: "In the Massachusetts Soldiers and Sailors in The War of the Revolution." A manuscript that consists of 17 volumes, and is recorded that Russell Greene's information is within the sixth volume on page 831. On this page, Russell is listed as serving in the Continental Army from 09 July 1780 through 06 December 1780, where pay for services and required travel was included with the town of Lansborough responsible for raising the money to pay all of the servicemen. The commanding officer over Russell Greene and the other men is stated as being Brigadier General Paterson, and his duty station was Camp Totoway.[102]

In addition to this, Revolutionary Rolls for the state of Massachusetts, Vol. 4 p 157, lists Russell of Hancock's and others as receiving pay. Wiltsee, p 143 lists the following in regards to a response for his request for information on Russel's Revolutionary War service: "Russell Green of Hancock, Mass. Common Wealth of Massachusetts. Office of Secretary, Boston April 1, 1892, Revolutionary Rolls Vol. 4 p. 157. In addition, a complete detail of his enlistments is included. Three separate enlistments are shown with the first listing as June 1780 for six months as a private under Captain Hitchcock, and Colonel Ebenezer Sproat of Massachusetts. The second is September 1781 for twenty days as a private under Captain William Douglass, the name of his Colonel is not listed. The third and final listing is November 1781 for a total of twelve days under a Captain Clark, and again his Colonel is not listed. According to all of these records, Russell did not participate in any battles.[103]

Other information about Russell Greene, along with his wife Patience, are provided through several census records between the years of 1790-1830, and in the records of the U.S. Pensioners, 1818-1872. The former records indicate that both are recorded as residing in Hancock, Berkshire, Massachusetts. The same location Russell Greene's father, Jeremiah is listed of being laid to rest. As for the latter records, Russell Greene stated as leaving behind a widow, Patience Greene, who is the benefactor to his military pension. This includes the location of where he is laid to rest, which is, Plainfield, Windham, Connecticut, in 1785. His wife, on the other hand, is listed of being laid to rest in Clarence, Erie, New York on 11 December 1845. A good sixty years following the death of her husband, where the reason of causes of his death is not known.[104]

---

[102] Secretary of the Commonwealth. Massachusetts Soldiers and Sailors of the Revolutionary War, A Compilation from the Archives, In Accordance with Chapter 100, Resolves of 1891. Volume 6, 831. Boston: Wright and Potter Printing Company, 1900.

[103] Secretary of the Commonwealth. Massachusetts Soldiers and Sailors of the Revolutionary War, A Compilation from the Archives, In Accordance with Chapter 100, Resolves of 1891. Volume 4, 157. Boston: Wright and Potter Printing Company, 1900; Wiltsee 143-144

[104] Church of Jesus Christ of Latter Day Saints, FamilySearch.org, Rhode Island, Births and Christenings, 1600-1914, index, https://familysearch.org/pal:/MM9.1.1/F83X-WRP, Accessed 28 March 2013, Russel Greene, 24 December 1760; Church of Jesus Christ of Latter Day Saints, FamilySearch.org, Rhode Island, Births and Christenings, 1600-1914, index, https://familysearch.org/pal:/MM9.1.1/F83X-WR5, Accessed 28 March 2013, Jeremiah Greene in the entry for Russel Greene, 24 December 1760; Church of Jesus Christ of Latter Day Saints, "United States Census, 1800", database with images, *FamilySearch* (https://familysearch.org/ark:/61903/1:1:XH55-Y9L: accessed 24 April

Having said all of the information above, it is important to note an interesting back story of Russell Greene and his wife Patience Straight Moon. Information that does not only provide and confirm details of Russell Greene, but perhaps sheds some light on the absence and minimal information of his wife, Patience. In the manuscript entitled: "The Memoir of Philippe Wiltsee," Philippe's wife Sarah Greene, is the daughter of Russell Greene and Patience Straight Moon. This memoir is documented as being written by Sarah Greene, the same Sarah that is the daughter of Russell and Patience, and wife of Philippe Wiltsee, where she recounts her heritage, alongside with that of her husband's.[105]

She accounts the arrival of John Greene of Quidnessett, and his exact location of present-day Salem, Massachusetts about 1620. Although this date of arrival is conflicting as other credible information suggests 1626, nonetheless, according to Sarah Greene Waltsee, the year of his arrival into the Boston, Massachusetts area was 1620. Regardless of this date, Sarah mentions the location of where in England he came from was Salisbury, England and was Quakers. Sometime in the 1630's John Greene of Quidnessett left the Boston area to Rhode Island, and that he had three sons. The names Sarah provides in the memoir are: John, James and Thomas, with James being the head of the Greene branch that produces Nathaniel Greene. This latter person going on to historically known as General Nathaniel Greene of the Revolutionary War. Whereas, the head of the branch of this line would be that of Thomas. There is discrepancy on this however, as further investigation of this family line points to James as the head branch, not Thomas. Also, there is no indication of John Greene of Quidnessett ever having a son by the name of Thomas and is likely confused with one of the other two John Greene's that settled the Rhode Island colony. As John of Quidnessett is confirmed through other credible information of having six sons, with James Greene and John Robert Greene often being confused as the same man; and out of all of the names of his six sons, none of them are named Thomas.[106]

Having said that, Sarah goes on to provide the names of the children of Thomas. Their names being: James, Jeremiah and Gardener. The problem with this information is on the basis of confirmation of being directly descended from James Greene, son of John of Quidnessett,

---

2016), Russell Greene, 1800; Church of Jesus Christ of Latter Day Saints, "United States Census, 1830," database with images, *FamilySearch* (https://familysearch.org/ark:/61903/1:1:XHP6-FG8: accessed 24 April 2016), Russell Greene, Providence West Side of River, Providence, Rhode Island, United States; citing 86, NARA microfilm publication M19, (Washington D.C.: National Archives and Records Administration, n.d.), roll 168; FHL microfilm 22,267; Church of Jesus Christ of Latter Day Saints, "United States Census, 1810", database with images, *FamilySearch* (https://familysearch.org/ark:/61903/1:1:XH2G-R78: accessed 24 April 2016), Russell Green, 1810; Church of Jesus Christ of Latter Day Saints, "United States Census, 1790", database with images, *FamilySearch* (https://familysearch.org/ark:/61903/1:1:XHKT-SGT: accessed 24 April 2016), Russell Green, 1790; Church of Jesus Christ of Latter Day Saints, "United States Census, 1790", database with images, *FamilySearch* (https://familysearch.org/ark:/61903/1:1:XHKT-3HG: accessed 24 April 2016), Russell Green, 1790; Church of Jesus Christ of Latter Day Saints, United States Pensioners, 1818-1872. Name: Russell Green, Widow's Name: Patience Green, Pension City: Albany, State: New York' year range 1836-1848; Wiltsee 143

[105] Wiltsee 143
[106] Wiltsee 142

whose son had a son he named James, who in return had a son named Jeremiah that had a son named Russell that married Patience Straight Moon, and had Sarah. Sarah's son being the author of the memoir. This highlights her outstanding knowledge to this branch of the Greene family, however; confusion on the correct number of children and the son this branch is actually descended from. Nonetheless, she does go on to mention that Russell Greene is her father and that he fought in the American Revolution on the Continental Army.[107]

She elaborates that her father's father moved to Western Massachusetts, near the colonial village of Hancock and established a tavern. A tavern that would be known as the "ax handle tavern." According to the memoir, Sarah states the tavern would go by that name because of the ax that is hung above the entry. She additionally states that all of James's sons, including her father were poorly educated and could hardly read or writes; and that all of Russell's children were born in the tavern with exception to one of the daughters. This daughter being Lydia, who was born in the town of Hancock.[108]

What Sarah does mention is that aside from her father's participation in the Revolutionary War, he worked mostly contracted jobs, and engaged in very little business. The business engagements likely being exclusively with the "ax handle tavern," that was built by Russell's father James. While working the contracting jobs, these same contractors are stated as often hiring his daughters to assist with housework. Like their father, Sarah points out neither that herself nor her siblings received adequate education; however, all of them would receive minimal understanding of the basics of education. These basics being limited knowledge of reading, writing and arithmetic. In addition to this, Sarah states that at some point, with exception to the youngest sibling, Lydia, all of them would re-locate to Eric County, New York. The county that contains the city of Buffalo, in upstate New York.[109]

As for Patience, the wife of Russell Greene. Sarah states that she was actually adopted by a family with the last name of Moon. According to the information provided in the memoir, Patience was a shipwreck survivor and was saved by a man with the last name Moon, and was raised as one of his children. Based on her full name, Patience Straight Moon, it is likely that documents may have been recovered within the shipwreck, along with her that stated her last name was "Straight." Although, Sarah does not state this in the memoir, nor does she state the name and location as to where the shipwreck occurred. It is believed however; this shipwreck was somewhere off the coast of present-day Massachusetts or Rhode Island area.[110]

---

[107] Wiltsee 143-146
[108] Wiltsee 146-150
[109] Wiltsee 143-146
[110] Wiltsee 21, Number 142

Chapter X:
The Greene Family and the American Revolution

The American Revolution:

By the start of the American Revolution, many early colonists had brought up their numerous children with an ideology that was completely different than the thoughts and practices going on in England. The taxes and laws the British empire loosely enforced on the profitable American colonies would come to head. This would happen slowly as the Americans colonists knew of their own in-experience in battle. An in-experience the British empire was fully aware of; and therefore, did not see the American colonies as a threat.[111]

During this time frame, and early stages of the Revolution, first generation Americans had already created their own militias. A militia that was mostly used as protection from indigenous people attacks, nonetheless; the American colonists had an army in the event of a possible battle. Unfortunately, the American colony has a whole was not at all prepared for a war that was going to be as historically significant and defining, not only to the American colonists; but a symbol that set precedence of other nations under colonial rule to eventually follow suit.[112]

As for the Green's involvement, many men from this line; as well as, the other distant related Greens of Rhode Island would send an overwhelming amount of men to the Continental Army. An army that was formed mostly through the command of George Washington, who would ultimately become the First President of the United States of America. This man is credited as bringing the colonists together with the assistance of many trusted advisors. These advisors include a cousin to this line General Nathanael Greene.[113]

Nathanael Greene was born not far from the Greene's of Quidnessett Rhode Island (the origin of this line) in Warwick. This makes him an extremely close cousin to this branch as his father Richard was the fourth child of Sir Robert Greene of Gillingham, who was additionally the younger brother to John.[114] The latter being the direct line to this Green family line.

---

[111] William J. Duiker & Jackson J. Spielvogel, 486; Leckie, Robert. *George Washington's War: The Saga of the American Revolution*. New York: HarperCollins Publisher Incorporated 1992, 10-21; Stokesbury, James L. *A Short History of the American Revolution*. New York: HarperCollins Publisher, Incorporated, 1991, 97-261

[112] Bailyn, Bernard. *Face of Revolution: Personalities and Themes in the Struggle for American Independence*. New York: First Vintage Books Edition, 1992, 153-184; Golway, Terry. *Washington's General: Nathanael Greene and the Triumph of the American Revolution*. New York: Henry Holt and Company, 2005, 12-28; Lackie 10-21

[113] Wood, Gordon S. *Revolutionary Characters: What Made the Founders Different*. New York: The Penguin Press, 2006, 29-64

[114] Golway 12-16

Nonetheless, Nathanael would go on to become a notable figure within the American Revolution. A figure that rose to the ranks quite unexpectedly and to the surprise to many other Rhode Islanders. This surprise was because of a permanent limp that is believed to be an injury he received while very young growing up on his family's farm.[115]

At an early age, Nathanael would assist his father on the farm and as he grew to adulthood would take on various roles as an ironmaster and merchant. A combination of the two occupations, his early childhood injury that left him with a permanent limp, and his family raising all of their children to be Quakers that were against war and conflict; made his choice to become a military soldier a surprise to everyone. A surprise, however, that really should have been seen long before he became a man. In several source materials found on Nathanael, it is documented that he would push aside his daily learning materials of religion and Quaker practices, in favor to reading books on military tactics and strategies. Books that included Julius Caesar, Fredrick the Great and others to understand ways to organize and deceive the attacking enemy, which will prove to be useful in the years to come.[116]

At the start of his military career he became credited as being one of the men that founded the Kentish Guard of Rhode Island, and began as a private. A rank that he would maintain and showed no signs of going up into higher rank, because of his childhood injury that prevented him to do many of the physical military training practices the other soldiers could do. In the year of 1775, and before the British siege of Boston, Massachusetts, it is recorded that Nathanael would be granted the rank of General. A rank that was mysteriously given to him by what appears to have occurred over night. Some historians have suggested through investigative findings that his quick and sudden promotion from private to general will most likely remain a mystery.[117]

Speculation of this promotion however, can be seen everywhere in literature of Nathanael. One of the most common speculative reasons is due to his family's strong political leadership throughout the Rhode Island colony. Whatever the reason may be, it was a title that he would quickly prove to everyone in Rhode Island that was well earned. Not long following his promotion of Rhode Island General of military observations, he would lead a number of Rhode Island patriots to Boston; in order to assist Brigadier General George Washington on the British siege of Boston, following the defeat at Concord and Lexington the American colonists endured from the British army.[118]

The support, strategic and tactical military understanding Nathanael possessed from all of his readings over the years of military conflict rose him to the rank of General in the Continental Army; and because of the military support he immediately provided to George Washington in

---

[115] Golway 1-10; Middlekauff, Robert. *Glorious Cause: The American Revolution, The*. London: Oxford University Press, 1982, 464-470; Shaara, Jeff. *The Glorious Cause: A Novel of the American Revolution*. New York: The Random House Ballantine Publishing Group, 2002, xiv-xv
[116] Golway 1-6
[117] Leckie 10-21; Stokesbury 97-261
[118] Golway 1-11; Leckie 10-21; Middlekauff 464-470

Boston led him to be one of Washington's most trusted advisors. A trust that would make Washington call on Nathanael on more than one occasion. This includes his request from Washington to protect Long Island, save West Point, on the Hudson River in upstate New York and to support the American colonists fight against the British Army in the Carolinas and Georgia colonies.[119]

Although Nathanael would never get the notoriety he apparently wanted and dreamed about growing up on a Rhode Island farm, he would prove to be extremely pivotal for the colonists' fight against the British empire. One of the reasons behind him not gaining the notoriety he was hoping to obtain, was his sudden and unfortunate illness in August of 1776, right before the British sack of New York that prevented him from leading the patriot soldiers and fight of the British troops; and whether or not Nathanael's absence made the deciding factor between victory or defeat will remain forever a mystery. The only thing that is for certain is the due to the poor fortification of an area along Long Island that would prove to be pivotal is what is blamed on the reason for America losing New York to the British.[120]

As for the other to mention requests Nathanael received from Washington, the protection to West Point came when Nathanael could see the that the fort was going to be overtaken by the British Army. This last minute support by Nathanael proved pivotal in the northern colonies. The preservation of West Point would allow the Continental Army an access point to continue supplying their men with weapons and other previsions. As a result of this success he would be called upon in 1780 to head down south and support General Haratio Gates with his failures in the Carolinas and Georgia colonies. Although it is recorded that Nathanael had strong hate and resentment to General Gates, he would ultimately head down south to support Gates in his series of defeats.[121]

Sadly, Nathanael would not win a single military battle; but his military tactics and strategies to deter the adversaries lead to no additional ground to be taken by the British in the final stages of the Revolutionary War. The success of Nathanael's ability to keep the British Army from acquiring more territory in the south ultimately led to their retreat with no one being declared a victor. Following the British retreat, Nathanael would receive a plantation in Georgia a place that he would live out the remainder of his days.[122]

In light of the Revolutionary war participants of this Green family line, Willett "Gardener" Greene, son of Russell Greene is recorded in military records as being a soldier in the Continental Army during the American Revolution. The two battles it is believed that he participated in are the Boston siege that lasted from 1775-1776, the battle of Rhode Island and

---

[119] Golway 1-6; Middlekauff 464-470
[120] Fast, Howard. *The Crossing*. New York: Open Road, 1971, 15-85; Middlekauff 464-470; Shaara 10-90
[121] Leckie 10-21; Middlekauff 464-470; Stokesbury 97-261
[122] Middlekauff 464-470

the Battle of Freeman's Farm in upstate New York. As for his military ranks, it is believed he went in as a private and finished his military career as a Corporal.[123]

The map graphic below, which is additionally featured in Appendix I, show some of the major battles fought during the Revolutionary war. This map provides information on the location of battles with the known locations of this Green family line. The purpose of this map, along with the limitation of military records, will assist in the likely battles this line participated in during the war.

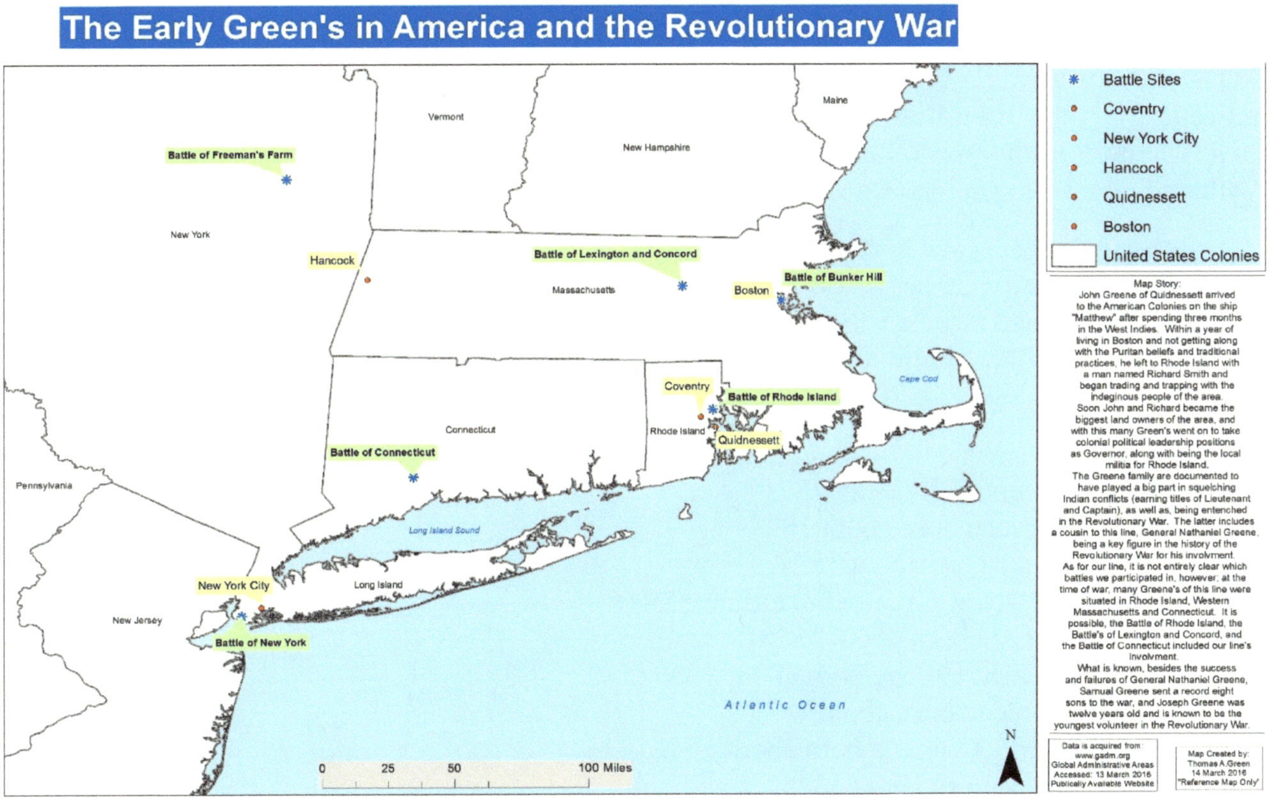

Figure 4: Green, Thomas A. 2016. Data collection acquired from www.gadm.org; accessed 13 March 2016

---

[123] Massachusetts Secretary of the Commonwealth, Volume 6, 831

Chapter XI:
The Greene's Settle A Newly Independent Nation

Generation VI: Willet "Gardner" Greene

Willet "Gardner" Greene was born 23 October 1799 in Hancock, Berkshire, Massachusetts to Russell Greene and Freelove Hopkins. Gardner married Polly Ann Mary Eldridge about 1819, and based on public records Polly was born in Hancock, Berkshire, Massachusetts as well. This means that Willet and Polly got married to one another prior to their move to Clarence, Erie, New York. A location that is mentioned in his sister Sarah's manuscript, "The Memoir of Philippe Wiltsee" that the entire family, with exception to the youngest sibling, Lydia, all moved to Clarence, a village about sixty miles due east of Buffalo, New York.[124]

His wife Polly was born on 01 January 1801 to parents that are not entirely known, however; information on her that is known is her marriage to Willett Gardner Greene, they are believed to have had at least ten children and are recorded as being laid to rest in present-day Michigan.[125] As for the child, they are listed below with the child that is directed descended to this family line is highlighted in bold:

1. Almira S. Greene born about 1820-1851
2. Nancy Greene born about 1821
3. Philena Greene born about 1823
4. Polly Greene born about 1824
5. **Samuel Watson Greene born about 1826**
6. Betsey Greene born about 1828
7. George Willett Greene born about 1830
8. Matilda Greene born about 1837
9. Willet Gardner Greene born about 1842
10. Eliza Greene born about 1845

Based on the records found, the last two children are listed as being born in Michigan. The reason for this further migration west deals with the 1823 completion of the Erie Canal and Michigan being referred to as the promised land for New Englanders. This last reason is because of the growing northern population with the average colonist having ten children, which resulted in limitation of land and resulted in a call by the colonists for more land. Aside from this, it is

---

[124] Church of Jesus Christ of Latter Day Saints, "Rhode Island Births and Christenings, 1600-1914," database, *FamilySearch* (https://familysearch.org/ark:/61903/1:1:F83X-4M7: accessed 24 April 2016), Jeremiah Greene in entry for Gardner Greene, 15 Dec 1763; citing Rhode Island, USA, reference v 1 p 141; FHL microfilm 925,978;
[125] Wiltsee 144

important to mention the next generation of this direct line will be back in New York with Samuel Greene, son of Willett, participation in the Civil War.[126]

In addition to this, records do indicate Willet Gardener was a Union Soldier Volunteer from the state of Michigan; and was assigned to the 8th Regiment of Michigan in the Infantry B Company with the rank of private. As a volunteer, it can be left to the assumption that Willett Gardner was only called upon, in the event of a conflict, most of these conflicts likely being with indigenous people based on the time period. An assumption that can explain why he is listed as joining and leaving as a private.[127]

The reason for Willett only being a Volunteer in the Michigan Union Army, is because of his age. As mentioned earlier, records indicate the first eight of his children are listed as being born in New York; whereas the last two children were born in Michigan. Based on the birth of these final two children, 1842 and 1845 respectively, this would have made Willett Gardner in his mid-40's, and was therefore; not likely necessary for him to enlist.[128]

Aside from Willett's volunteering in the Michigan Union military, the only other information is he was farmer. The farm that he owned is somewhere in the vicinity of Clinton, Michigan. This is the same town that he is presently listed as passing away in and being laid to rest on 17 August 1880. His wife, Polly, is listed as passing away on 08 May 1878. Two years before her husband, and being laid to rest in Clinton, Michigan as well.[129]

---

[126] Church of Jesus Christ of Latter Day Saints, "United States General Index to Pension Files, 1861-1934", database with images, *FamilySearch* (https://familysearch.org/ark:/61903/1:1:KDYP-ZRN: accessed 24 April 2016), Willett G Green, 1863; Dempsey, Jack, Michigan and the Civil War: A Great and Bloody Sacrifice, History Press, 2011; Ingall, David & Kevin Risko, Michigan Civil Landmarks, 2016, History Press

[127] Church of Jesus Christ of Latter Day Saints, "United States Civil War Soldiers Index, 1861-1865," database, *FamilySearch* (https://familysearch.org/ark:/61903/1:1:F9T8-F2R: accessed 24 April 2016), Willet G. Green, Private, Company B, 8th Regiment, Michigan Infantry, Union; citing NARA microfilm publication M545 (Washington D.C.: National Archives and Records Administration, n.d.), roll 16; FHL microfilm 881,929; Church of Jesus Christ of Latter Day Saints, "United States Civil War Soldiers Index, 1861-1865," database, *FamilySearch* (https://familysearch.org/ark:/61903/1:1:F9T8-FTL: accessed 24 April 2016), Willett P. Green (alias: Willet G. Green), Private, Company B, 8th Regiment, Michigan Infantry, Union; citing NARA microfilm publication M545 (Washington D.C.: National Archives and Records Administration, n.d.), roll 16; FHL microfilm 881,929; Church of Jesus Christ of Latter Day Saints, "United States Civil War Soldiers Index, 1861-1865," database, *FamilySearch* (https://familysearch.org/ark:/61903/1:1:FSHG-LPF: accessed 24 April 2016), Willett C. Green (alias: Willet G. Green), Private, Company B, 8th Regiment, Michigan Infantry, Union; citing NARA microfilm publication M545 (Washington D.C.: National Archives and Records Administration, n.d.), roll 16; FHL microfilm 881,929.

[128] Church of Jesus Christ of Latter Day Saints, "United States Civil War Soldiers Index, 1861-1865," database, *FamilySearch* (https://familysearch.org/ark:/61903/1:1:F9T8-F2R: accessed 24 April 2016); Church of Jesus Christ of Latter Day Saints, "United States Civil War Soldiers Index, 1861-1865," database, *FamilySearch* (https://familysearch.org/ark:/61903/1:1:F9T8-FTL: accessed 24 April 2016); Church of Jesus Christ of Latter Day Saints, "United States Civil War Soldiers Index, 1861-1865," database, *FamilySearch* (https://familysearch.org/ark:/61903/1:1:F9T8-FTL: accessed 24 April 2016)

[129] Church of Jesus Christ of Latter Day Saints, "United States General Index to Pension Files, 1861-1934", database with images, *FamilySearch* (https://familysearch.org/ark:/61903/1:1:KDYP-ZRN: accessed 24 April 2016), Willett G Green, 1863.

Generation VII: Samuel Watson Greene

Samuel Watson Greene was born 23 February 1826 in New York to Willet "Gardner" Greene and Polly Ann Mary Eldridge. He married twice. The first wife is believed to have been a woman by the name of Catherine Clark, as indicated in 1870 census records. Records that were likely from old information, as other records state he had already been married to Julia, since the mid-1850. The name of Catherine's parents is not known nor is it known whether or not the two of them had any children. There is belief the two had one child together, a girl, however; the name of this child is not for certain. The only other information of this first wife is she re-married and lived out the rest of her life with her second husband in St. John's, Michigan.[130]

His second marriage is recorded. This marriage is in public records of taking place in Clinton, Dallas, Michigan sometime in 1855. The name of this second wife, depending on sources, is Julia Dutton or Julia Dayton. She is the daughter of Anson Dutton (Dayton) and Sarah Adams. Julia was born 13 May 1836 in Grand Blanc, Genesee, Michigan.[131] Together Samuel and Julia had four children. These four children are listed below and the name of the child that is the direct descendant to this line is highlighted in bold:

1. Ella Green born about 1856
2. Edmund Green born about 1858
3. **George Willett Green born about 1860**
4. Mary Green born about 1862

The absence of the "e" at the last name of the children is important to notice, as it is Samuel Watson Greene, who is responsible for making the change to this Green family branch. According to source, these sources most of them being information passed down from one generation to the next, is Samuel Greene did not want the northern Greene's to be associated with the distant southern Greene cousins that were slave owners and were for the continuation of

---

[130] Church of Jesus Christ of Latter Day Saints, FamilySearch.org, United States Census Records, 1860, https://familysearch.org/pal:MM9.1.1/MCHJ-W8T, Accessed 23 July 2012, Records of Samuel W Green, Oswego, New York. Church of Jesus Christ of Latter Day Saints, FamilySearch.org, Michigan, Marriages, 1868-1925, index and images, https://familysearch.org/pal:/MM9.1.1/NQ7B-JVX, Accessed 20 July 2012
Church of Jesus Christ of Latter Day Saints, FamilySearch.org, United States Census Records, 1880, index, https://familysearch.org/pal:/MM9.1.1/MWS9-2RQ, Accessed 20 July 2012, Samuel Green, Dallas, Clinton, Michigan. Church of Jesus Christ of Latter Day Saints, FamilySearch.org, United States Census Records, 1870, index and images, https://familysearch.org/pal:/MM9.1.1/MHHF-W22, Accessed 20 July 2012, Samuel Green in household of Samuel Green, Michigan, United States.
Church of Jesus Christ of Latter Day Saints, United States City Directories, 1821-1989, Provo, Utah, USA: Ancestry.com Operations, Inc., 2011, Accessed 22 July 2012.
[131] Church of Jesus Christ of Latter Day Saints, FamilySearch.org, United States Census Records, 1860, https://familysearch.org/pal:MM9.1.1/MCHJ-W8T, Accessed 23 July 2012, Records of Samuel W Green, Oswego, New York. Church of Jesus Christ of Latter Day Saints, FamilySearch.org, Michigan, Marriages, 1868-1925

slavery. This remove of the "e" of the last name was his way to show his stance on slavery and support to the north.[132]

Despite this change, records of Samuel Watson Greene and his involvement in the Civil War is not entirely known. All that is known is it is stated he participated in the Civil War; but the military company of the Union Army in Michigan is not known. While it is possible he may have gone into the same company as his father, Infantry B Company, of the 8th Brigade, this cannot be confirmed. This additionally includes the name of the battle or battles that Samuel was involved in. The only other information known of Samuel Greene is was a farmer, and at some point he moved to New York, and then returned to Michigan prior to his death.[133]

The reason for the knowledge of this migration to New York and back to Michigan is based on the public records that state his last two children, George Willett Green and Mary Green as being born in New York. It is likely; their birth place in New York was around the same area their father had initially migrated from to his own arrival in Michigan. This town being Clarence, Erie, New York. Nonetheless, it is recorded that he died on 09 May 1883, and was laid to rest in St. John's, Michigan, along with his wife Julia.[134]

This place of rest however, must be known that after thorough investigation of records and first-hand travels to the St. John's area, it has been discovered that Samuel Watson Greene's resting place is not in St. John's, Michigan. In fact, he and his son George are often confused between a different Samuel and George that have completely different birth dates. The correct Samuel and George Green are buried next to each other in Pewamo, Ionia, Michigan. In addition to this, investigation additionally uncovered that Samuel Greene had apparently divorced from his second wife Julia as well. Thus the reason why Samuel is buried next to his son.[135]

---

[132] Green, Iva A., Personal Green Family Archives and Records, 1800's-2016
[133] Church of Jesus Christ of Latter Day Saints, FamilySearch.org, United States Census Records, 1860, https://familysearch.org/pal:MM9.1.1/MCHJ-W8T, Accessed 23 July 2012, Records of Samuel W Green, Oswego, New York. Church of Jesus Christ of Latter Day Saints, FamilySearch.org, Michigan, Marriages, 1868-1925, index and images, https://familysearch.org/pal:/MM9.1.1/NQ7B-JVX, Accessed 20 July 2012
[134] Church of Jesus Christ of Latter Day Saints, FamilySearch.org, United States Census Records, 1860, https://familysearch.org/pal:MM9.1.1/MCHJ-W8T, Accessed 23 July 2012, Records of Samuel W Green, Oswego, New York. Church of Jesus Christ of Latter Day Saints, FamilySearch.org, Michigan, Marriages, 1868-1925, index and images, https://familysearch.org/pal:/MM9.1.1/NQ7B-JVX, Accessed 20 July 2012
[135] Green Family Records 1880-2016

Chapter XII:
Settling the Frontier

Generation VIII: George Willet Green

George Willet Green was born 31 August 1861 in Clarence, Erie, New York. There is some source information that lists his birth year as being in 1860 or 1862. These recorded years of birth are going to be presumed to be in-correct, despite his headstone stating his date of birth as 31 August 1860. The reason behind the likely headstone discrepancy will be explained in the preceding paragraphs. George is the third of four children and second son of Samuel Watson Greene and Julia Datton/Dayton (both spellings found), and according new numerous sources was born in New York. In fact, he is apparently the only child of Samuel and Julia's four children to be born in New York with all of the others being born in Michigan.[136]

The likely reason behind the headstone discrepancy; as well as, being the only child of the four siblings to be born in New York is as follows: First, indication of the timeframe is of extreme importance. By 1860, the United States was on the brink of Civil War as the south had

---

[136] Green, Personal Green Family Archives and Records, 1800's-2016; Church of Jesus Christ of Latter Day Saints, FamilySearch.org, Michigan, Deaths and Burials, 1800-1995, Index, https://familysearch.org/pal:/MM9.1.1/FHN2-H89, Accessed 20 July 2012, Samuel Green in entry for George Green, 1860; Church of Jesus Christ of Latter Day Saints, FamilySearch.org, Michigan, Marriages, 1868-1925, index and images, https://familysearch.org/pal:/MM9.1.1/NQ7B-JV6, Accessed 20 July 2012, George W. Green, 1889; Church of Jesus Christ of Latter Day Saints, FamilySearch.org, United States Census Records, 1900, index and images, https://familysearch.org/pal:/MM9.1.1/M911-TPT, Accessed 20 July 2012, George W Green, ED 18 Victor Township, Clinton, Michigan, United States.
Church of Jesus Christ of Latter Day Saints, FamilySearch.org, Michigan, Marriages, 1868-1925, index and images, https://familysearch.org/pal:/MM9.1.1/NQ7B-JVF, Accessed 20 July 2012, Julia A. Dutton in entry for George W. Green and Lena A. Harter, 1889; Church of Jesus Christ of Latter Day Saints, FamilySearch.org, Michigan, Marriages, 1868-1925, index and images, https://familysearch.org/pal:/MM9.1.1/NQ7B-JVX, Accessed 20 July 2012, Sam W. Green in entry for George W. Green and Lena A. Harter, 1889.

already succeeded the union to create the United Confederate States. A time that clearly shows that America was divided and it was going to take a lot of administrative and heavy combat fighting with no guarantee of success to bring the nation back together. While the American Civil War would never make it as far north into the state of Michigan, the state was one of the most vocal states in the entire nation that opposed slavery.[137]

A combination of Michigan's strong opposition to slavery and far northern geographic location is which resulted in the state being one of the first to recruit a large number of volunteers. Volunteers that are recorded as coming from all over the state of Michigan, to Detroit for processing and making their tribe to battle. This first wave is suggested to be in the thousands, and was in response to the President of the United States, Abraham Lincoln's request for all northern states to send all abled men to fight. A request that George Green's father Samuel responded to; and in doing so, is believed to have taken his family as far as New York to be closer to relatives. Relatives that had not left Clarence, Erie, New York.[138]

According to the manuscript written by David Ignall and Karin Risko, the first wave of military troops sent out to fight in the Civil War, were sent out sometime in May of 1861. This would make Samuel's wife about six months pregnant with George, at which time was born in August. It is believed George's father fought in Pennsylvania and New York, and perhaps as far

---

[137] Green, Personal Green Family Archives and Records, 1800's-2016; Church of Jesus Christ of Latter Day Saints, FamilySearch.org, Michigan, Deaths and Burials, 1800-1995, Index, https://familysearch.org/pal:/MM9.1.1/FHN2-H89, Accessed 20 July 2012, Samuel Green in entry for George Green, 1860; Church of Jesus Christ of Latter Day Saints, FamilySearch.org, Michigan, Marriages, 1868-1925, index and images, https://familysearch.org/pal:/MM9.1.1/NQ7B-JV6, Accessed 20 July 2012, George W. Green, 1889; Church of Jesus Christ of Latter Day Saints, FamilySearch.org, United States Census Records, 1900, index and images, https://familysearch.org/pal:/MM9.1.1/M911-TPT, Accessed 20 July 2012, George W Green, ED 18 Victor Township, Clinton, Michigan, United States.
Church of Jesus Christ of Latter Day Saints, FamilySearch.org, Michigan, Marriages, 1868-1925, index and images, https://familysearch.org/pal:/MM9.1.1/NQ7B-JVF, Accessed 20 July 2012, Julia A. Dutton in entry for George W. Green and Lena A. Harter, 1889; Church of Jesus Christ of Latter Day Saints, FamilySearch.org, Michigan, Marriages, 1868-1925, index and images, https://familysearch.org/pal:/MM9.1.1/NQ7B-JVX, Accessed 20 July 2012, Sam W. Green in entry for George W. Green and Lena A. Harter, 1889

[138] Green, Family Records 1880-2016; Green, Family Records 1880-2016; Church of Jesus Christ of Latter Day Saints, FamilySearch.org, Michigan, Deaths and Burials, 1800-1995, Index, https://familysearch.org/pal:/MM9.1.1/FHN2-H89, Accessed 20 July 2012, Samuel Green in entry for George Green, 1860; Church of Jesus Christ of Latter Day Saints, FamilySearch.org, Michigan, Marriages, 1868-1925, index and images, https://familysearch.org/pal:/MM9.1.1/NQ7B-JV6, Accessed 20 July 2012, George W. Green, 1889; Church of Jesus Christ of Latter Day Saints, FamilySearch.org, United States Census Records, 1900, index and images, https://familysearch.org/pal:/MM9.1.1/M911-TPT, Accessed 20 July 2012, George W Green, ED 18 Victor Township, Clinton, Michigan, United States.
Church of Jesus Christ of Latter Day Saints, FamilySearch.org, Michigan, Marriages, 1868-1925, index and images, https://familysearch.org/pal:/MM9.1.1/NQ7B-JVF, Accessed 20 July 2012, Julia A. Dutton in entry for George W. Green and Lena A. Harter, 1889; Church of Jesus Christ of Latter Day Saints, FamilySearch.org, Michigan, Marriages, 1868-1925, index and images, https://familysearch.org/pal:/MM9.1.1/NQ7B-JVX, Accessed 20 July 2012, Sam W. Green in entry for George W. Green and Lena A. Harter, 1889.

south as Northern Virginia; however, the battles he participated in are not for certain. Something else that is not for certain is within a year it is believed that he was injured enough in one of the battles to be honorably discharged and allowed to return home to Michigan. This latter part explains the reason for George's sister and the youngest child of Samuel and Julia to be born in Michigan. Overtime, many other Michigan men would volunteer as it is recorded that the state sent an estimated ninety thousand men to fight in the Civil War. Of these men that would fight in battles, estimates indicate fifteen thousand dead, in battles that took place in southern Indiana, Ohio, West Virginia, Pennsylvania and New York.[139]

Despite being born in New York; George grew up as a Michigander. On 09 March 1889, he married Lena Amanda Harter in Ithaca, Michigan. At the time of their marriage, George was twenty-eight-years-old, while his wife was sixteen. Based on personal family records, the two of them had their first child out of wed lock, as the child was born in January with the wedding taking place in March. This is a very surprising revolution as cultural customs at the time seriously frowned upon any woman to have a child out of wed lock.[140] Nonetheless, the two of them would have a total of three children. These children are listed below and the child that is the direct descendant to this family line is highlighted in bold:

1. **James Samuel Green born 15 January 1889**
2. Virgil Green born 1890
3. Cordelia Green born

While the two of them were married, George is recorded as being the head livestock foreman for Naldrett Farms, a farm that was located somewhere in the Ithaca, Michigan area. As the head livestock foreman, the limited records state he carried for the animals; and would have likely been considered a veterinarian without a veterinarian degree. The reason for this likelihood is based on the level of care it is suggested he provided to the animals, while

---

[139] Ingall, David & Kevin Risko, Michigan Civil Landmarks, 2016, History Press; Dempsey, Jack, Michigan and the Civil War: A Great and Bloody Sacrifice, History Press, 2011

[140] Green, Personal Green Family Archives and Records, 1800's-2016; Church of Jesus Christ of Latter Day Saints, FamilySearch.org, Michigan, Deaths and Burials, 1800-1995, Index, https://familysearch.org/pal:/MM9.1.1/FHN2-H89, Accessed 20 July 2012, Samuel Green in entry for George Green, 1860; Church of Jesus Christ of Latter Day Saints, FamilySearch.org, Michigan, Marriages, 1868-1925, index and images, https://familysearch.org/pal:/MM9.1.1/NQ7B-JV6, Accessed 20 July 2012, George W. Green, 1889; Church of Jesus Christ of Latter Day Saints, FamilySearch.org, United States Census Records, 1900, index and images, https://familysearch.org/pal:/MM9.1.1/M911-TPT, Accessed 20 July 2012, George W Green, ED 18 Victor Township, Clinton, Michigan, United States.
Church of Jesus Christ of Latter Day Saints, FamilySearch.org, Michigan, Marriages, 1868-1925, index and images, https://familysearch.org/pal:/MM9.1.1/NQ7B-JVF, Accessed 20 July 2012, Julia A. Dutton in entry for George W. Green and Lena A. Harter, 1889; Church of Jesus Christ of Latter Day Saints, FamilySearch.org, Michigan, Marriages, 1868-1925, index and images, https://familysearch.org/pal:/MM9.1.1/NQ7B-JVX, Accessed 20 July 2012, Sam W. Green in entry for George W. Green and Lena A. Harter, 1889.

employed at Naldrett Farms. It is while employed their and caring for the animals in the winter of 1912 that he caught pneumonia and died.[141]

At the time of his death, records indicate he and his wife had divorced and she was already re-married and had other children with her new husband. This final finding was only discovered after taking a personal trip to Michigan to learn more about George W. Green, the father of James S. Green, who is the father of George W. "Bud" Green, which is the father to this author. The finding included the location and visit to his grave site in Pewamo, Michigan on 19 July 2015. At his grave site, and following meeting distant relatives in the area on that same day, it was learned the reason why both George W Green and his father Samuel W. Green were buried together with in a location without wives. This is because both men at some point divorced, and their former wives were buried elsewhere with their current husbands.[142]

There is still some mystery, as three other gravestones were clustered with the two men, however; these three other headstones had no words, only carvings of leaves. Pictures were taken of the grave site by the author and the author's oldest child. As for George W. Green's ex-wife, Lena Amanda Harter, all which is known is she was born 27 November 1873, and after the death of George, she married a man with the last name of Briggs, and died in Milwaukee, Wisconsin, 20 March 1969. As for Lena's parents, they are listed as being James T. Harter and

---

[141] Green, Personal Green Family Archives and Records, 1800's-2016; Church of Jesus Christ of Latter Day Saints, FamilySearch.org, Michigan, Deaths and Burials, 1800-1995, Index, https://familysearch.org/pal:/MM9.1.1/FHN2-H89, Accessed 20 July 2012, Samuel Green in entry for George Green, 1860; Church of Jesus Christ of Latter Day Saints, FamilySearch.org, Michigan, Marriages, 1868-1925, index and images, https://familysearch.org/pal:/MM9.1.1/NQ7B-JV6, Accessed 20 July 2012, George W. Green, 1889; Church of Jesus Christ of Latter Day Saints, FamilySearch.org, United States Census Records, 1900, index and images, https://familysearch.org/pal:/MM9.1.1/M911-TPT, Accessed 20 July 2012, George W Green, ED 18 Victor Township, Clinton, Michigan, United States; Church of Jesus Christ of Latter Day Saints, FamilySearch.org, Michigan, Marriages, 1868-1925, index and images, https://familysearch.org/pal:/MM9.1.1/NQ7B-JVF, Accessed 20 July 2012, Julia A. Dutton in entry for George W. Green and Lena A. Harter, 1889; Church of Jesus Christ of Latter Day Saints, FamilySearch.org, Michigan, Marriages, 1868-1925, index and images, https://familysearch.org/pal:/MM9.1.1/NQ7B-JVX, Accessed 20 July 2012, Sam W. Green in entry for George W. Green and Lena A. Harter, 1889.

[142] Green, Family Records 1880-2016; Green, Family Records 1880-2016; Church of Jesus Christ of Latter Day Saints, FamilySearch.org, Michigan, Deaths and Burials, 1800-1995, Index, https://familysearch.org/pal:/MM9.1.1/FHN2-H89, Accessed 20 July 2012, Samuel Green in entry for George Green, 1860; Church of Jesus Christ of Latter Day Saints, FamilySearch.org, Michigan, Marriages, 1868-1925, index and images, https://familysearch.org/pal:/MM9.1.1/NQ7B-JV6, Accessed 20 July 2012, George W. Green, 1889; Church of Jesus Christ of Latter Day Saints, FamilySearch.org, United States Census Records, 1900, index and images, https://familysearch.org/pal:/MM9.1.1/M911-TPT, Accessed 20 July 2012, George W Green, ED 18 Victor Township, Clinton, Michigan, United States.
Church of Jesus Christ of Latter Day Saints, FamilySearch.org, Michigan, Marriages, 1868-1925, index and images, https://familysearch.org/pal:/MM9.1.1/NQ7B-JVF, Accessed 20 July 2012, Julia A. Dutton in entry for George W. Green and Lena A. Harter, 1889; Church of Jesus Christ of Latter Day Saints, FamilySearch.org, Michigan, Marriages, 1868-1925, index and images, https://familysearch.org/pal:/MM9.1.1/NQ7B-JVX, Accessed 20 July 2012, Sam W. Green in entry for George W. Green and Lena A. Harter, 1889.

Catheriana Stnac, and were born in Newark, Gratiot, Michigan. Aside from the information found of their divorce and her re-marriage prior to her first husband, George, death; court records found additionally show that she had re-married at least two more time after her divorce from George Green. The last husband as the last name of Briggs, as mentioned earlier. Thus the reason as my siblings and me were growing up, all we knew was she lives in Milwaukee, Wisconsin, and was referred to as Grandma Briggs.[143]

---

[143] https://familysearch.org/pal:/MM9.1.1/FC6P-QF2, George W. Green, birth: 1861, place Michigan. Age 28, Spouse's name: Lena A. Harter; Spouse's date of birth: 1873. Spouse's birth place Michigan. Spouse's age: 16, Event Date: 9 March 1889. Event Place: Ithaca, Gratiot Co., Michigan. Father's Name: Samuel W. Green. Mother's Name: Julia A. Dalton. Spouse's father's Name: James T. Harter. Spouse's Mother's Name: Catheriana Stnac. Race: White. Indexing Project (batch) number: M73660-5. System Origin: Michigan-EASy gs film number: 985694, reference id: BK 1866-1903 V. A-C. Collection: George W. Green, "Michigan, Marriages, 1822-1995" https://familysearch.org/pal:/MM9.1.1/F4R5-9QV. https://familysearch.org/pal:/MM9.1.1/F4R5-9QV. Name: James S. Green, gender: Male birth date: 15 January 1889. Birthplace: Dallas, Clinton, Michigan. Father's Name George W. Green, Mother's Name Lena. Indexing project (batch) Number: C73354-4. System origin: Michigan-CDM, gs film number: 987079. Collection: George W. Green in entry for James S. Green, "Michigan, Births and Christenings, 1775-1995" https://familysearch.org/pal:/MM9.1.1/MHCL-N4M. George Green, birth year (estimated) 1861, gender: Male, Age (original) 9 years. Race: White, birth place: Michigan. Event place: Michigan. James, Virgil and Cordelia.

Chapter XIII:
A Spotlight on a Modern American Military Hero

Generation IX: James Samuel Green

James Samuel Green was born in Ithaca, Michigan to George Willet Green and Lena Amanda Harter. He was born 15 January 1889, as stated on his birth certificate. A document that was found in the possession of the author's aunt, who was the older half-sister of George Willett Green, the son of James Samuel Green. This birth certificate was found with many other keep sake items that belonged to James Green; which include numerous military records of re-enlistments. Many of these records, particular his military records shed light on the reason behind the confusion of his birth date. These records, along with letters that were either written by him or to him, indicate that he lied about his age to join the military.[144]

His decision to join the military was something that he had his younger brother do with him, in order to ensure of their own well-being; as well as, their mother and younger sister. At the time of their enlistment, James and Virgil's parents had divorced and is believed this divorce took place sometime when the boys were about ten to twelve-years-old. Although there is belief that James and his younger brother Virgil remained in contact with their father George, even after the divorce, the revelation of these two boys only being about fourteen and fifteen-years-old at the time of their enlistment suggests otherwise.[145]

In addition to the military records, letters and paperwork that were kept inside an old army trunk were photographs. In one photograph, both James and his younger brother Virgil are pictured together in their military uniforms (Appendix J). This photo of these two young men

---
[144] Green, Personal Green Family Archives and Records, 1800's-2016
[145] Green Family Records 1800's-2016

provides evidence of their deception, in order to join the military for the purpose of sending half of their earnings to their mother to ensure the well-being of her and their young sister. Just at first glance of this photo, there is no doubt both boys (James Green and Virgil Green) were approximately fourteen and fifteen years of age, and posing as young men that were at least seventeen and eighteen. Thus the reason for one military record of his 1908 reenlistment at the age of nineteen, with a birth date of 06 January (Appendix G, Figure 14). This date although wrong, confirms of his enlistment at the age of about fifteen, which makes his brother who is one year younger to have been about fourteen.

Prior to finding these military records, verbal information about grandfather James Green, father of Georgia and George Green, only joined the military along with his younger brother following the death of their father. These initial pasted down stories however, proved to be in-correct as their father died in 1912. If both James and Virgil did in fact join the military after their father's death, they would have been about twenty-three and twenty-four, respectively. Therefore, neither boys would have had to lie about their ages to join. This latter statement, additionally being a part of the story. Instead, James Green and his brother went off to the military prior to their father's death.

This revelation leads to a second discovery, which is James's younger brother is likely to have served one military tour with his brother; and once over, returned back home to Michigan. It is at this point in time that both brothers are assumed to have parted ways. The reason for this likelihood is because the information on Virgil, although limited, has him back in Michigan. James, on the other hand, had a re-enlistment at the age of 19 and is listed as experienced on his paperwork, where he is assigned to Fort Sill Oklahoma. As for his brother Virgil, there is evidence that he was already back in Michigan at the time of both boys' fathers passing in 1912, as he is the one giving the information for the death certificate.

As for Lena Harter, James and Virgil Green's mother, she is recorded as remarrying and later moving to Milwaukee, Wisconsin with the boys' younger sister Cordelia sometime after 1912. This re-location is believed to have occurred within the same year or not long after the passing of her ex-husband George Willet Green. By remaining in the area, before her ex-husband's death suggests the possibility that all three children remained in contact with their father.[146]

Returning back to James Green, his first enlistment had him stationed at Washington Barracks, in the state of Washington. Evidence that was found to support this is available within the United States Registry of Enlistments, 1794-1914. In this registry, documents state that James Green was stationed at Washington Barracks, where he stayed for two years. The interesting thing about the records found with all of his records in my possession, is there is no record of the first enlistment. Only the mention on the enlistment I have at the age of 19 is he is experienced. Information states of his enlistment in 1908; sent him to Fort Sill, Oklahoma. A military base that is directly north of Lawton, Comanche, Oklahoma. I have been unable to locate enlistment papers for the underage enlistment. I have only proof of him first in the Michigan Militia and the two years at Washington Barracks. These records are apparently in-complete, as personal artifacts in the author's possession that are shown in Appendix G, point

---

[146] Green Family Records 1800's-2016

out that his 1908 enlistment at the age of nineteen is a re-enlistment as an experienced private into the United States Army. Military records that have him at Fort Sill, Oklahoma; which is something that was correct in the United States Registry of Enlistments. A military post that he will remain serving for more than thirty years.

Throughout his military career, James Samuel Green work in ordinance and in the motor pool. The latter job being his primary duty. During the early years of his serves, there are no records that indicate he fought in World War I, despite being old enough to go. In fact, there are no records to indicate he participated in a military conflict of any kind. This could be the reason as to why he was so determined to participate in World War II, along with his two step-sons. An event that will be discussed latter in this chapter.

While stationed at Fort Sill, Oklahoma he would become very acquainted and friends with the two men. The names of these men being Robert Sinclair and James O'Connell. These two men and he will end up having one thing in common. All three of them fall in love with a woman by the name of Abbie Glenn. A woman that will eventually become the wife of James Green. All three men will become very close during their time at Fort Sill. A bond that will be broken due to one of the men's infidelity and the others untimely death. All of which being discussed in the following chapter.

The marriage to Abbie Glenn occurred sometime around 1922 or 1923. This will be the first marriage for James, but the third marriage for Abbie. Abbie was born in Saint Joseph, Missouri in 05 March 1891 with her full name being Abbie Lusina Glenn. Her parents were Robert Neff Glenn and Estella (Stella) Elizabeth Jordon.[147] Together James Green and Abbie Glenn would have two children. Both children are listed below with the child that is the descendant to this direct line being highlighted in bold:

1. Georgia Green born 08 October 1925, Fort Sill, Lawton, Comanche, Oklahoma
2. **George Green born 03 April 1931, Fort Sill, Lawton, Comanche, Oklahoma**

A couple years prior to his marriage to Abbie Glenn, personal records of James Green that are still in this families' possession, indicate in 1921 he traveled to Magdalena, Socorro, New Mexico by rail to purchase a homestead. A state that had only been granted statehood for a mere decade. Pictures of this homestead are still in existence and can be seen in Appendix J. Although the pictures are dated as being taken in 1932, when James and Abbie's youngest child was a year old, paperwork provides proof of the land acquisition as occurring in 1921.[148] In addition to this, the map graphic at the top of the next page shows the present location of Lawton, Oklahoma and Magdalena, New Mexico. This same map graphic is additionally featured within Appendix I, which is at the back of this manuscript. The purpose for this is to allow the reader to better view the supportive narrative that is located to the right side of the image.

---

[147] Green Family Records 1800's-2016
[148] Green Family Records 1800's-2016

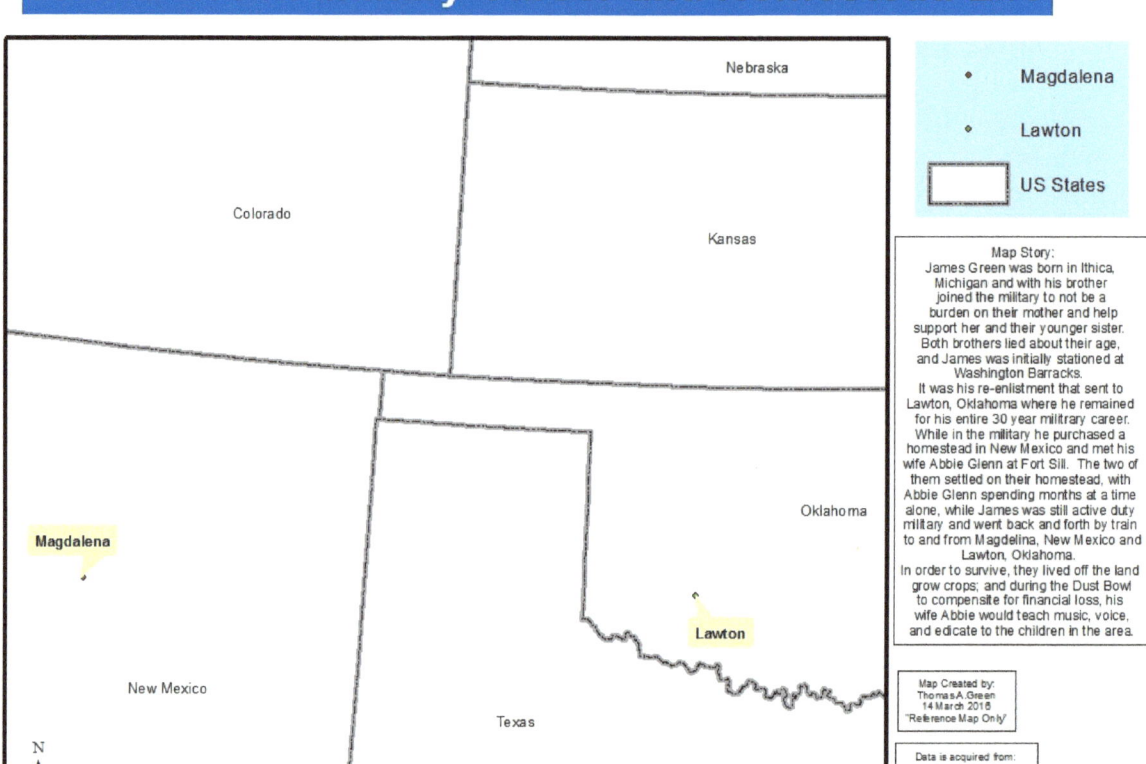

Figure 5: Green, Thomas A. 2016. Data collection acquired from www.gadm.org; accessed 13 March 2016

     Based on the dates listed on the land acquisition and the gap between the first known photographs of the homestead, it is clear James Green went back and forth by rail from his military station in Fort Sill to his homestead. A trip that likely occurred several times per year, as part of the contract of the homestead purchase included the construction of permanent structure i.e., livable dwelling, and indication that someone is living off of the land. By 1932 however, James Green continued his service, while his wife, children and step-children began to reside full time on the homestead. Thus the likely reason for the first known picture taken of the homestead in 1932 could potentially be the very first photograph.[149]

     As for the last years of his military service, his military records indicate that he retired with the rank of Sergeant in 1939. At this time, he would be approximately fifty-years-old. Aside from this, it is imperative to note the time frame of the year he retired; in relation to, the year of 1939. During this time a European conflict was on the rise that was being caused by Germany; as well as, a land and sea invasion on the opposite of the world by the hands of Japan that would ultimately lead to a global conflict known today as World War II. This was additionally a time, when the United States was recovering from a "Great Recession" that was in

---

[149] Green Family Records 1800's-2016

part blamed on World War I (1914-1919), along with the interior section of the United States that were still re-building from the aftermath of the "Dust Bowl."[150]

In reference to the latter event, i.e., the "Dust Bowl," by this time James had moved his wife likely right before this event would pledge the entire interior section of the United States. An event that would lead to mass migration out from the interior to further western areas, such as, California, Arizona; and to a certain extent New Mexico. These areas either did not experience the effects of the Dust Bowl or if the effects were felt as in New Mexico, they were minor in comparison to the Central United States of Nebraska, Kansas and Oklahoma. Nonetheless, based on these two events, the United States as a whole was not entirely interested in being thrusted or volunteering for another war of the same proportions of World War I. A war that was still referenced in the late 1930's as the "Great War" that many Americans were still blaming for the Great Depression.[151]

Throughout the 1930's, despite the interior United States being put through even more hardship due to the Dust Bowl, The Green family lived off of the homestead. They would proceed to add additional land to the initial purchase. It is estimated by the time James retired to his homestead in 1939, he had acquired more than one hundred acres of land to go with the initial homestead purchase of 1921 (Appendix G, Figure 21). By 1941, with the attack on Pearl Harbor in the United States territory of Hawaii, thus thrusting the nation into a new World War, James was clearly already regretting his retirement. It is likely this reason to this twofold. The first and mostly likely reason is one the basis that throughout his entire thirty plus military career, he had never gone to a war. Although he was old enough and able to have gone to World War I, there are no records to support it; and it is not out the realms of possibility that he never went. As for the second reason, was sharing the patriotism of other Americans and his want to participate in a war that he knew his two step-sons were going to be in. Step-sons that were at this time, twenty-five and twenty-one respectively. Sons, he claimed as his own.[152]

Based on these two likely reasons, with the first being the mostly likely reason of the two, he would attempt to re-enlist in 1942, shortly after the attack on Pearl Harbor. Instead of being able to re-enlist, he would receive a letter by the United States Army (Appendix G, Figure 9), which states that based on his age that he was not needed; and to basically enjoy retirement on his homestead. After reading this it made me think of one of my favorite Christmas movies, White Christmas, staring Bing Crosby and Danny Kaye. This was an incredible movie that is a

---

[150] Adams, Michael C.C. The Best War Ever: America and World War II, 1st edition. Baltimore: John Hopkins University Press, 1994, 1-44; McElvaine, Robert S. The Great Depression: America 1929-1941. New York: Radom House, 1984, 3-24, 72-91 & 170-195; Egan, Timothy. The Worst of Time: The Untold Story of Those Who Survived the Great American Dust Bowl. New York: Houghton Mifflin Company, 2006, Chapter III, 145-308; Nash, Gerald D. The Critical Era: The Great Depression and World War II 1929-1945. 2nd ed. Prospect Heights: Waveland Press Incorporated, 1992, 1-9 & 38-45.

[151] Rothbard, Murray N. America's Great Depression, Fifth Edition. Auburn: The Ludwig von Mises Institute, 2000, 3-80, 279 & 328.

[152] Adams 2, 21, 26, 36 & 40; Egan 91-102 & 171-175; Green Family Records 1800's-2016; Szasz, Ferenc Morton. Albuquerque: University of New Mexico Press, 1984, 13, 24 & 29; Worster, Donald. Dust Bowl: The Southern Plains in the 1930's. Oxford: Oxford University Press Incorporated, 2004, 10-25 & 118-138

must see by everyone that deals with patriotism, and presents a cheery disposition of the United States post World War II era.

In this movie, the general wants to re-enlist to return to the Army; but is told he is too old and the military does not have anything for him. Reading the letter, the United States Army sent to James Green, brought tears to this author. As the first thing that came to mind was that amazing movie, and how one of the songs in the movie says "What can you do with a General, when he stops being a General," but instead, "What can you do with a Sergeant, when he stops being a Sergeant." Nonetheless, he did not get to re-enlist and participate in World War II as his two step-sons, Robert Sinclair and William O'Connell, the latter, earning the rank of Colonel.[153]

Around the time his step-son, William received his ranks of Colonel based on the efforts and success him and his Army Company had at the Battle of the Bulge and other battles that followed, resulted in the United States War Department to send his step-father James a letter stating that he was promoted to Colonel (Appendix G, Figure 10). It is believed this took place as the United States Army knew of his intent to re-enlist to participate in World War II and was declined; as well as, the knowledge that his step-son had earned the title of Colonel. It is these two reasons that likely caused the United States Army wanted to grant him with the title of Colonel, based on years of service, and his leadership for veterans. A title that James Green would not use, as family stories, particularly from one of his step-children and son, that would say "he did not go by the title of Colonel, because he felt he did not earn it."[154]

His refusal to use the title of Colonel that was given to him long after his retirement from the military only increases my admiration. Thus making him a person this author would have liked to have enjoyed spending time with as an adult, rather than a toddler. This is because any man that refuses a title, they felt was not earned deserves respect. As it shows James Green was not a man of entitlement, instead he was a man that believed in providing his civic duty to his country. As well as, ensure the security and wellbeing to his mother and younger sister, thus the primary reason he joined with his brother in hopes of possibly earning a better opportunity he could pass on to his children.[155]

As mentioned earlier, during my grandfather's enlistment in the military, he purchased a home stead in present-day New Mexico. This purchase was conducted during the existence of the Homestead Act of 1862. An act that was designed to provide adult citizens, or those

---

[153] Dolan, Robert Emmett. White Christmas. Curtiz, Michael. Los Angeles: Paramount Pictures, 1954; Green Family Records 1800's-2016

[154] Balkoski, Joseph. *Utah Beach: The Amphibious Landing and Airborne Operations on D-Day*. Mechanicsburg: Stackpole Books, 2005; Beevor, Antony. *Ardennes 1944: The Battle of the Bulge*. New York: Penguin Random House, 2015; Caddick-Adam, Peter. Snow & Steel: The Battle of the Bulge 1944-1945, 1st ed. London: Oxford University Press, 2015; Green Family Records 1800's-2016; Kershaw, Alex. The Longest Winter: The Battle of the Bulge and the Epic and the Epic Story of World War II's Most Decorated Platoon. Cambridge: First De Capo Press, 2004.

[155] Green Family Records 1800's-2016

intending to become citizens, whom had never raised against the United States government the ability to claim 160 acres of government surveyed land.[156]

In order to claim land, they were required to build a home and cultivate the land for five years. Once this was completed, the land would be free and clear. However, a small registration fee would be required. A title to the land may be acquired after just six months with land improvements such as the building of a home and a fee of $1.25 per acre. That is $200.00 and a $10.00 registration fee. This was considered a very large chunk of change in those days, but was something my grandfather was able to come up with early on during his military career.

When the Homestead Act of 1862 was passed, only a limited amount of farmers and laborers were able to take advantage of it. Even fewer could afford to uproot their families moving hundreds of miles away by railroad. This huge endeavor was something, both my grandparents thought was a chance worth taking, and did something most Americans felt as being risky. Something that made this even more of a risk, is knowing that my grandmother would often spend months at a time on the homestead alone with her four children and one other female companion without the presence of a man. This is something that a woman did not do, especially at this particular timeframe.[157]

I believe it was the latter rules that apply to my grandparents, based on the multiple records in my possession that state my grandfather paid $1.37 per acre and a $10.00 registration fee for a total of $19.20 more than the governments set price. I remember my Aunt Elizabeth telling me how the family camped under an old army tent and made their first Adobe house at the homestead one summer. The pictures in my possession are of the second Adobe home. I have been to the site as a young girl; we walked around the area and found both the old home sites. The first home site had only a few Adobe bricks near the corners of the construction that was once the family home. The second home site had all four walls standing with a partial roof. My father found a few family items, including his old baby spoon.[158]

An interview James gave to ABC Radio, when his blind daughter Georgia, at the age of 18, witnessed the Atomic Bomb blast. This interview is also playing in the background at the Trinity Site Tours, still today. In this interview, it is quite obvious that James has become tired of answering questions by reporters in regards to his daughter's eyewitness account, as he verifies she saw the flash and states, "And that's all I have to say about that!" before he answers the reporter's question and describes his own eyewitness account. His daughter Georgia was fifty miles north of Socorro, New Mexico, on Highway 85. Her brother-in-law Lieutenant Joe Wills was driving her to Albuquerque for a music lesson. The description of the Atomic bomb is described in the Socorro Chieftain, as "Intensely white and seemed to fill the entire

---

[156] United States Government. National Park Service, Homestead Act, website. http://www.nps.gov/home/learn/historyculture/abouthomesteadactlaw.htm. Accessed: 25 March 2016; Green Family Records 1800's-2016
[157] Green, Personal Family Records, 1800's-2016
[158] Green, Personal Family Records, 1800's-2016

world…followed by a crimson glow." Not only was the flash seen, but sound and shockwaves were seen, heard and felt more than a hundred miles away.[159]

      While Georgia Green may always be a controversy in college classrooms and on line, let me clear this miss conception here and now. Before Georgia was even in school, she lost the sight in one eye, when childhood epidemics swept the area of the homestead in the 1930's. It doesn't take much to see the devastation. Just visit all the graveyards in the area to see the generation of lost children. However, it was not until the age of seven that my Aunt Georgia became blind. One morning while opening the refrigerator door, which had a pull down handle, she somehow caught her good eye on the door handle and popped it out. After the loss of her seeing eye, Georgia was left with the eye damaged by childhood epidemics. It was with this single eye, that Georgia could only distinguish the difference between light and dark. It is important to understand that there are different classifications of blindness. A definition of how blindness is classified can be found at Visionaware.org.[160]

---

[159] ABC Radio interview 17 July 1945 of James S. Green. Albuquerque Journal. "Explosives Blasts Jolts Wide Area." 17 July 1945; Socorro Chieftain. 17, July 1945.
[160] Green, Iva A.; Visionaware.org/info/your-eye-condition/eye-health/low-vision/low-vision-terms-amd-descriptions/1235.

Chapter XIV:
Spotlight on a Modern American Woman

Abbie Lusina Glenn

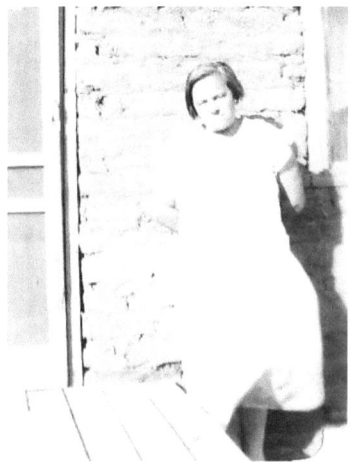

Abbie Lusina Glenn was born in St. Joseph, Missouri, to Robert Neff Glenn and Estella (Stella) Elizabeth Jordan. Abbie attended public school in St. Joseph, Missouri and graduated from St Joseph High school in 1909. While in St. Joseph, Abbie was active in the Methodist church and often assisted with Sunday school classes. After high school Abbie attended Missouri Methodist, earning a degree in music. Despite her degree being in music, it is important to note Abbie accomplishment, in a time when few women attended, much less earned a college degree.[161]

At some point after graduation, for reasons unknown to me, Abbie moved to Lawton, Oklahoma, taking a position at Fort Sill Army base as a civilian. Abbie worked in both the Officer's Club and Mess Hall on base. It was here that Abbie met and married her first husband Robert Sinclair. After the marriage, Abbie moved on base with Robert. Robert was from Ireland, but to avoid religious persecution his family had fled to Germany. Robert had come to America with a close friend William O'Connell, from his home town. Both men joined the American Army, and both were stationed together at Fort Sill. It was these two friends as well as another who tried to court Abbie in an attempt to win her hand in marriage, yet it was Robert she chose.[162]

Abbie and Robert had two children; Mary Alice born 1915, died 1960 and Robert "Glenn" born 1917, died 1990. While pregnant with their son, Robert was injured in an accident on base. While at the hospital by his side two more wives arrived. Not only was Abbie shocked to learn of his bigamy, so were his two closes friends. It was learned that Abbie was his second

---

[161] Green Family Records 1800's-2016
[162] Green Family Records 1800's-2016

wife and therefore, not legally married. He had married his first wife only a few months' prior off base, to marrying Abbie on base. His first wife had one child with him, a daughter. Robert was given the option of a dishonorable discharge and return to his family in Germany, return by himself to Ireland or be prosecuted and placed in Fort Leavenworth, Kansas. Robert chose the dishonorable discharge and the one-way ticket to Germany.[163]

Vowing to ensure Abbie's well-being, Roberts's closest friend who had joined the Army with him William O'Connell vowed to marry her and care for her and Roberts Children. Two years later, Abbie married William O'Connell. Abbie and William had two children; Elizabeth "Beth" Rebecca, born 1919 and William "Bill", born 1921, died 2008. While pregnant with Bill, William was injured in a munitions explosion on base. He died three days later. Abbie next married the third friend in the group, my grandfather James Samuel Green, in May of 1923.[164] Together, they had two children: Georgia Willetta born 1925, died 1960, and my father, George Willett.

The most amazing thing about this woman is the hardships she endured. Not only was her life that of a strong, non-traditional woman, she was a survivor. After she married her third husband, she had the courage to up-root her family and move to a homestead alone with four of her children. While her oldest two children stayed behind with their step-father to complete their education, the younger four were moved out west by train.

On her husband's homestead alone with a female companion she grew crops, raised animals for food and traded and bartered with distant neighbors. For money she taught locals music voice and poise lessons. As a young girl and well into my thirties people would come up to me to tell me about the music lessons and kindness they, or their parents received from this woman. They would say how their family would take a wagon to her homestead and she would teach the children in the morning, when she lived on the homestead. At noon they had a large picnic with all the families bringing food and sharing. Then in the afternoon they would all return home. It was a day long trip that families made twice a week due to the distance. This was a glimpse at her daily life on a homestead for over a decade. She taught lessons Monday through Saturday, taking Sunday off to devote her time to the local Methodist Church.

In the 1940's after my grandfather retired, they later chose to sell their homestead and move to a nearby town, Socorro, New Mexico. Both Abbie and her husband James became much more involved in the community and became members of many different local and national organizations. At the time of her death Abbie was heavily involved in the Methodist church, and ran the youth programs, including Rainbow and Sunshine Girls. Those in the program received music, voice and poise for free as she had completely retired.

Mary Alice Sinclair Brooks married after high school and moved to Washington State. In a letter sent to Abbie in regards to her daughter Mary Alice, on May 22 1960: " *Dear Mrs. Green: I am writing this letter on behalf of your daughter Mary. She has been very ill with a rare blood disease. It's a disease that the doctors around here haven't heard of for 12 years. She became very anemic and was in bed for about two months off and on going to the doctors.*

---

[163] Green Family Records 1800's-2016
[164] Green Family Records 1800's-2016

she got so weak her legs wouldn't hold her up and they finally had to take her to the hospital. it took them a week of taking tests to find out what she has. She <u>does not have leukemia</u> and will get well though she will need care for some time as far as I have found out she has Pur-Puro, which the membranes of the tissues break and bleed and caused the ends of her fingers and toes and the end of her nose to look like they had been smashed. They were deep purple and she had splotches all over her. These have cleared up pretty well on the outside, but she has them internally too. She is feeling quite a bit better and is leaving the sanitarium where I work, Sunday she told me today. One of the head nurses told me she is likely to be in and out of the hospital for some time though she doesn't know this so don't mention it to her when you write. As soon as she feels well enough she is going to Arizona for a visit and rest up time. I understand she will have to take medications for quite a while.... Sherrie is fine and growing up. I am Mary's Aunt by marriage and think a lot of her. God Bless you, Mrs. Earl Brooks." By the time Abbie received this letter, Mary Alice had died (see Appendix H, figure 28-29).[165]

        one daughter, living
Robert "Glenn" Sinclair, Married Vinita
    son, living
Elizabeth O'Connell
    two children
    Betty Gale Green Robertson Deceased
        one son, living
    living
        two sons
        Condon Hulgan Deceased
        living
William "Bill O'Connell
    three daughters living
Georgia Green deceased, no children.

Abbie Lusina (Glenn) Green, passed away on 12 July 1969 (Appendix H, Figure 33). While this author has in her possession, multiple copies of Abbie's Last Will and Testament. The only Will in Testament is that of her husband's James, that is featured in this manuscript (Appendix G, Figures 23-24).

---

[165] Green Family Records 1800's-2016

Chapter XV:

The Far Western Frontier

Generation X: George Willett Green

George Willett (Buddy/Bud) Green was born in Lawton, Oklahoma, to James Samuel Green and Abbie Lusina Glenn on April 3, 1931, while his father was stationed at Fort Sill. At less than a year old he moved to the homestead outside Magdalena, New Mexico. The homestead is situated just off present day U. S. Highway 60 between Socorro, New Mexico and Magdalena, New Mexico, heading west the homestead was located just before and to the right of the current Water Canyon turn off.[166]

Looking through the old photographs of my father on the homestead I realize how difficult it was being so detached from civilization. I also have a better understanding why the older children chose not to join the family in New Mexico.[167]

During their time on the homestead, they had to endure the effects of the disastrous "Dust Bowl" that devastated much of the interior part of the United States. An event of disastrous proportions that many people are unaware had its effects as far West as Central New Mexico. The stories that were told to the author from an aunt, recalls days when the wind and dust were so bad their mother would keep them indoors as much as possible; and the amount of dirt accumulating on the door way and window seals were in inches. This includes thick string being attached from the house to the out buildings, in order to not become disoriented when these storms were at their worst. The two books from the authors Egan and Worster, do not account for the effects of the Dust Bowl in New Mexico, however; both books do represent very similar accounts that were passed down to this author from their aunt.

---

[166] Egan 91-102 & 171-175; Worster 10-25 & 118-138; Green Family Records 1800's-2016
[167] Green Family Records 1800's-2016

Only to make matter worse, prior to the Dust Bowl, a devastating epidemic of childhood diseases swept through the area in 1929-30. While according to the high amount of child graves in the area for this period, my Aunt Elizabeth was correct, and few families were spared. This aunt described it as one of her worst childhood memories. She said her mother placed dark curtains over all the windows to keep the light out. The reason for this drastic measure to keep a room as dark is possible is based on the timeframe. It was common belief for at home remedies and in the field of medicine to keep as room as dark as possible in the event that your child or children contract scarlet fever, mumps, chicken pox and small pox; something that her brother Bill, half-sister Georgia and herself caught and one right after the other. While everyone survived, Aunt Georgia lost her sight in one eye. This disease outbreak that pledged the area, is suggest by this aunt as the reason they would eventually leave the Homestead, as locals were very angry that all of Abbie's children survived, when so many households in the area lost one or more children.

When he was old enough to start school, my father, spoke more Spanish than English, and was enrolled in Private school, in Socorro, New Mexico. He attended the Mount Carmel School, through eighth grade, before enrolling in Socorro Public Schools. During this time, he would join the Boy Scouts of America and earn the rank of Eagle Scout, the highest honor within that association (Appendix H, Figure 30). In addition to his achievement of Eagle Scout with the U.S. Boy Scouts of America, Bud would conduct yard maintenance for the old lady that lived on his street for exchange for antique figurines, salt and pepper shakers, gravy boat, etc…

As Bud got into high school age, he would assist ranchers as a ranch hand. This included participation in cattle drives. In the summer of 1948, between his junior and senior year of high school, he signed up to the local U.S. National Guard with the occupation of cook (Appendix H, Figures 31-32). According to these records, Bud was honorably discharged from the National Guard on 14 February 1950 after serving one year, seven months and twenty days. While in the U.S. National Guard, he continued to attend Socorro High School where graduated in May of 1949. During both his junior and senior year of high school, he played football for the Socorro High School, Warriors and helped clench the high school's First State Championship Trophy during the 1949 season. The significance of this win is Socorro High School would not win another Football State Championship title until Bud's fifth child was senior in the 1978 season.[168]

After High School, he attended the University of Oklahoma, in Norman, for a degree in Drafting Engineering. While attending college, he worked for Norman Lumber Company, which was owned by his two older brothers, Glenn St. Clair and William (Bill) O'Connell. In April, his junior year, he met and married his wife, Phyllis Florine Crockett. After the birth of their first two children, he had a falling out with his brothers and moved to Tulsa, near his wife's family. He worked in construction with his father-in-law, then after the birth of his third child, he moved to Albuquerque, New Mexico. While in Albuquerque, he worked in construction. Later in life, he enjoyed showing his children the subdivisions, restaurants and churches he built during this time. Many still stand today. During this time, his in-laws joined him and his wife in Albuquerque,

---

[168] Green Family Records 1800's-2016

New Mexico. He also added to his family three more daughters. In 1963, he moved to Cuba, New Mexico.

While in Cuba, he worked in the construction field, the local Saw Mill, drove a semi-truck, and taught English to the Native Americans at Choco Canyon. He later gave all that up and ran a restaurant. During this time his "Buddy Burgers" and fried chicken brought people in from all around. In 1967 an executive from the Kentucky Fried Chicken franchise after eating at my father's diner called up a large group of executives to come try my father's fried chicken. They accused my father of stealing the recipe from the Kentucky Fried Chicken Company, issuing an order preventing him to sell his fried chicken. After an in-depth investigation and learning my father never worked for the company and had no relatives that had worked for the company, they demanded he show them how he made his chicken. I was present and have a clear memory of these men standing around my father in their suits in the kitchen of the restaurant as he demonstrated how he prepared his chicken. He was cleared of any wrong doing, because he used twenty-three herbs and spices. My father learned his cooking skills from his mother and in the Army National Guard when he was a cook. Unfortunately, this investigation took a toll on his business and he had to close his restaurant.

He moved his family again in 1968 to Lemitar, New Mexico, located within Socorro, County to be closer to his mother during her failing health. He took a job with his brother-in-law, Sherman Ingram at the Coke-a-Cola Bottling Distribution Center, delivering to vendors throughout several counties within the state. After he completed deliveries he would work construction jobs well into the night.

In 1971 he purchased a home, located at 704 Lucero Street in Socorro, using the money left to him and his children by his mother (Appendix H, Figure 34). During one of my visits in 2007, I drove by and learned the house had been torn down. After the death of his wife, Phyllis, who passed in the home, he decided to sell the home. He purchased a small trailer, as many of his children had grown and left for college or military careers. After the death of his wife, he took a job with the City of Socorro as the City Building Inspector. This was short lived as the local politics became unacceptable to him, asking him to violate laws and his personal principles, and passing favors.[169]

He then became a building inspector for the State of New Mexico, where he worked until 1990, when his health did not allow him to continue. He was also the State of New Mexico's first Multiple Inspector. He not only inspected buildings, but conducted electrical, plumbing, gas, LP gas, and mechanical inspections. His territory included the following counties: Torrance, Socorro, Sierra, Lincoln, De Baca, Curry, Roosevelt, Chaves, Eddy, Lea, Otero, Grant, Catron, Hidalgo, Luna, and Guadalupe. He was very proud of having the largest territory out of all state inspectors and being the only multiple inspector. While working for the state, in 1985, he moved back to Lemitar where he resided until his death in 1991.[170]

---

[169] Green Family Records 1800's-2016
[170] Green Family Records 1800's-2016

Phyllis Florine Crockett 1934-1976

Phyllis Florine Crockett was born in Vinita, Oklahoma on September 26, 1934, to Elza Isaac Crockett and Iva Iona Powell. Raised mainly on a farm, as the oldest of four children she often assisted her father outside; as there are pictures in my collection of her sitting on her dad's lap on a tractor and one standing next to him as he drives the tractor, in rural Oklahoma. It is important to note, however, they did not always live on a farm. During the "Great Depression," her family moved to Tulsa, Oklahoma to find work as farming became nearly impossible. Nonetheless, Phyllis wound up not having as much experience in house chores as she preferred to work outside with her dad and younger brother, thus leaving her two younger sisters to assist the mother with the daily inside house work.

She graduated from High School in 1952 in Tulsa, Oklahoma. She attended the University of Oklahoma in Norman, majoring in Education. While she attended college for a teaching degree, it was apparent her real intention of going to college was to find a husband. It is important to note; it was common for women to attend college for the purpose of finding a husband. It often was strongly encouraged for women of this time to go to college and find an educated man. They were not necessarily expected to finish, but to collect enough classes at the collegiate level to carry on a conversation with her husband.[171]

After leaving college she often worked small menial positions. Sometimes answering phones in a small office, sorting and rolling coins, and as a waitress. She typically worked the morning shift at small family owned restaurants, in order to be at home with the children in the afternoon and evenings. By the time the seventh and final child was born, she began to work from 2pm to 10pm as a waitress to cut the cost of child care. This was because the two oldest children were 15 and 14 years old respectively, and could watch the younger children as both

---

[171] Green, Personal Family Records, 1800's-2016

parents worked. With my dad often working two and three jobs, verses my mother working one this seemed like an ideal situation as it limited the time they paid for a sitter.

It was often difficult not having parents there as being watched by older siblings that constantly had power struggles of who was in charge, made after school at home un-inviting. This went on until the two oldest in 1973 went off to college. During this time, if we were able to see our mother it was late in the evening to have her sign report cards, permission slips, get help with homework or have the younger children, myself included, to count her tips that she earned for that day.

In 1969 she was diagnosed with Melanoma Cancer. This was something that she only learned after going to the doctor at the insistence of her oldest daughter. A mole that was located on her calf that would ooze blood and pus. During her visit she learned a piece of good news. That was she was pregnant with her seventh and final child. Unfortunately, bad news was to soon follow.

Within a few weeks the results were back in from the mole scrapping, and it was cancer. The doctor provided her with instructions if she terminated the pregnancy and began cancer treatment immediately there would be a very strong chance of getting rid of the cancer, in order to live a long healthy life. Just the thought of terminating the pregnancy made my mother very upset, and she refused to go with her doctors' orders. Instead she went through with the pregnancy and gave birth to a very healthy baby girl. After the baby was no longer breastfeeding and about a year old, our mom began cancer treatment sometime in 1971. It was immediately stated to her by her doctor and other medical staff that because of the delay in treatment the odds would not be in her favor.[172]

In 1974 she took a less strenuous job as a part-time teacher's aide. 1976, she quickly was promoted to math specialist at the local elementary school. Her primary task was to assist the students that were struggling in math and get them back up to speed. In early 1976 she was given a clean bill of health and was 100% cancer free. Unfortunately, this was very short lived. By spring of 1976 she began to feel very tired and called her doctor in Albuquerque New Mexico, to schedule an appointment. Since her last visit had been less than three months, and she was considered cancer free at her last appointment, getting an appointment was very difficult. They refused to see her until September, and by then it was a struggle for her to do much of anything. When she went to get into the vehicle so we could drive her to the doctors, we heard a loud pop. As she put her hand down to steady herself, her arm broke.

She insisted on going straight to her appointment in Albuquerque some 76 miles away so she would not miss her appointment. Once at the doctors in Albuquerque, now with a broken arm, an x-ray was conducted immediately. It was discovered the bone in her arm had degraded and her cancer was back. This time she had development multiple types of cancer and was informed; as well as, her family that she would lose this battle and may not even make it to see the end of the year. Indeed, the medical staff was correct as Phyllis died December 12, 1976.[173]

---

[172] Green Family Records 1800's-2016
[173] Green Family Records 1800's-2016

George Willet Green + Phyllis Florine Crockett=

Private male 1954 bn. Norman, Oklahoma (living) Attended Highlands University in Las Vegas, New Mexico for teaching shop, left school to return home and aid in the support of family at his father's request. Occupations: construction, ranching, disabled in a fire in 1984. Burns suffered on face, chest and hands. Active member of the Knights of Pythian. Never married.

Private female 1955 bn. Norman, Oklahoma (living) Attended New Mexico State
    University, Las Cruces, New Mexico for teaching elementary education. Earned
    her M.S. in Science New Mexico Institute of Mining and Technology, Socorro,
    New Mexico. Occupations: waitress, secretary, current position elementary
    teacher, Socorro, New Mexico. Active member of the Pythian Sisters and Eastern
    Star. divorced

Private male 1957 bn. Tulsa, Oklahoma (living) Attended New Mexico State University
    for Wildlife Science, left school to return home and aid in the support of family at
    his father's request. Occupations: Construction, owns his own company, also
    worked at local college for many years. Currently runs his construction company,
    semi-retired. never married.

Private female 1959 bn. Albuquerque, New Mexico Entered into the United States Army
    after graduating from high school. Attended college at Eastern New
    Mexico University in Roswell, New Mexico as well as Highlands
    University Albuquerque branch. Completer her degree in Special
    Education. Occupations: waitress, soldier, teacher. Current position
    Special Education teacher, Belen New Mexico. (living)
    married m. Private bn. PA two children, one female 1979 living and one male 1980

Private female 1960 bn. Albuquerque, New Mexico Occupations; secretary, fast food,
    retail, construction, retired from local college as property manager. Never
    married. (living)

Private female 1962 bn. Albuquerque, New Mexico (living)
        m. divorced, three male children 1981, 1982, 1984 (living)
            male 1981 no children, divorced
            male 1982 three biological children, Married
                Four children bn. Columbia Missouri
                      male bn. 2002 (living) (Step-son)
                      female bn. 2006 (living)
                      female bn. 2007 (living)
                      male bn. 2011 (living)
            male 1984 three children, Divorced
                      female bn. Ft Benning, Georgia, May 24

> deceased Died May 24 Ft Benning, Georgia, Buried New Town, Missouri Cemetery, May 24, 2004
> male bn. 2012 (living)
> male bn. 2016 (living)

Private female 1969 bn. Socorro, New Mexico. Attended New Mexico State University for Acting, left school 1990. Returned to education attending University of Missouri to earn a BS in Archeology and Classics, then earning her MS in Classics. Occupations; waitress, title company sales, current position, Latin teacher Garland Texas (living)
> m. Private female, bn. 1993 Palm Springs, California[174]

---

[174] Green Family Records 1800's-2016

Chapter XVI:
About the Author

The Author:

Growing up in a large family in a rural community with working class parents, often meant little to no supervision. Like others in this era, the streets were played in; the parks were full of baseball, frisbee or soccer games. We spent hours riding our bicycles around town with friends or all afternoon at the local swimming pool. There were no computers, no cell phones and we only had 3 channels, unless you counted the learning channel, then we had four.

It was a little different for me. My father often worked two or more jobs at a time. My mother, waited tables at the Ma and Pa type restaurants. I remember my father taking us to work with him at the old saw mill. My two sisters just older than I, and me would sit in the car while he worked when school was in session. He positioned the car so we could watch him and the other men work. When a loud whistle would blow for breaks and lunches my father would let us out of the car to use a port-a-potty, and eat with him and his co-workers, then back to the car we went. As time went by, my sisters started school, leaving me alone in the car. I cried and cried, without my sisters. I remember my parents complaining about having to hire a babysitter for the first time.

At the time, my mother worked the morning shift, at a small restaurant. My father worked at the old saw mill full time, he worked a construction job full time and worked part-time teaching English as a second language. During summer months the older children were left in charge of caring for the younger children. There was actually no supervision. I remember my childhood as a bunch of children fighting and no parents.[175]

---

[175] Green Family Records 1800's-2016

By second grade decided I wanted to sell the local newspaper, which came out three days a week, eventually changing to twice a week. I was granted permission by my Mother, who allowed me to sell the paper alone on the streets. I often took the papers I had left door to door until I ran out. It didn't matter how late I was out, as my only rule was to be home before my father. I continued to sell the local newspaper until I started in high school. Once I started high school, I felt like I was too old to sell newspapers on the streets, yet too young to have a real job. So I focused on school and after school sports.

In spring and fall during harvest season, we were dropped off in a field to pick crops. My oldest brother and sister were in charge. Our parents left us a gallon jug of water, and a small ice chest containing a sandwich for each of us and a piece of fruit. The older children told us when it was time to get a small drink of water every hour. At noon one of our parents would come and check on us and we ate our lunch. We would have dinner once we were home. It often consisted of the crops of the day. I really did not like picking corn all day, just to go home and have corn on the cobb for dinner. We often picked crops from sun up to sun down. If we didn't pick enough during the day, they would bring in flood lights. We often picked corn, chili, jalapenos, tomatoes and other vegetables. However, sometimes we were in the orchards picking apples, peaches, grapes and apricots. My parents were paid a small amount for our work and we were given some of what we picked to sell or eat. After my mother's death we no longer picked crops.

I attended public school earning my diploma in 1980, but one thing was sure, I was ready to get out of town. I worked fulltime waiting tables my junior and senior year to avoid being home. With more free time, my home life became too difficult for me. I was seventeen and chose to walk away from everything. This is because my job was not giving me enough hours, and the difficulties that surrounded me at home. So one night in August 1980 I literally walked away in the middle of a rain storm. I ended up at Little Mormon Lake, Arizona. Where I spent two stress free weeks. The friend I convinced to go with me was married and had just turned eighteen. Her husband was at his annual two-week National Guard training. Since her husband was returning, it was time for her to return to the community as well. I decided to go back with her. It was two weeks before my eighteenth birthday, and less then twenty-four hours later I was picked up from her house and returned to my father. My father took her to court, but I told the judge the truth. I was leaving; she just chose to come along with me when she could not convince me to stay. All charges against her were dropped.[176]

Surprisingly, my job never knew I was gone and I worked a few hours a week for the next month. I switched restaurants and began getting all the hours I wanted, often working double shifts. It was there that I met the manager's son, who had been taken by an Aunt at an early age. Together, we were just too lost teens that bonded, due to our personal difficulties. Together, we had my oldest child, and fate kept us apart, and we went our separate ways. It is with son that the Green line will continue, as my brothers have no children.

---

[176] Green Family Records 1800's-2016

Once I returned to work, after the birth of our son, I met the father of my second two sons. I had actually met him my senior year when he was attending a church retreat at a camping area just west of my hometown. The marriage did not last and I soon found myself alone, twenty- one, and with three children. Struggling to support my family I often worked one full time job and two-part time jobs. It is also with these two sons this Green line will continue. I have never legally taken their fathers last name when I married him. So all three of my sons carry my last name.

While my children were young, I began taking classes at the local college. But it wasn't until they were all in pre-school and school that I met my second husband. Let's just say I am thankful we never had children together. While he was in the service, I began attending trade school, against his wishes. By the time I completed my A.A.S. in Law, he was out of the picture. Struggling to support my children, I went back to college to earn my B.S. in History and Political Science. I primarily supported my children with work study jobs, PELL Grants and Scholarships and a few student loans.

Still struggling to support myself and children on my own, I returned to College and earned my M.Ed. in Education in Counseling. A degree I was recruited for by the director of the program. The school agreed to pay one half the tuition if I was admitted to the program. This program was an excelled fourteen-month program. I completed this program at the same time my two youngest sons completed high school.

While attending college for this program I also worked two jobs. One in retail and the other a Dual Diagnosis Treatment Center. I often worked double shifts at the treatment center and chose to leave the retail position for unlimited overtime. This would come to an end a few years later and I took a position as an officer for the department of corrections, until the facility that employed me was shut down and I was forced to transfer. During my time working for correction I applied for other positions outside the prison. I left the prison to work at an Independent Living Center as an Independent Living Specialist.[177]

After relocating and leaving this position, I returned to working two fulltime jobs. One retail and one in education. In less than two years I decided I want more, so I returned to College and earned my second master's degree. This being a field I was passionate about, History. Clearly, I earned my college education for non-traditional reasons. Several reasons come to mind, the first being what I perceived as a poor education I received growing up in a small rural town, which made me feel inadequate in the workforce. This may also be contributed to no adult supervision in my home life until after the death of my mother. However, the main reason was fear. Fear of not being able to keep my children together and with me.

Through this all, I continued to research my family independently through the years. While I have lots of cousins, I am happy to have found, I began because I just wanted to know about the family I didn't know as a child. Growing up, we stopped visiting my cousins after the

---

[177] Green Family Records 1800's-2016

death of both my grandmothers and great grandparents in the summer of 1969. The only cousin who visited with us this had two sons, one my age and one two years younger. Sadly, she didn't live close by.

It has taken years for me to realize I am educated, I am fine, I survived and I have let go of all that held me back. I surround myself with those who enjoy my company and except me for who I am today. I found happiness within the family I have created for myself. This is not limited to my children and grandchildren. My family is not all made up of blood related members. Family is the people we choose to admit into our lives. Some may come and go but all served a purpose to assist us as we move to the next level of our lives.[178]

---

[178] Green Family Records 1800's-2016

Chapter XVII:

The Present Lines

Generation XII: Your children

The Oldest Child:

All three of my children were born in the same American Southwestern town not far from where the original homestead was located, which was purchased by my grandfather James Samuel Green. My first child was a twin, however, since the doctor that delivered him did not believe a baby was actually human until it breathes its first breath, it is nothing more than a tumor, he is listed on his birth certificate as a single birth. (This Dr. was later sued by multiple individuals and can no longer deliver babies without another doctor present.) The child that did survive, was a healthy seven pound fourteen-ounce baby boy, despite being a month away from my nineteenth birthday, I was looking forward to being a mom.[179]

My first child was very advanced when it came to walking and to my surprise did many things earlier than children in his age group. However, he did not learn to crawl until he was a year old after he was already walking. Nor did he talk much until after the age of two, but when he did, it was complete sentences. Additionally, he was considered big for his age and was constantly confused for being older. This caused many difficulties in his childhood. This son was very active; despite being ruled by his stomach. Growing up he enjoyed building cities with his enormous collection of Lego's and hot wheels, and miniature people collection and action

---

[179] Green Family Records 1800's-2016

figures. Other activities included playing basketball, a sport my second husband who was in the military would play, with all of us as a family as it was his favorite sport.

This son did not appear to like sports when he was young; however, as he developed and got older this attitude changed. His interests included Soccer, Baseball, Football and Golf. Of these sports, the one that he played the longest and got the best at doing was golf. However, by the age of 9 he could kick a football halfway across a football field through the goal posts. In addition, his ability to throw a football at an impressive distance was also noted by many locals, who began harassing him for not joining little league and playing football in local leagues.

One of the funniest memories of him as a child was when my younger sister had a flat tire. He took it upon himself to assess the situation. He walked around her pinto and kicked the tire a few times. While the jack and spare were retrieved, he calmly said "I see what the problem is. If you turn the tire over I think it will drive just fine auntie, it's just flat on one side."

This child was primarily homeschooled. He attended one year of Head start, and kindergarten through fourth grade in a public setting. He then attended a private Christian school for a year. He spent one more year in a public educational system, before returning to homeschool. He then attended community college and earned his G.E.D. After he earned his G.E.D. he attended community college and earned his associate degree in General Studies, before entering college.

Despite his change of interests when it came to sports, his true passion was in science and geography. This is what he would go on to college for and make his career in. With all of our moving around, instead of moving out of state, he chose to stay in-state to save money and earn his degree within the present state of residency in the Midwestern United States. He completed his Bachelor's Degree in the mid-2000's (Bachelors of Science) in Geography. Even being awarded the highest award given by the University he attended, the "Golden Globe". It was within two years of earning this degree; he accepted a job out in the American Southwest with the United States Federal Government. After being employed with the Federal Government, he decided to return to college to earn his Master's Degree. This decision resulted in his re-location to the Great Lakes area of the United States, where he completed his Masters of Science in Geography in the early 2011's.[180]

This son made many sacrifices no child should have to make. He made a deal with me that he would work and assist me in financially supporting his younger brothers, if I allowed him to earn his G.E.D., he would earn at least a Bachelor's degree. He kept his promise, and exceeded it. He is doing what he always wanted to do. He has also been accepted into a program where he will begin earning a second master's degree. I am very proud of this son for all the sacrifices he has made, his difficult journey and his successes. I look forward to see what the future holds as he sets and achieves his goals.

---

[180] Green Family Records 1800's-2016

At the present time, he is currently employed with the United States Federal Government. However, he is employed within a different agency and resides in the Midwestern United States, about three and half hours away from where he earned his bachelor's degree.[181]

The Middle Child:

My second child is best described as being the curious, wanting to be the military hero or astronaut. As a child, he would take toys, telephone and televisions apart; especially if he thought there was something wrong with it. What amazed me the most was his ability to have a conception of time and dates, as without fail he would always know when the space shuttle would be launching or landing! It did not matter the time of day; he would be sitting in front of the television at 5am or 11pm, at the age of three, and watching the entire televised event. Even with the 1986 Challenger explosion that occurred on live television 38 seconds after take-off, the only response he had was "I will have to fix it before I can go up." He also would say, "Someday I am going to guard the president!" and "When I grow up I will be just like Tom Brokaw". In elementary school he was voted artist in residence for his artistic talent. Sadly, he became disinterested after he was always being asked to draw something by teachers and students alike. It became common to see his artistry in the hallways of his elementary school every time you walked down a hallway. This is a talent he possesses has today.

In addition, every family member wanted to spend time with this son. Everyone who met him loved his attention span, even for old World War II movies. His ability to sit, quietly and watch any John Wayne movies, and World War II movies, my father would be watching on that particular day, made him his favorite movie watcher. Overtime, the childhood games all three of my children would play were typically from what they saw in the movies. For this one, it was anything that dealt with military, war and fighting re-enactments. Still today, one of the funniest

---

[181] Green Family Records 1800's-2016

memories was when all three of my boys went outside and the oldest simply said he will be the travel guide; while the other two shouted: I AM KELLY!", and the other, "I AM HERO!"

One of my father's favorite movies, aside from John Wayne Westerns and war movies was a movie called: Kelly's Hero starring Clint Eastwood and Donald Sutherland. By this age, it was clear; my middle child was going to be in the military. He began to live and breathe everything military. This led my middle son to be extremely close to his step-father, an officer in the United States Army.

As time went on and we found ourselves moving to various areas throughout the United States, and he decided he wanted back in public school, primarily for social interaction and the possibility of playing sports. This son more than either of his brothers craved socializing. Once back in the public system, he joined Air Force ROTC, at the high school and tried out for the drill team and was admitted as the youngest member while attending public school on the East Coast, and began he slowly began to decide which branch of military he was going to join. While on the East Coast and seeing how much he enjoyed Air Force ROTC, this is not the branch of military he would pick. Instead, after leaving the East Coast and moving to the Midwest, he decided to join the Marines on delayed entry. He completed his education January 2001, a semester early. However, he did not walk for commencement until May 2001. Shortly thereafter, he left for Camp Pendleton, California where he completed his basic training.

He graduated from boot camp in the fall of 2001 and returned home on September 10th waking up the next morning to the September 11, 2001 terrorist attacks and the need to return to base. Although, my instincts led me to believe this child would be in the next war, and I did all I could to talk him out of it and give college a try first, it was clear the military was his choice over college. This son served as a Presidential Guard at the White House and traveled to the Middle East on Air Force One with the President. He served in 2nd Battalion/1st Marines, Fox Company 3rd Platoon. His Iraqi tour placed him in Fallujah.[182]

The morning of September 11, 2001, I spoke briefly to my oldest child on his way to the University for school, as I was watching the morning news. The events of this morning, well…let's just say everyone has heard different stories on this for a thousand times, so to spare such a story, it was a morning that went by so quickly and slowly all at the same time. Before I knew it, my oldest son was calling me on the cell phone saying they have closed school because of the attacks. At the same time, I was calling my middle child who was with friends, at which time, found myself only waking him up to tell them to turn on the television because we are under attack. It was at this instance I knew my two youngest children were going to war, whether I wanted them to or not; and all I could do was pray. Pray they would make it back safely. Pray they would come back in one piece without missing any body parts, or worse, getting that dreaded knock on the door that all parents and spouses of military personnel never want.

---

[182] Green Family Records 1800's-2016

Thankfully, at first he did not have to go war, as he was offered the opportunity to train as a Marine Presidential Guard for the nation's current President, George W. Bush. This was a job that sadly did not last for his entire military enlistment. With less than a year remaining on his five-year enlistment he was sent to the war in the Middle East, in order to serve the remaining part of his five-year sign-up on delayed entry contract.

Like many men of his age that went into the military, most of them took part in the post war baby boom. By the mid 2000's he was married and had his first child, a girl. It was a very proud moment for all of us, and I was so very happy to be a grandmother! Within 15 months, he and his wife would have their second child, a second girl. Now having two grand-daughters, let's just say I finally got the girls I had secretly always wanted, but instead they came in the form of grandchildren.

This marriage ended in divorce and he later re-married his current wife. In this marriage he took on an additional child and became a step-father to a son, she had from a previous relationship, and from this marriage had his third child (her second child) in the early 2010's. This time, he will have a son. A son that can continue the line of Green. At the moment he learned he was having a son, he was on the phone with me. This was clearly an exciting moment in his life.

Today, my middle son is attending college and enjoying his time with all four of his quickly growing children and wife. This son has always been naturally studious. He continues to set goals and challenge himself, while setting a good example for his children. I am very proud of him and all his accomplishments. While the effects of the war plague him in the form of injuries, hearing loss and PTSD, he continues to work for the goals he sets for himself, while providing for the next generation.[183]

---

[183] Green Family Records 1800's-2016

The Youngest Child:

My third son was always the funny one, a natural country boy. As a child, this one would play along with the middle child's war game re-enactments; i.e., their G.I. Joe action figures; or if alone, would play farmer or doctor. As he would say, in his adorable three-year-old New York accent: "I am going to be a farmer…or doctor, a doctor for animals." Out of all of my children, this one was the most country. While the other two would talk about living in the cities or suburbs of a city, my youngest never had any interest of doing so.

The youngest would occasionally help my two brothers who worked construction, when we lived nearby to them; if not, he would take turns hanging out with both of his older brothers. When hanging out with the oldest, it never failed it had to do with Lego's and hot wheel, during the winter. In the warm months, it was superhero games, usually Batman because that was my oldest son's favorite superhero or it was re-enacting some movie like Indiana Jones or the Goonies, where they would hunt for buried treasure.[184]

While hunting for buried treasure a game which would be of interest to the middle child, with all three hunting for treasure or imaging they are exploring some far off land, the middle child would typically go back to his war games. The one game my youngest would play by him was with his Tonka farming tracker, his toy chain saw, hot wheel cars, or his Teenage Mutant Ninja Turtles. Nonetheless, all three of my children were very close, and it appeared when they were young my youngest was the bridge between the other two, while growing up. This was because the oldest did not like war games and found his Lego's, hot wheels and extensive map collection than pretending to blow things up. Whereas the middle child thought the exact opposite, and with my youngest son would re-enact together and end the game as the hero.

My funniest memory of this child occurred when he was three years old. Fruit by the foot had just come out that year and he and his brothers loved them. One hot summer New Mexico day, he came inside from playing for a drink of water. The way he came in is something

---
[184] Green Family Records 1800's-2016

that I will remember forever, as it is still the funniest thing I have seen he do to date. He entered the house all hot and sweaty, saying "water" water" like in a dried up desert seen of an old western movie. He had placed a cherry fruit by the foot against his tongue and was dragging it between his legs, making it look like an extension of his tongue.

Like my middle son, my youngest chose to return to the public education system. During high school, he decided to go into the military, and give up his dream of caring for animals. I believe this stems from the public school he attended. While earning my Master's degree in Education in Counseling I was often told that as a public school counselor it would be my job to learn as much as possible about a student's family dynamics. If the students' parent/parents did not hold a college degree and or a professional position within the community, the student was to be discouraged of attending college. I was told it would be my job, to tell them it will be a waste of money and time. This is something I could never do, and is the reason I chose to utilize my degree in the rehabilitation and recovery arena rather than the education system its self.

This is something that was pushed on my children by the local public education system. While I accepted the fact my middle child was most likely going to join the military, then attend college, I was hoping the youngest would go to college like the oldest. Instead he joined the military; it was this son who would choose the Army.

My youngest son graduated a year early from high school. He graduated with A/B honor roll. This may not seem like much, but my youngest son had an I.E.P. He not only spoke with a heavy New York accent, making it difficult for others to understand, but he is extremely dyslexic. But on subject he learned to excel at was mathematics. This son was able to solve mathematical equations using a calculator that even his teachers did not have the ability to solve, nor did they know a calculator could be used to solve the equations. This is partly because when he was younger and bored, he enjoyed studying calculator math. He is extremely smart, but his ability to place it on paper has always been a challenge. He graduated in May 2001. He was able to walk at commencement with his older brother.[185]

Unfortunately, unlike my middle child that did not immediately have to go to war following the September 11, 2001 terror attacks. This one, my seventeen-year-old baby, was a part of the first wave. This son was 3rd Division, 3rd Brigade 1/15th Infantry. The same unit as the famous Audie Murphy, who was idolized after World War II. It was this son, who spent almost all his time in the United States Army, in the Middle East. While in the Middle East, he was stationed in Kuwait twice, Pakistan once and the invasion of Iraq. He participated in Operation Desert Shield, Operation Enduring Freedom, Operation Inspired Gambit and Operation Enduring Freedom. While serving his country he was injured in a transport accident, in Kuwait, a river fording accident, in Pakistan, where he ended up and a tank accident Kuwait, and broke both feet in the march to Bagdad. He turned down a Purple Heart, because at the time he witnessed other soldiers, from other units, receiving Purple Hearts for meaningless actions, such as "driving through smoke." He feels a Purple Heart should be reserved for those who were

---

[185] Green Family Records 1800's-2016

injured in battle or patrol. In addition, it is a disgrace to all soldiers who actually earned the medal past and present, for these individuals to accept a Purple Heart under these conditions and worse, their commanding officers to put them in for one. Thankfully, he made it home safely each time and did not lose any body parts. He too like many men and women who served in this war and others suffers from PTSD. After returning from the Middle East, with a year left on his Enlistment, he married an old high school acquaintance and had his first child.

Sadly, I would never get the opportunity to see or hold, this beautiful child as she died just six hours after her birth. For reasons unknown to me, they allowed my son to remove her from the morgue and hold her, for the week before she was flown to the Midwest for burial. This may have been in order to assist him with his grief, but for a week until her corpse smelled too bad for him to handle the stench, was a little much.

This was very hard on my youngest son who always told me he wanted lots of children, and would tell me when he was a small child, that he would be the first to make me a grandma. The death of this beautiful Angel effected all of us as a family. However, the effect it had on my son, who has witnessed so much death at such a young age, and was now seeing death again, was unbearable. It pained me, each time he would call and tell me just how much he wished she would have opened her eyes just once so he could look into her eyes. He would just say "Mom, I wanted her to see how much I love her, I just want her to know I love her!"

This devastating ordeal led my son to not want any children, and being only 19 years old at the time of this incident, a divorce from this wife was inevitable. It took him a half a decade to heal emotionally enough to attempt having another child. In the early 2010's, he decided to marry his old high school sweetheart, he initially wanted to be with, and they had their first child, a boy. In addition to this, he took on the role of step-father to the son she had six years before, whom would have been close to a year younger than his daughter, if she had survived. While the marriage ended in divorce, he is happily taking care of his now four-year-old son, and three-month old son.[186]

After he left the military, he worked in construction, and then owned his own construction company. He also worked as a police officer at the same time. He currently works for the Federal Government, with the Department of Veterans Affairs, at a Veterans Hospital, and is looking to locate rural property to purchase and live on with his two sons. This is because, as I said before, this one has always loved the country and never had any desire to live in the city. This is what makes me so proud as a mom. Knowing that all three of my children has lived up to achieve their dreams in one-way or another.

---

[186] Green Family Records 1800's-2016

Generation XIII: Your Grandchildren

Grandson, age 14: This grandson is very tall, which is handy for someone short like myself. He attends public school in a small rural town. He is taking fitness and weight training classes. He is excelling in school and is growing up nicely. Funniest memory at the moment is when one of his uncle's showed him a YouTube clip of a Will Smith music video "Getting Jiggy Wit It," and he quickly stated: Will Smith was a singer! I always thought he was an Actor?" Let's just day, this uncle of his, my oldest son, felt really old at that moment.

Granddaughter, Georgie Verla Green Deceased. This granddaughter is my first grandchild. She was born to my youngest son on 24 May 2004 and died on 24 May 2004 in Columbus, GA at Fort Benning Army Post. She was born premature and lived only six hours. She is buried at the Newtown, Missouri cemetery, in Newtown, Missouri.[187]

Granddaughter, age 10: This granddaughter is my oldest living grandchild. She attends public school in a small rural town. Custody is shared between both parents, with her father having primary custody. She is excelling at school and working above grade level. This granddaughter is very elegant. On my recent visit with her, I asked her how she describes her family and relatives, using one word. She described her daddy, as being "strong" her step-mom, as being "pretty" her step-brother, as "smart" because he reads eighth grade books, her sister as "wild" as she is always running around, her younger brother as "rough" as he is always kicking and hitting, her four-year-old cousin "loving" because he is always trying to cuddle and hug everyone, her new baby cousin "sleepy" as all he does is sleep. As for her uncles, the one that works for the federal government as the "rich one", because he has a nice house and her other uncle as "funny", because he is always making jokes and making people laugh with his pranks; and finally, grandma (me) as the "soft and loving," since I was soft to lay on and kind and have unconditional love for her and all my grandchildren's. My favorite funny memory of her at an early age, was the moment you turned on music, she would crawl to the nearest wall, pull herself up and dance. This granddaughter was often in my care during her first two years of life. She had a rough start, with water in her lungs and then developing an infection. She was in and out of the hospital her first year of life. From an early age she stayed the night with me. When she was extremely ill and released from the hospital to die, my son brought her to me crying, asking for help. I set up with her for days as she could only breathe in a sitting position. When I needed sleep my oldest son stepped in. A few days later she was able to lay down and sleep without turning blue and choking on her mucus. She wore a heart monitor until the age of one.

Grand-daughter, age 9: This granddaughter attends public school in a small rural town. Custody is shared between both parents, with her father having primary custody. She too is excelling in school and working above grade level. This granddaughter is very energetic. The funniest memory I have of this grandchild was when we were returning from a week-long trip in the Southwest, we stopped in Oklahoma for dinner. There were flies everywhere. Several joined us in my car. We drove with the windows down to get them all out. Once we believed them to all

---

[187] Green Family Records 1800's-2016

be out, she began to say in the most adorable Midwestern accent, "There's a bug (buuug) in my chair.

Grandson, age 5: This grandson will be starting Kindergarten next year. He is the youngest child of my middle son and the first male of the new generation to carry on the Green line. One of the sweetest things he most recently said was, It's my uncle, I love my uncle. It's grandma, O love my grandma upon our arrival.

Grandson, age 4: This grandson belongs to my youngest son. He is his second child and oldest living. This grandson can best be described as a real sweetheart. He and his father lived together with me for a couple years. He is a very loving child and has the ability to really watch things around him and analyze everything. He is advanced for his age in many things. He can sit for hours playing with his cars. He is filled with love and happiness. I pray he never loses his happy and loving disposition. He enjoys music and learning. While cautious, once he gets to know someone and care for them he is all cuddles, kisses and has the most manners I have ever seen in such a young child. There are two funny memories that immediately come to mind. First when his uncle purchased his home, he immediately picked the first bedroom you come to stating it was his room. He then picked the biggest bedroom for his uncle. It wasn't until he realized his uncle had his own bathroom that he didn't have one in his room and wanted one added. That evening, and ever since, when his dad puts their items in his room, he pulls his dads bags out and says, "Daddy, I don't want your stuff in my room. The second was when he decided he wanted to sit on his uncle's ottoman. He calmly walked up and said, "Uncle, if you don't give me that chair, I think I will cry.

Grandson, age three months: This grandson is the newest member of our family and my youngest sons' third child. His second child living. At this time all I can say about this sleeping Angel is he loves to be held, he laughs in his sleep, he has personality, he is difficult to burp and on my first meeting he spewed in my hair. It was instant love.[188]

---

[188] Green Family Records 1800's-2016

Chapter XVIII:
Conclusion

As a researcher, historian and genealogist I am happy to share my journey of this particular Green line. A line that originated in present day France, which was well documented for its direct alignment with the Charlemagne (Charles I, King of the Franks). It is because the direct ancestry to Charlemagne, this line found themselves within a continual legacy of being vassals of their territories that will follow them to present-day England. A migration that occurred sometime in the 1150's and where this line would remain for the next five hundred years. Throughout this time, the Greens would earn numerous titles that include the roles of Knights, Dukes, Justice of the Kings Bench and more. They created beautiful gardens, and were great sportsmen. The Green's fought for their King, their country and beliefs, even when it meant being locked in a tower, or losing their head. A family so ingrained in history, even the famous William Shakespeare can't help but write about them. Through all the generations of the Green family they would defend their country, work the land, create massive estates and make themselves known to history.

When I began my research, I wanted to know more about my grandfather and his family. I have not only succeeded in this endeavor, but I have learned more than I ever expected. I am honored to be in this line of Green. I am amazed at the strength of both my grandfather James S. Green and his wife Abbie L. (Glenn) Green, who helped shape the west. While I have in my possession the last will in testament of both James and Abbie, I am impressed by James's will, where he lists not only his biological children but his step-children as well. When it comes to the division of property, his words, "share and share alike" shows his love for all the children he raised. He was a man who refused the title of Colonel, with the belief he did not earn it. However, I am equally impressed by his wife Abbie Glenn and her ability to survive on a rural homestead for more than a decade, with just four young children and a female companion.

What is clear is this line would have died with the eleventh generation, if the author had not kept her maiden name, and passed it to all three of her sons, as no males from the eleventh generation have an heir. It is with the twelfth and thirteenth generation the hope of the line continues.

Appendix A

De La Zouche: Charlemagne to Geoffrey De La Zouche Ancestry Line

THE DE LA ZOUCHE AND GREENE ROYAL DESCENT

Image 1: Eudo de la Zouche, brother of Alexander de la Zouche he leads the Powell line later on into this Green line, a topic to be discussed in a later manuscript

1. Alfred the Great, King of England bn. 871 d. 901 AD

2. Edward the elder, King of England bn. 901 d. 925 AD

3. Henry I, Count de Vermandois bn. 1005 d. 1060 AD
    m. Anna?

4. Herbert, fourth Count de Vermandois bn. 1097 d.? AD
    m. Lady Adelaide of Valois

5. Hugh the Great, Count de Vermandois bn. 1120 AD France, Commander of the Crusade
    m. Lady Adelaide

6. Lady Isabel de Vermandois bn. 1085 d. 1131 AD France to England
    m. Robert de Beaumont, First Earl of Leister, Lord Justice of England bn. 1096 d. 1118 AD

7. Robert de Beaumont, Second Earl of Leister, Lord Justice of England bn. 1104 d.? AD
    m. Amicia de Guade or de Gael.

8. Robert de Beaumont, third Earl of Leister, Stewart of England bn. 1121 d. 1190 AD
    m. Countess Petronella Greatemesnil

9. Margaret de Beaumont bn. 1156 d. 1235 AD
    m. Saher de Quincey, Earl of Winchester bn. 1150 d. 1219 AD

10. Robert de Quincey, Second Earl of Winchester bn.? d. 1264
    m. Helen McDonald

11. Lady Eline de Quincey bn.? d. 1269
    m. Sir Alan, Baron de la Zouche

12. Lord Eudo de la Zouche
    m. Lady Millicent Cantilupe[189]

de la Zouche pedigree:
(1) Robert strong either the son or grandson of Wittekind, the famous Saxon chief who defied Charlemagne. Charles the Bold, the grandson of Charlemagne called on Robert the Strong of Germany to aid him in his fight with his brothers. In return for his services, Robert was rewarded the titles Count of Anjou and Duke of the Isle de France, in addition to territorial grants in 861. Robert the Strong later married the granddaughter of Charlemagne. He fell in battle with the Norsemen who were harassing the Frankish kingdom.

(2) Duke Robert, the son of Robert the Strong and his brother Duke Eudes, are sometimes considered among the kings of France because of the great power the exercised.

(3) Count Hugo the White, or Hugo the Great, became Duke of France and was king in all but name. He was the son of Duke Robert

(4) Hugh the Capet, the son of Hugo the Great seized the throne of France from the weak descendant of Charlemagne 987 and was crowned king at Rheims. He was the start of a long line of kings that reigned in France down to 1848. He married a sister of Guilhelm Fier-a-Bras (William the Iron Arm). Duke of Aquitaine.

(5) Robert the Pious, Hugh's son came to the throne in 996 and reigned until his death in 1031. He was a good man but a weak king. He married Constance of Provence.

(6) King Henry, who became king in 1031 after the death of his father, was the third of the Capetian line. His twenty-nine-year reign was a continuous struggle between him and his nobles. Guerilla warfare was carried out to the point the Church proclaimed a "Truce of God." This truce included no hostilities could take place from Thursday evening until Monday morning, on feast days, during lent and Advent. King Henry married as his second wife, and the mother of his children Anne of Russia, the daughter of the Grand Duke Jaroslav and descendant of Jaroslav the Great.

(7) Hugh Magnus, Count of Vermandois, known as the Great Crusader, was the first of
    the great leaders to reach the Holy Land in 1096. He was the second son of King Henry. He died in the city of Tarsus in 1102.

(8) Lady Isabel, daughter of Count Hugh, married Robert de Bellemont, Earl of Mellent and the first Earl of Leicester.

---

[189] Universal Encyclopedia, Vol. 12, Pgs 4370-4373

(9) Earl Robert, the younger, married Aurelia de la Ware, daughter of Ralph, Earl of Norfolk. Earl Robert was the Lord Chief Justice of England.

(10) Earl Robert, third Earl of Leicester, married Petronella, daughter of Hugh de Grantes-Mismil.

(11) Lady Margaret de Bellemont married Sieur de Quincy. He was in the Crusades of 1118-1192, under Richard Coeur de Lion, King of England. One of his fellow crusaders was Robert, the third Earl of Leicester, afterward, his father-in-law. In 1207, King John nobleman Earl of Winchester. Unfortunately, the Barons rose up against King eight years later; he was one of the twenty-five great barons who signed the magna charter.

12) Earl Roger, second Earl of Winchester married Helen daughter of Alen, Lord of Galway. (13) Lady Elene de Quincy married Alan, Lord de la Zouche, Governor of the castle of Northampton, who died in 1260.

14) Eudo de la Zouche.

(15) Lady Lucy de La Zouche married Sir Thomas, fifth Lord Greene.

Appendix B
De Vere Family Line and its Ties to De La Zouche

Hugh Capet

Hugh Capet   King of France, 987
Spouse Lady Adela, daughter of Duke William of Aquitaine
Children Princess Hedewige

Princess Hedewige   Spouse Raginerus IV., Count of Hainault
Children Lady Beatrix

Lady Beatrix   Spouse Eblo I., Count of Rouci and Reimes
Children Adela, Countess de Rouci

Adela, Countess   Spouse Hildwin IV., Countde Rouci and Montdider
Children Lady Margaret De Rouci

Lady Margaret   Spouse Hugh, Count de Clermont and de Beauvais
Children Aeliza De Clermomt

Lady Aeliza De Clermont   Spouse Gilbert de Tonsburg, 2nd Earl of Clare
Children Adeliza De Clare

Lady Adeliza De Clare   Spouse Alberic, 2nd Baron de Vere
Children Alberic 3rd Baron in 1135, Earl of Oxford and great high chamberlain, d 1194
Spouse Lady Lucia, daughter of William 3rd Baron d' Abrancis
Children Robert De Vere, 3rd Earl of Oxford; one of the twenty-five Barons selected to enforce the Magna Charta

Robert De Vere 3rd   Spouse Lady Isabel, daughter of Hugh 2nd Baron de Bolbee
Children Hugh De Vere 4th Earl of Oxford, great high chamberlain crossing into the Greene line
Spouse Lady Hawise, daughter of Saher de Quincey, Earl of Winchester, one of the twenty-five Magna Charta Barons
Child Robert De Vere 5th Earl of Oxford which crosses into the line of Greene

Robert De Vere 5th   Spouse Alice, daughter of Gilbert, Baron Saundford, chamberlin in fee to Eleanor Queen of Henry III

	Children Alfonso De Vere 2nd son
Alfonso De Vere	Spouse Lady Jane, daughter of Richard Foliot, a Knight
	Children John De Vere 7th Earl of Oxford, killed in Rheims
John De Vere	Spouse Lady Maud, daughter of Bartholomew 1st Baron Badlesmere, were executed in 1322, and widow of Robert Fitz-Payn
	Children Aubrey De Vere
Aubrey De Vere	2nd son (uncle of Robert, 9th Earl of Oxford, and Duke of Dublin, declared a traitor to King Richard, and outlawed). His honors, titles and estates of Oxford were retored making him the 10th Earl of Oxford
	Spouse Lady Alice, daughter of John, Lord Fitz-Walter
	Children Richard De Vere, 11th Earl of Oxford, crossing into the Greene line
Richard De Vere	Spouse Lady Alice, daughter of Sir John Sergeaux, a knight, of Cornwall
Robert De Vere	2nd son
	Spouse married Lady Joan, daughter of Sir Hugh Courtney, a knight, also of Royal Descent
	Children John De Vere
John De Vere	Spouse Alice, daughter of Walter Kelrington
	Children Sir John De Vere
Sir John De Vere	Kings Guard succeeded the 5th Earl of Oxford; great lord high chamberlain of England
	Spouse Elizabeth daughter of Sir Edward Trussel, of Cublesdon
	Children Lady Anne De Vere ending the line of De Vere, which crosses into the Greene line and inherits Greene's Norton

Appendix C

Powell line and its multiple crossing into the Green Ancestry Line

Image 2: Great-Grandfather James "Bolo" Powell, who is the father to Iva Iona Powell; the grandmother to the author.

John Powell
    Born
    Father unknown
    Mother Unknown
    Spouse Mary Unknown
    Children Thomas Powell

Thomas Powell
    Born
    Father John Powell
    Mother Mary
    Spouse Sarah Mnu
    Children Joseph Powell

Joseph Powell
    Born 1754, Died 1832
    Father Thomas Powell
    Mother Sarah Mnu
    Spouse Rachel McCoy b 1758, Died 1832
    Children Dr. Joseph A. Powell

Dr. Joseph A. Powell

Born 1786, Died 1839
Father Joseph Powell
Mother Rachel McCoy
Spouse Eleanor Wheeler Neely
Children Dr. John Alvin Powell

Dr. John Alvin Powell

Born 1822 Died 1882
Father Dr. Joseph A. Powell
Mother Eleanor Wheeler Neely
Spouse Mary Polly Welch
Children Robert Welsh Powell

Robert Welsh Powell

Born 1842, Died 1898
Father Dr. John Alvin Powell
Mother Mary Polly Welsh
Spouse Iva Ann Parker/Taylor*
Children James Welsh "Bolo" Powell

James Welsh Powell

Born 1882, Died 1969
Father Robert Welsh Powell
Mother Iva Ann Parker/Taylor*
Spouse Bertha Lattimore
Children Iva Iona Powell*

Iva Iona Powell*

Born 1911, Died 1974
Father James Welsh Powell
Mother Bertha Lattimore
Spouse Elza/Elzia (Pronounced Ell-Zee) Crockett*
Children Phyllis Florene Crockett

Phyllis Florene Crockett

Born 1934, Died 1976
Father Elza/Elzia Crockett*
Mother Iva Iona Powell
Spouse George Willet Green
Children Living

*Iva Ann Parker/Taylor, the reason for both Parker and Taylor is because she is located in many different records with both last names. Taylor is her mother's name and Parker her father's last name. It is clear her parents did not marry. In court documents I have located her and her sisters were unaware her father was living in Indian Territory. It was brought to her attention when an older half-sister attempted to contest the division of property after his death. This ancestor through her mother is directly related to Zachary Taylor "The Elder" and a cousin to the former President Zachary Taylor.

*Iva Iona Powell it is my Native American connection through her father. She is registered with the Cherokee Nation.

* Elzia/Elza Crockett is my connection to Davy Crockett the Great Frontiersman

Appendix D

The Glenn Family line and Connection to the Green Family Line

John Glenn
  Born
  Died
  Father
  Mother
  Spouse

William Glenn
  Born 1788 Kirchubin, Down, Ireland
  Died
  Father John Glenn
  Mother
  Spouse

William Armstrong Glenn
  Born 1811 Scotland, PA
  Died
  Father William Glenn
  Mother
  Spouse Jane Middleton

William Armstrong Glenn II
  Born Aug 1844, Franklin County, PA
  Died 1899 St. Joseph, Buchannan, MO
  Father William Armstrong Glenn
  Mother Jane Middleton
  Spouse Mary Abigail Neff

Robert Neff Glenn
  Born 9 Apr 1868 Godfrey, Madison, Missouri
  Died 31 Mar 1942, St. Joseph, Buchannan, Missouri
  Father William Armstrong Glenn
  Mother Mary Abigail Neff
  Spouse Estella "Stella" Elizabeth Jordan (twin)

Abbie Lusina Glenn
  Born 5 Mar 1891, St. Joseph, Buchannan, MO
  Died July 1969
  Father Robert Neff Glenn
  Mother Estella "Stella" Elizabeth Jordan (twin)

George Willet Green

NM

Author

Spouse	James Samuel Green	
Born	3 April, 1931, Lawton, (Fort Sill) OK	
Died	18 April 1991, Socorro, Socorro,	
Father	James Samuel Green	
Mother	Abbie Lusina Glenn	
Spouse	Phyllis Florine Crockett	
	Private	

Appendix E

The Crockett Family Line and Connection to the Green Family Line

Gabriel Gustave de Crocketagne
    Born 12 Oct 1672, Montanbon, Haute-Garonne, Midi Pyrenees, France.
    Died   1708 France
    Father
    Mother
    Spouse Michelle Harney

Antoine de Saussure Peronette de Crocketagne
    Born 10 July 1643, Montanbon, Haute-Garonne, Midi Pyrenees, France
    Died 1735 County Londonberry, North Ireland
    Father Gabriel Gustave de Crocketagne
    Mother Michelle Harney
    Spouse Louise Saix

Joseph Louis Crockett
    Born 9 Jan 1675, Kenmore County, Kerry, Munster, Ireland
    Died Aug 1746, South Branch, Roanoke, Virginia
    Father Antoine de Saussur Peronette de Crocketange
    Mother Michelle Harney
    Spouse Sarah Stewart
    Born Abt. 1676 Ireland
    Died 1776 South Branch Roanoke, VA

William D. Crockett
    Born 10 August 1709 Huguenot Colony New Rochelle, NY
    Died 9 June 1777
    Father Joseph Louis Crockett
    Mother Sarah Stewart
    Spouse Agnes Richie, Children, Lois May Brewer Spouse Eliza Boulay, Children David "the Elder" Crockett
    Spouse Hannah, Children John David Crockett, William Crockett, Joseph Crockett and James Crockett

David "The Elder" Crockett	Born 10 Aug 1727 Cumberland County, PA Died Aug 1777 Crockett's Creek, Rogersville, Hawkins, TN (Indian attack) Father William D. Crockett Mother Hannah Spouse Elizabeth Hedge Born Jan 1730 Died Aug 1777 Crockett's Creek, Rogersville, Hawkins, TN
Robert Edward Crockett	Born 13 Aug 1755, Frederich County, Colony of VA Served in Revolutionary War Died 26 Feb 1836, Cumberland County, TN Father David "The Elder" Crockett Mother Elizabeth Hedge Spouse Margaret Rayburn m. Green County, NC Children William Crockett, b abt.1782, Elizabeth Crockett, b 1784, Mary Polly Crockett, b 1787, David B. Crockett, b 18 Aug 1796, James Martin Crockett, April 1801, Robert Crockett
James Martin Crockett	Born April 1801 Father Robert Edward Crockett Mother Margaret Rayburn Spouse Margaret Couch Children William Crockett, b 1823-1910, Mary Polly Crockett, b 1827-1913, Margaret Jane Crockett, b 1828-1906, Emiline Crockett, b 1831-1897, Emily Crockett, b 1831-1903, Martha Crockett, b 1833-1903, Sarah Elizabeth Crockett, b 1835-1871, David Crockett, b 1839-1864, Clamanza Jane Crockett, b 1840-1931, James Robert Crockett, b 1842-1930
William Crockett	Born 19 Oct 1823

	Died 29 Nov 1910
	Father James Martin Crockett
	Mother Margaret Couch
	Spouse Elizabeth Reed
	Children Thursa/Theresa Crockett, b 1849, James Denton Crockett, b 1852, Mary Bird Crockett, b 1855, Martha Jane Crockett, b 1857-1888, Edmond Gibbon Crockett, b 1859-1926, John C Crockett, b 1860, Joseph Crockett, b 1861, Elizabeth Crockett, b 1864, Clamanza Crockett, b 1866-1951, William David Crockett, b 1870-1941
Edmond Gibbon Crockett	Born 20 June 1859 Clinton, Kentucky
	Died 29 Jan 1926 Vinita, Oklahoma
	Father William Crockett
	Mother Elizabeth Reed
	Spouse Mary Ann Parmley
	Children James Issac Crockett, b 1882-1956, Elizabeth "Lizzie" E Crockett, b 1883, William "Willie" E Crockett, b 1885, Robert Andrew Crockett, b 1888-1959, Mary S Crockett, b 1894, Amanda "Mandy" B Crockett, 1897, Joseph David Crockett, 1899-1962
James Isaac Crockett	Born 1881
	Died May 1956
	Father Edmond Gibbon Crockett
	Mother Mary Ann Parmley
	Spouse Laura Ellen Stevens
	Children Tommy Gibbon Crockett, b 1907, Velva Delora Crockett, b 1908, Elzia Isaac Crockett, b 1911, Kenneth Elmo Crockett, b 1914, Alma Marie Crockett, b 1919
Elza/Elzia Isaac Crockett	Pronounced ELL ZEE
	Born 13 Sept 1911, Yale Craig Oklahoma

	Died 7 Feb 1985, Tulsa, Tulsa Oklahoma Father James Isaac Mother Laura Ellen Stevens Spouse Iva Iona Powell b 8 Nov 1911 Oklahoma Died Jan 1974 Tulsa, Tulsa, Oklahoma Children Phyllis Florene Crockett, b 1933, Norma Jean Crockett, b James Elzia Crockett b Laura Jane Crockett b
Phyllis Florene Crockett	Born 26 Sept 1933 Vinita, Oklahoma Died 12 Dec 1976 Socorro, Socorro, New Mexico Father Elza/Elzia Crockett Mother Iva Iona Powell Spouse George Willet Green Children Male, 1954, Living Female, 1955 Living, Male, 1957 Living, Female, 1959, Female, 1960, Female, 1962, Female, 1969.
Author	Living Father George Willet Green Mother Phyllis Florene Crockett Spouse Private Children Living, Male, 1981, Living, Male, 1982, Living, 1984
Male 1	Spouse Private Children Private
Male 2	Spouse Private Children Private
Male 3	Spouse Private Children Private

Appendix F

The Charlemagne Connection

Charlemagne, King of France and Emperor of the West	Spouse Hildegard 3rd wife, daughter of Childebrand Duke of Suabia
	Children Pepin, King of Lombardy and Italy, 2nd son
Pepin, King of Lombardy and Italy	Spouse Lady Bertha, daughter of William Count of Thoulouse
	Children Bernard, King of Lombardy
Bernard, King of Lombardy	Spouse Cunegonde
	Children Pepin, Count of Vermandois and Peronne
Pepin, Count of Vermandois and Peronne	Spouse unknown, a lay abbot, 840
	Children Pepin De Senlis De Valois, Count Berengarius,
Pepin De Senlis De Valois	Spouse unknown
	Children Lady Poppa De Valois
Lady Poppa De Valois	Spouse 1st wife of Rollo the Dane, founder of the Royal House of Normandy and England, 1st Duke of Normandy
	Children William the Longsword, 2nd Duke of Normandy
William Longsword	Spouse not listed
	Children Richard 1 3rd Duke of Normandy
Richard I	Spouse not listed
	Children Godfrey, Count of Eu and Brion, in Normandy
Godfrey	Spouse not listed
	Children Giselbert-Crispin, Count of Eu and Brion
Giselbert-Crispin	Spouse not listed
	Children Baldwin De Brion
Baldwin De Brion	He accompanied his relative William of Normandy, to England, and became high scheriff of Devonshire.

Richard D. Auveranche de Redvers	Spouse Lady Albreda, daughter of Richard-de gros d'Abrancis, Viscount d' Auveranches (who accompanied William the Conqueror and was granted the Earldom of Chester Emme, half-sister, to King William the Conqueror Children Richard D. Auveranche de Redvers, Baron of Oakhampton, created the Earl of Devon Lady Adeliza, daughter of William Fitz-Osborne, Count of Bretoille, lieutenant and steward in Normandy, created Earl of Hereford Note: It is this line that crosses in multiple times to the Greene line through the De Sayer, Fitz-Walter, and Baldwin lines, linking Charlemagne, William the Conqueror and Robert the Strong This line as well as the de la Zouche, De Sayer and Fitz-Walter lines also intercept multiple times with the Powell line within the scope of this research

Americans of Royal Descent Reprinted by Genealogical Publishing Company, Baltimore, 1969

Appendix G

Green Family Select Letters, Military Records & Certificates

James Samuel Green Military Records

```
STATE OF OKLAHOMA )
                  ) SS
COUNTY OF COMANCHE)
```

Personally appeared before me, the undersigned authority for administering oaths in cases of this character, one, W. C. Wandell, Civillian Armament Foreman, Ordnance Department, U. S. A. Who, after being duly sworn according to law, deposes and says:

That on May 23, 1923, I was present during a field problem when Corporal James S. Green was hurt about 9:00 A. M. I was within 10 feet of him at the time of the accident and was watching him repair the track of a 10-ton tractor. He was using a heavy hammer to drive the track pin in the link when a fragment of either the pin or the hammer struck him in the left eye. He staggered and almost fell. I personally looked at the eye but could see nothing. Therefore, thinking that he had only received a blow on the outside of the eye, he was permitted to continue repairs to the tractor which he did under difficulties due to the pain in his eye. After having repaired the tractor and driving aome three (3) or four (4) miles, my attention was again called to him as he sat upon the tractor, pale and apparently in pain. I went up to him and recommended that he permit me to take him in my Dodge Light Repair Truck to the Post and to the hospital. He finally consented and came down from the tractor. I put him on the seat beside me in the Dodge and started with him to the Post. I noticed that he was suffering a great deal and was apparently "light headed" or on the verge of fainting before I got him to the hospital about 4:00 P. M. He was received in the hospital and remained there.

Further the deponent sayeth not.

W. C. Wandell,
Armament Foreman.

Subscribed and sworn to before me this 7th day of November, 1928.

J. D. Balmer,
1st Lt., 1st F. A.
Summary Court.

Figure 6: Green Family Collection, James Samuel Green, Military Records, Report of on base (Fort Sill, OK) injury that occurred 23 May 1923 to Corporal James S. Green.

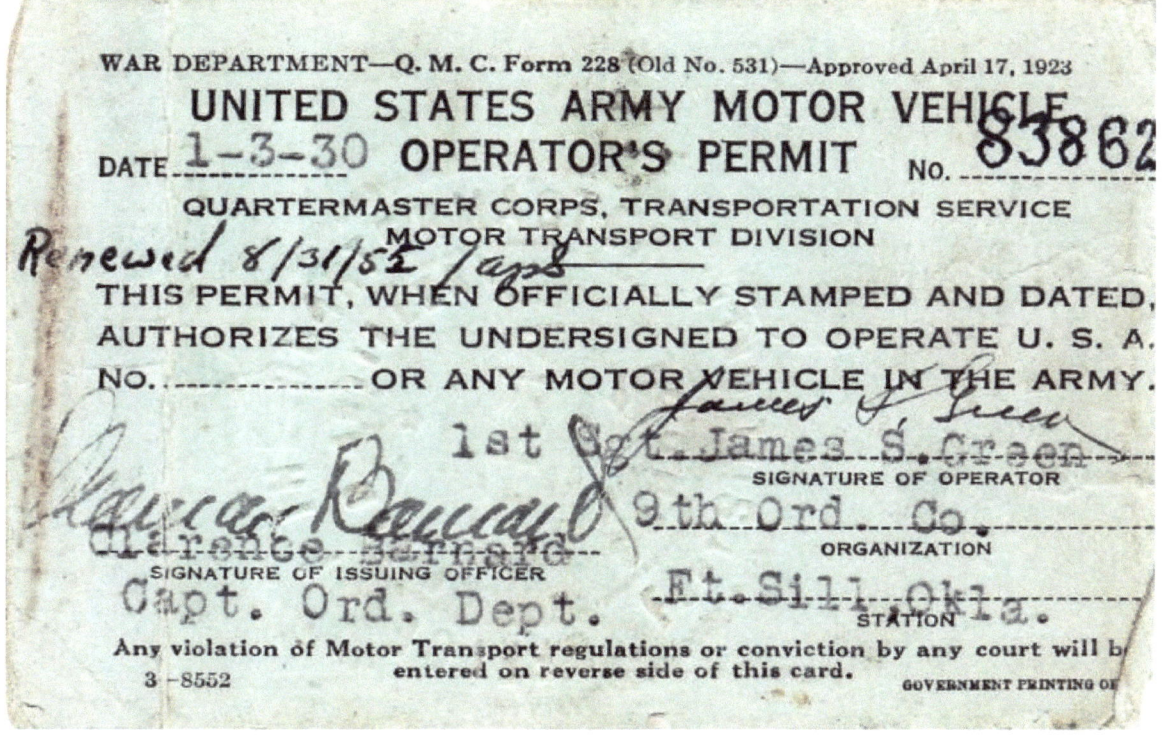

Figure 7: Green Family Collection, James Samuel Green, Military Records, War Department, 1930.

HTC/mbb

July 17, 1942

M/Sgt James S. Green
U. S. Army, Retired
P. O. Box 936
Socorro, New Mexico

My dear Sergeant Green:

    Your letter addressed to the Commanding General, 8th Corps Area, dated June 30, 1942, has been referred to this office for reply, by rubber stamp indorsement. I suspect that your letter was misunderstood at headquarters, and that it was considered to be a request for enlistment. I suggest that you write a second letter to Commanding General, 8th Corps Area, and specifically state that you are applying for a return to active duty from the retired list. I have no information on this subject relative to the possibility or probability of your request being granted, but certainly this is the proper procedure to have your request receive consideration.

    I remember you very distinctly when you were 1st Sgt. of the 9th Ordnance Company, and I wish you the best of success in your attempt to return to active duty.

                   Very sincerely yours,

                   H. T. CLARK, Major, C.A.C.
                   Dist. Ret. & Ind. Officer

Figure 8: Green Family Collection, James Samuel Green, Military Records. Letter written by Master Sergeant James S. Green to request for re-activation into active duty to be of service to the U.S. Army for World War II.

HEADQUARTERS EIGHTH CORPS AREA
OFFICE OF THE CORPS AREA COMMANDER

SAM
FORT SAM HOUSTON, TEXAS.

AG 201 (Enl) Green, James S.   July 29, 1942

Subject: Active Duty.

To : Master Sergeant James S. Green (Retired), Box 936, Socorro, New Mexico.

---

    1. Receipt is acknowledged of your letter of July 24, 1942, offering your services in the present emergency.

    2. The assignment of retired enlisted men to active duty is not contemplated at the present time.

    3. Your patriotic offer is fully appreciated.

    By command of Major General DONOVAN:

P. E. FELTER,
Captain, Corps of Engineers.
Actg. Asst. Adjutant General.

Figure 9: Green Family Collection, James Samuel Green, Military Records, War Department, Denial of Re-enlistment, 1942.

BRIGADIER GENERAL RAY ANDREW
THE ADJUTANT GENERAL

STATE OF NEW MEXICO
OFFICE OF THE ADJUTANT GENERAL
SANTA FE

22 June 1945

Colonel James S. Green
Box 936
Socorro, New Mexico

Dear Colonel Green:

    Acting Governor Jones has instructed me to transmit the attached commission as a Colonel Aide-de-Camp.

    I sincerely congratulate you upon receiving this commission, and I assure you of my hearty cooperation in all matters pertaining to this office.

Sincerely,

RAY ANDREW
Brigadier General
The Adjutant General

Figure 10: Green Family Collection, James Samuel Green, War Department, Letter of Promotion to Colonel, 1945.

SPECIAL ORDERS No. 264, List of 1939 SERIES.
HEADQUARTERS THE F. A. SCHOOL,
Fort Sill, Oklahoma.

SPECIAL ORDERS: December 30, 1939.

No.   264:

E X T R A C T

1. The following promotions in the F.A.S. Det. (Colored) are announced, effective
    January 1, 1940:

    TO BE MASTER SERGEANT
    1st Sgt.   JAMES C. JOHNSON,   R-1140581

    TO BE FIRST SERGEANT
    Staff Sgt. WILLIAM WASHINGTON,   R513699

    TO BE STAFF SERGEANT
    Sergeant   FRANK BRAZIER,   R-313337

    TO BE SERGEANT
    Corporal   CLARENCE JOHNSON,   6226507

    TO BE CORPORAL
    Pvt.1cl Specl 4cl PURLEY W. HAMILTON, Jr. 6266647

2. Par. 18, S.O., 262, this Hq., c.s., is revoked.

    The following-named enlisted men are transferred to C. Tn., 1st Bn., 77th F.A.
    and are attached to F.A.S. Det. (White) for administration and duty,
    effective before breakfast January 1, 1940:

    Pvt.   JAMES H. LIGON,   6295958,   Btry H, 1st F.A.
    Pvt.   THOMAS R. PHILLIPS, Jr. 6295878,   Btry H, 1st F.A.
    Pvt.   QUENTIN REID,   6294158,   Btry H, 1st F.A.
    Pvt.   HAROLD W. MOWRY,   6118646,   Btry H, 1st F.A.
    Pvt.   BYFORD D. BLACK,   6295877,   Btry G, 1st F.A.
    Pvt.   PICKETT E. CHAMBERS,   6293865,   Btry G, 1st F.A.
    Pvt.   WILLIAM D. SMITH,   6292117,   Btry G, 1st F.A.

3. The following-named enlisted men are transferred to C.Tn,1st Bn.,77th F.A.and
    will remain on special duty with the Fort Sill Fire Department, effective
    before breakfast January 1, 1940:

    Pvt.   CLINTON F. COLLINS,   6287703,   Btry B, 1st F.A.
    Pvt.   JAMES H. DUDLEY,   6282997,   Btry I, 1st F.A.

4. Pvt. R. B. WALLACE, 6294213, Co. A, 38th Inf., is transferred to Det. Q.M.C.
    effective January 2, 1940.

5. M.Sgt. JAMES S. GREEN, R-2132246, F.A.S. Det. (White), will upon retirement
    proceed to his home, Magdalena, New Mexico. (par. 11, S.O.300, WD.,AGO.,
    12-28-39).
    The QMC will furnish the necessary transportation.
    Travel by privately owned conveyance is authorized.

Figure 11: Green Family Collection, James Samuel Green, Fort Sill Special Orders Document, Announcement of military promotions, transfers and retirement, 1939.

Army of the United States

To all who shall see these presents, greeting:

Know ye, that reposing special trust and confidence in the fidelity and abilities of James S. Green, R-2132246, 1st Sgt. 9th Ord. Co, I do hereby re-appoint him * Sergeant, 9th Ordnance Co, ARMY OF THE UNITED STATES, to rank as such from the sixteenth day of May one thousand nine hundred and twenty-eight. He is therefore carefully and diligently to discharge the duty of † Sergeant by doing and performing all manner of things thereunto belonging. And I do strictly charge and require all Noncommissioned Officers and Soldiers under his command to be obedient to his orders as Sergeant. And he is to observe and follow such orders and directions from time to time, as he shall receive from his Superior Officers and Noncommissioned Officers set over him, according to the rules and discipline of War.

Given under my hand at The Field Artillery School, Fort Sill, Oklahoma this tenth day of January in the year of our Lord one thousand nine hundred and thirty.

Colonel, First Field Artillery
Commandant

W. D., A. G. O. Form No. 58
March 25, 1924

* Insert grade, company, and regiment or branch; e.g., "Corporal, Company A..."
† Insert grade.

Figure 12: Green Family Collection, Army of the United States Document of James Samuel Green Promotion, 16 May 1928 to Sergeant.

ENLISTMENT RECORD

OF

Green, James S., R-2132246, First Sgt.
(Last name) (First name) (Middle initial) (Army Serial No.) (Grade)

Enlisted ~~or inducted~~, October 27, 1925, at Fort Sill, Oklahoma.

Completed 12 years, 11 months, 17 days service for longevity pay.

Prior service: * Co. "B" 1st Inf. 5-12-08 to 5-11-11, Musician, "Ex." E.T.S. Co. B. 1st Inf. 6-13-11 to 4-19-14, Pvt. "Ex." Unknown, 1st G.M.O.D.S. 10-15-15 to 10-26-19, Sgt. "Ex." Almost 9th Ord. Co. 10-27-19 to 10-26-22, Sgt. "Ex." per E.T.S. 9th Ord. Co. 10-27-22 to 10-26-25, 1st Sgt. "Ex." per E.T.S.

Noncommissioned officer: 1st Sgt. 6-10-25 Cont'd to 5-15-28, Sgt. 5-16-28 to 8-17-28, 1st Sgt. 8-18-28

Qualification in arms:† Rifle Sharpshooter 10-5-28

Horsemanship: Not mounted.

Knowledge of any vocation: Clerk, Motor Mechanic

Attendance at: None.
(Name of noncommissioned officers' or special service school)

Battles, engagements, skirmishes, expeditions: None

Decorations, service medals, citations: None

Wounds received in service: None.

Physical condition when discharged: Good

Date and result of smallpox vaccination:‡ 3-3-26, Vaccinia

Date of completion of all typhoid-paratyphoid vaccinations:‡ Completed 12-29-22

Date and result of diphtheria immunity test (Schick):‡ None

Date of other vaccinations (specify vaccine used):‡ None

Married or single: Married

Character: Excellent. Very

Remarks: No time lost under 107th A.W.

Signature of soldier: James S. Green

W. M. Eyerly
2nd Lieut., Field Artillery
~~Commanding~~ Personnel Adjt.

* Give company, regiment, and branch, with inclusive dates of service in each enlistment.
† Give date of qualification, and number, date, and source of order announcing same.
‡ See par. 6, AR 40-215.

Figure 13: Green Family Collection, Enlistment Record, Indicates years of service and re-enlistment of James Samuel Green, 1928.

CUT HERE

1. DESIGNATOR'S LAST NAME - FIRST NAME - MIDDLE NAME: GREEN, James S.
2. PRESENT SERVICE NUMBER: R 2132246
3. GRADE/RANK: Mr. Sgt
4. DATE OF BIRTH: 1/6/1890
5. DATE: 7/22/60

6. HOME ADDRESS AT TIME OF LAST ENTRY INTO SERVICE (City, County & State): 9th Ord. Co., Ft. Sill, Okla.
7. DATE OF LAST ENTRY: 10/27/37 PRIOR SERVICE ☒ YES ☐ NO
8. SOCIAL SECURITY NUMBER: 525-42-3009
9. FORMER SERVICE NUMBER: None

10a. WIFE OR HUSBAND (First Name - Middle Name - Last Name) (If deceased, so state; if none, so state): Abbie L. Green
b. ADDRESS: Box 936, Socorro, N. Mex.

11. NAME OF CHILDREN (If none, so state; if step or adopted, so state)

NAME OF CHILDREN	ADDRESS	MARRIED YES	MARRIED NO	SEX	DATE OF BIRTH
Georgia Green	Box 936, Socorro, N. Mex.		x	F	10/23/25
George W. Green	%2825 Valencia Dr., N.E. Albuquerque, N. Mex.	x		M	4/3/31

12a. FATHER (First name - Middle name - Last name) (If deceased, so state): Deceased
b. ADDRESS:

13a. MOTHER (First name - Middle name - Last name) (If deceased, so state): Lena Briggs
b. ADDRESS: 824 A. W. Rogers St. Milwaukee, Wis.

14a. ADULT NEXT OF KIN NOT NAMED IN ANY OTHER ITEM AND RELATIONSHIP: Elizabeth Ingram, Step Daughter
b. ADDRESS: 2825 Valencia Dr., N.E. Albuquerque, N.Mex.

15. PERSON(S) NAMED IN OTHER ITEMS WHO ARE *NOT* TO BE NOTIFIED DUE TO ILL HEALTH: Lena Briggs

16. ORGANIZATION AND ADDRESS OF DESIGNATOR (To include Service): 9th Ord. Co., Ft. Sill, Okla.
Served 30 4/12 years in U. S. Army 9th Ord. Co. from 7/4/19 to 12/31/39

17. SIGNATURE OF WITNESS: Mrs Alice Collins
18. SIGNATURE OF DESIGNATOR: James S. Green

DD FORM 1 DEC 56 93 — REPLACES PREVIOUS EDITIONS OF DD FORM 93, AND DA FORM 1626, 1 FEB. 56, WHICH ARE OBSOLETE. — RECORD OF EMERGENCY DATA

Figure 14: Green Family Collection, James Samuel Green, Record of Emergency Data, 1937

DUPLICATE

RETIRED PAY CHANGE SLIP

NOTICE.—Each time your pay changes you will receive a new slip with an explanation under remarks. Keep it for future reference.

LAST NAME	FIRST NAME	MIDDLE INITIAL	GRADE	ARMY SERIAL NO.	P/R NO.
Green	James	S.	M/Sgt.	R2,132,346	7

ADDRESS	SUBJECT TO TAX	PAY PERIOD	COMPONENT	SLIP NO.
	☒ YES ☐ NO	April 1951	Army	51

	BASE PAY	OTHER	GROSS PAY	TAX	N INS	D INS	E ALMT.	BONDS	OTHER	NET PAY
OLD NORMAL PAY	220.50						10.00			210.50
ACTUAL PAY THIS PERIOD	220.50			10.00			10.00			200.50
NEW NORMAL PAY	220.50			10.00			10.00			200.50

REMARKS:

Tax Change

DA WFO FORM 1 DEC 49 4-06a — U. S. GOVERNMENT PRINTING OFFICE 16—62070-1 — FORM PRESCRIBED BY COMPTROLLER GENERAL, U. S. DECEMBER 5, 1949

Figure 15: Green Family Collection, James Samuel Green, Retirement Pay Slip, 05 December 1949.

DESIGNATIONS	FIRST NAME - MIDDLE NAME - LAST NAME	ADDRESS	RELATIONSHIP
19. BENEFICIARY FOR GRATUITY PAY IN EVENT THERE IS NO SURVIVING SPOUSE OR CHILD (Name Parents or Brothers or Sisters ONLY) (PL 881, 84th Congress)	Lena Briggs,	824 W. Rogers St., Milwaukee 4, Wisc.	Mother
20. BENEFICIARY FOR UNPAID PAY AND ALLOWANCES (PL 147, 84th Congress) (% of shares must total 100%) — SHARE %, SHARE 100, SHARE %	Abbie L. Green,	P. O. Box 936, Socorro, New Mexico.	Wife
21. PERSON TO RECEIVE ALLOTMENT IF MISSING — % OF PAY EA. MO.			
22. INSURANCE POLICIES IN FORCE - INCLUDING NSLI AND USGLI (Companies to be notified in case of death in Active Service)			
FULL NAME AND ADDRESS OF COMPANY		OFFICE RECEIVING PAYMENT	POLICY NUMER

FOR INSTRUCTIONS ON PREPARATION AND DISPOSITION REFER TO:
ARMY (Including Army Reserve) - AR 640-40
ARMY NATIONAL GUARD - NGR 29
AIR FORCE - AFR 35-38
AIR NATIONAL GUARD - AFR 35-38

DO NOT FORWARD THIS FORM TO VETERANS ADMINISTRATION

Figure 16: Green Family Collection, James Samuel Green Military Record for Insurance Policy

HEADQUARTERS THE F. A. SCHOOL
Fort Sill, Oklahoma.

November 1, 1939.

SPECIAL ORDER:

NO 220: E X T R A C T

1. 1st Sgt. JAMES S. GREEN, R-2132346, 9th Ordnance Co., is transferred in grade of Private to the F. A. S. Detachment (White), and is appointed Master Sergeant.
   M. Sgt. GREEN is attached to the 9th Ordnance Co., for administration and duty.

2. The following promotions in the 9th Ordnance Co., are announced:

   TO BE FIRST SERGEANT
   Sergeant GUSTER R. YORK,   6229622.

   TO BE SERGEANT
   Corporal ZEB T. PANGLE,   6076905.

   TO BE CORPORAL
   Pvt. specl 3cl MARVIN STEVENS, 6334470.

3. 1st Lt. PAUL R. WEYRAUCH, 1st F.A., is, in addition to his other duties attached to the Staff and Faculty, The F. A. School, as Instructor, effective this date, and will report to the Assistant Commandant, for duty, accordingly.

4. Captain JOHN C. OAKES, 1st F.A., is, in addition to his other duties attached to this Hq., for duty as Assistant Adjutant.

5. 1st Lt. MERVYN MACL. MAGEE, 18th F.A., is, in addition to his other duties attached to this Hq., for duty as Assistant Adjutant.

6. Pvt. specl 6cl. ALEX C. COOK, 6287501, Hq. Btry. 1st F.A., will be discharged and reenlisted in grade of Private and without specialist rating for Quartermaster Corps (Unasgd), Panama Canal Dept., in time to report to the C.O. OD&RD, Brooklyn, N.Y., between April 1st & 10th, 1940. Soldier being entitled to subsistence at Govt. expense the Fin. Dept. will pay in lieu thereof the money value of the garrison ration at the rate prescribed in WD. Cir. #33, 6/7/39, for one (1) man for two and two-thirds (2 2/3) days, the time required to perform the travel. Sixty (60) days delay enroute is authorized. (AR 615-275). Waiver of travel pay upon discharge will be enforced. (WD. Cir. #28, 5/5/39). (7th Ind. Hq. 8'CA; 10/30/39).
   Except for the above allowance no expense to the Govt. will be incurred.

7. Staff Sgt. SAM J. TETER, 6433046, Hq. Btry. 18th F.A., will proceed from this station to Ft. Moultrie, S.C., in time to report to the C.O., OD &RD, not earlier than three (3) days prior to sailing, nor later than 9:00AM of the day prior to sailing of the transport scheduled to leave Charleston, S.C. on or about February 9, 1940, for the Panama Canal Dept., as replacement for Staff Sgt. FOTIS A CUNNINGHAM, 6362536, F.A., being assigned this station.

Figure 17: Green Family Collection, James Samuel Green Military Record, Promotion to Master Sergeant 01 November 1939.

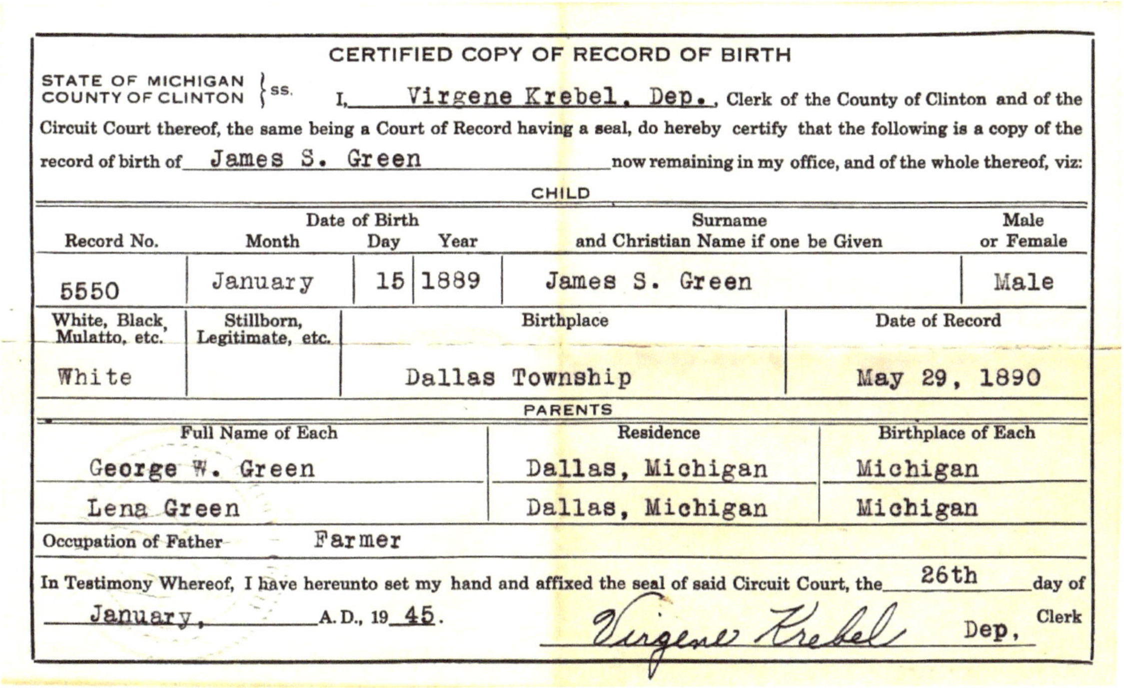

CERTIFIED COPY OF RECORD OF BIRTH

STATE OF MICHIGAN
COUNTY OF CLINTON } ss.

I, __Virgene Krebel, Dep.__, Clerk of the County of Clinton and of the Circuit Court thereof, the same being a Court of Record having a seal, do hereby certify that the following is a copy of the record of birth of __James S. Green__ now remaining in my office, and of the whole thereof, viz:

CHILD

Record No.	Date of Birth Month	Day	Year	Surname and Christian Name if one be Given	Male or Female
5550	January	15	1889	James S. Green	Male

White, Black, Mulatto, etc.	Stillborn, Legitimate, etc.	Birthplace	Date of Record
White		Dallas Township	May 29, 1890

PARENTS

Full Name of Each	Residence	Birthplace of Each
George W. Green	Dallas, Michigan	Michigan
Lena Green	Dallas, Michigan	Michigan

Occupation of Father — Farmer

In Testimony Whereof, I have hereunto set my hand and affixed the seal of said Circuit Court, the __26th__ day of __January,__ A.D., 19__45__.

Virgene Krebel Dep. Clerk

Figure 18: Green Family Collection, James Samuel Green Birth Certificate, 26 January 1945.

James Samuel Green Select Real Estate & Travel Records and Last Will in Testament

DEPARTMENT OF THE INTERIOR
GENERAL LAND OFFICE
4—131
Form approved by Comptroller General U. S.
November 22, 1929
MGA

RECEIPT

№ 3115421

U. S. LAND OFFICE, Las Cruces, N.M., April 6,1932
(Date)

Received of James S. Green, 9th Ord. Co., Fort Sill, Oklahoma.
(Name) (Address)

in connection with Add'l Homestead Appln Act 12-29-16 045699
(Kind of application and act under which made; number and date of lease, etc.) (Serial number)

THE SUM OF Ten & 00/100-- DOLLARS
in ~~cash or~~ by U. S. Postal Money Order

and/or

THE SUM OF ________ DOLLARS

by ________, SUBJECT TO COLLECTION.*
(Indicate form of remittance—check, draft, etc.)

Fees	10	00
Total,	10	00

*When tender is by check, draft, or form other than cash or U. S. Postal Money Order, this receipt will not become an acquittance until collection is made.

V B McCoy
Register, U. S. Land Office.

This Receipt is evidence only of the receipt of the amount indicated, and must be issued at the time the remittance is received, without regard to the subsequent allowance or rejection of the application, entry, etc., due notice of which will be given.
In case of error in this Receipt, notify the Register where issued, and the Commissioner of the General Land Office, Washington, D. C.
In writing to the local land office or the General Land Office concerning the application or entry in connection with which this Receipt issued, always give the above Serial Number and the Receipt Number.

6—11688 U. S. GOVERNMENT PRINTING OFFICE. 1929

Figure 19: Green Family Collection, James Samuel Green, Land Record, 06 April 1932

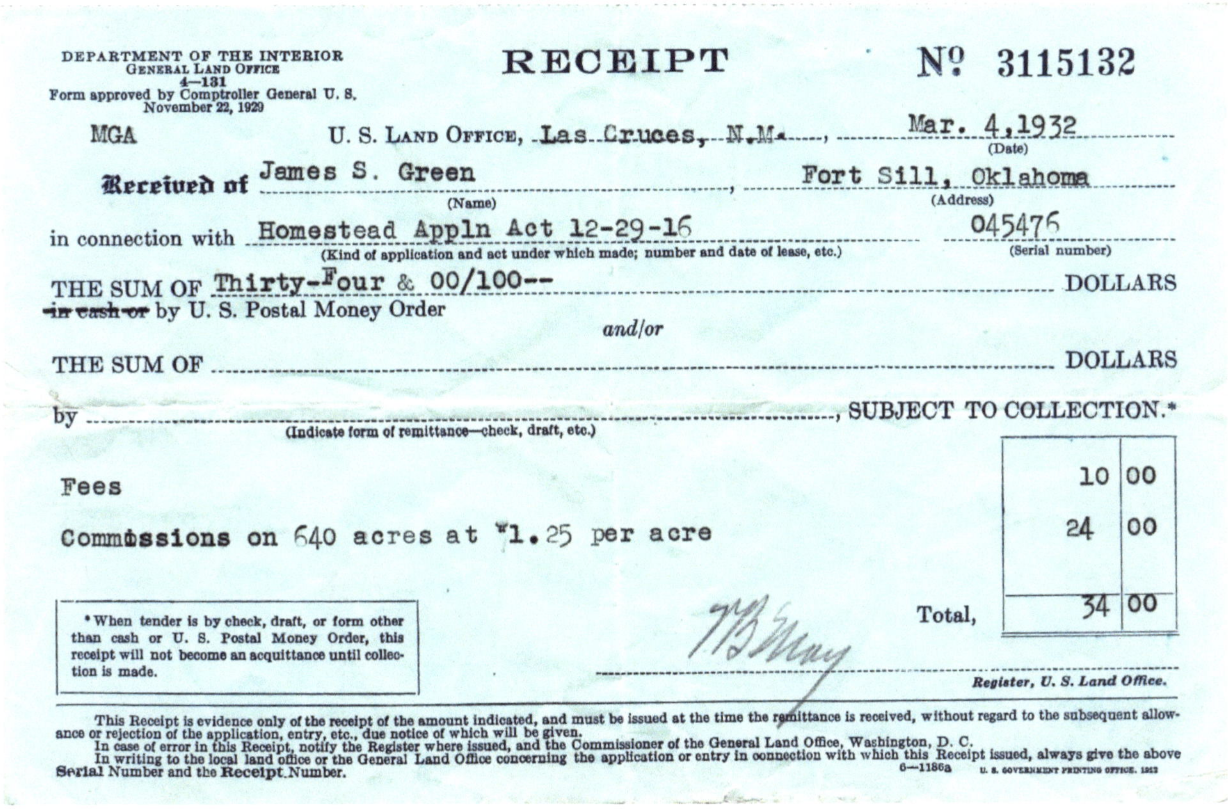

DEPARTMENT OF THE INTERIOR
GENERAL LAND OFFICE
4—131
Form approved by Comptroller General U. S.
November 22, 1929

RECEIPT

No. 3115132

MGA U. S. LAND OFFICE, Las Cruces, N.M., Mar. 4, 1932 (Date)

Received of James S. Green (Name), Fort Sill, Oklahoma (Address)

in connection with Homestead Appln Act 12-29-16 (Kind of application and act under which made; number and date of lease, etc.) 045476 (Serial number)

THE SUM OF Thirty-Four & 00/100-- DOLLARS
~~in cash or~~ by U. S. Postal Money Order

and/or

THE SUM OF .... DOLLARS

by .... (Indicate form of remittance—check, draft, etc.), SUBJECT TO COLLECTION.*

Fees	10	00
Commissions on 640 acres at $1.25 per acre	24	00
Total,	34	00

*When tender is by check, draft, or form other than cash or U. S. Postal Money Order, this receipt will not become an acquittance until collection is made.

WB May
Register, U. S. Land Office.

This Receipt is evidence only of the receipt of the amount indicated, and must be issued at the time the remittance is received, without regard to the subsequent allowance or rejection of the application, entry, etc., due notice of which will be given.
In case of error in this Receipt, notify the Register where issued, and the Commissioner of the General Land Office, Washington, D. C.
In writing to the local land office or the General Land Office concerning the application or entry in connection with which this Receipt issued, always give the above Serial Number and the Receipt Number.
6—1186a U. S. GOVERNMENT PRINTING OFFICE. 1912

Figure 20: Green Family Collection, James Samuel Green, Land Record, 04 March 1932.

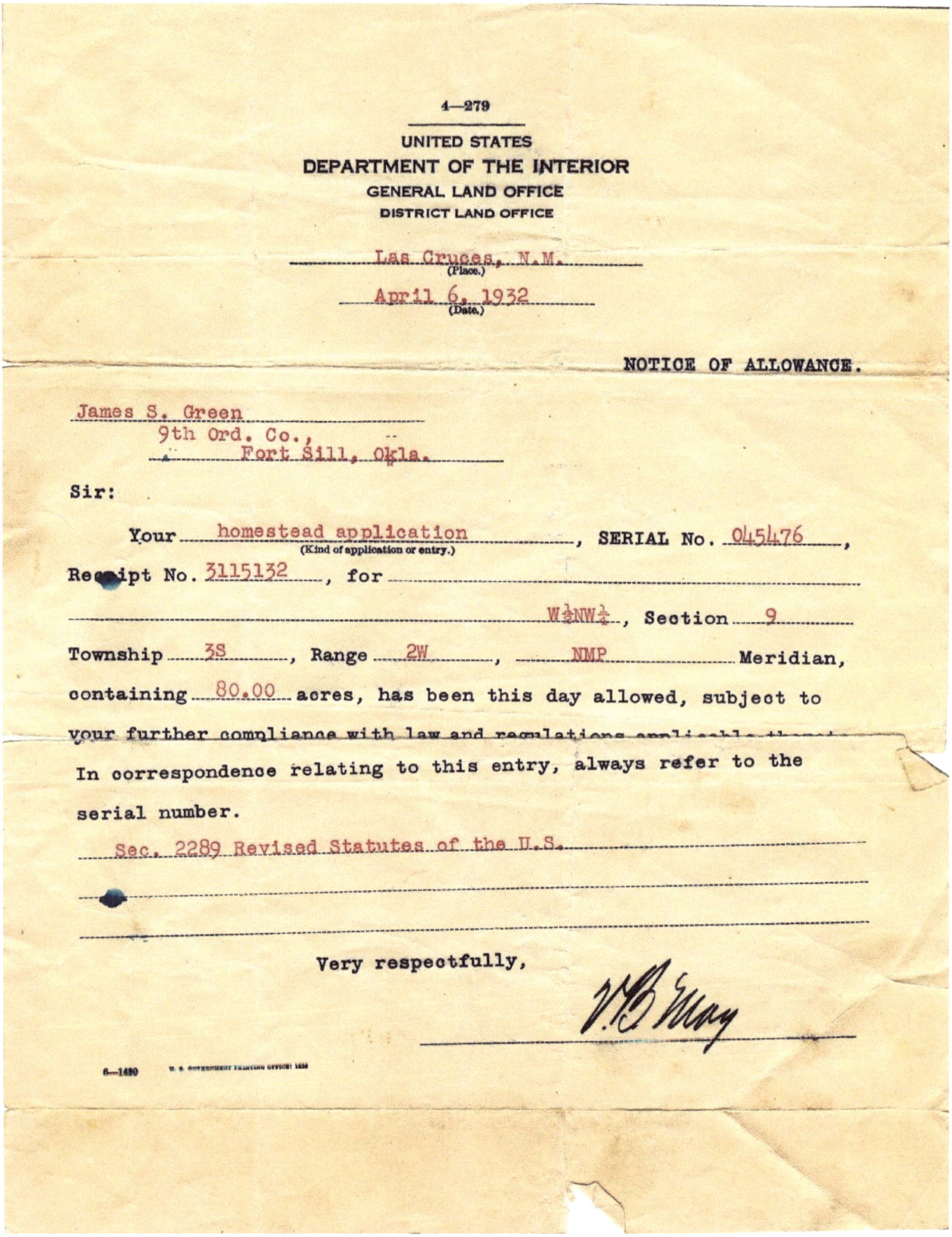

4—279

UNITED STATES
DEPARTMENT OF THE INTERIOR
GENERAL LAND OFFICE
DISTRICT LAND OFFICE

Las Cruces, N.M.
(Place.)

April 6, 1932
(Date.)

NOTICE OF ALLOWANCE.

James S. Green
9th Ord. Co.,
Fort Sill, Okla.

Sir:

Your homestead application (Kind of application or entry.), SERIAL No. 045476,
Receipt No. 3115132, for
W½NW¼, Section 9
Township 3S, Range 2W, NMP Meridian,
containing 80.00 acres, has been this day allowed, subject to
your further compliance with law and regulations applicable thereto.
In correspondence relating to this entry, always refer to the
serial number.

Sec. 2289 Revised Statutes of the U.S.

Very respectfully,

V. B. May

6—1490 U. S. GOVERNMENT PRINTING OFFICE: 1930

Figure 21: Green Family Collection, James Samuel Green, Homestead Application, 06 April 1932.

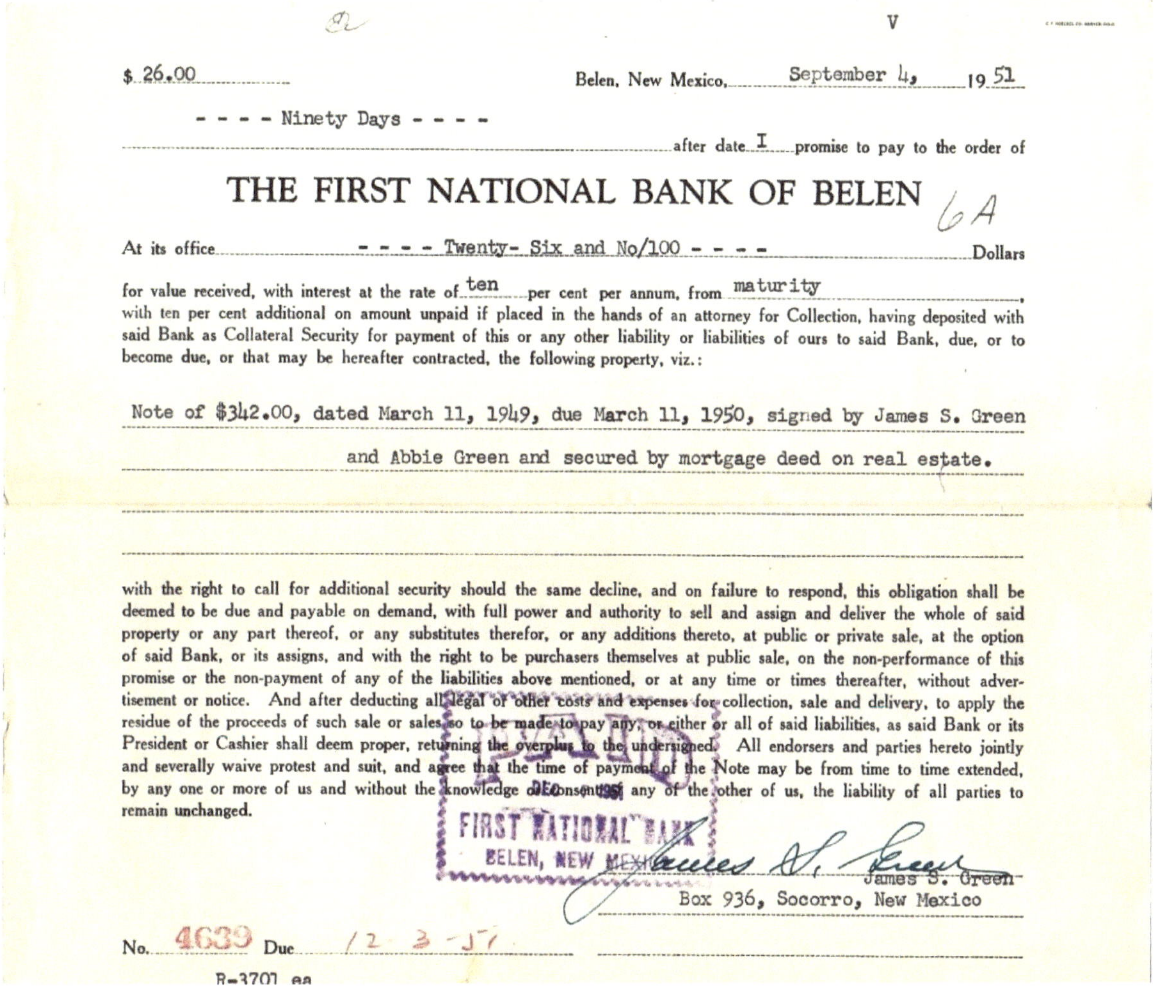

V

$ 26.00 Belen, New Mexico, September 4, 1951

---- Ninety Days ---- after date I promise to pay to the order of

THE FIRST NATIONAL BANK OF BELEN 6A

At its office ---- Twenty- Six and No/100 ---- Dollars

for value received, with interest at the rate of ten per cent per annum, from maturity, with ten per cent additional on amount unpaid if placed in the hands of an attorney for Collection, having deposited with said Bank as Collateral Security for payment of this or any other liability or liabilities of ours to said Bank, due, or to become due, or that may be hereafter contracted, the following property, viz.:

Note of $342.00, dated March 11, 1949, due March 11, 1950, signed by James S. Green and Abbie Green and secured by mortgage deed on real estate.

with the right to call for additional security should the same decline, and on failure to respond, this obligation shall be deemed to be due and payable on demand, with full power and authority to sell and assign and deliver the whole of said property or any part thereof, or any substitutes therefor, or any additions thereto, at public or private sale, at the option of said Bank, or its assigns, and with the right to be purchasers themselves at public sale, on the non-performance of this promise or the non-payment of any of the liabilities above mentioned, or at any time or times thereafter, without advertisement or notice. And after deducting all legal or other costs and expenses for collection, sale and delivery, to apply the residue of the proceeds of such sale or sales so to be made to pay any, or either or all of said liabilities, as said Bank or its President or Cashier shall deem proper, returning the overplus to the undersigned. All endorsers and parties hereto jointly and severally waive protest and suit, and agree that the time of payment of the Note may be from time to time extended, by any one or more of us and without the knowledge or consent of any of the other of us, the liability of all parties to remain unchanged.

PAID DEC 1951 FIRST NATIONAL BANK BELEN, NEW MEXICO

James S. Green
James S. Green
Box 936, Socorro, New Mexico

No. 4639 Due 12-3-51

R-3701 ea

Figure 22: Green Family Collection, James Samuel Green Bank Record, 04 September 1951.

Last Will and Testament
of
JAMES S. GREEN

I, JAMES S. GREEN, of the City of Socorro, County of Socorro, and State of New Mexico, being of legal age and of sound and disposing mind do make, publish, and declare this to be my Last Will and Testament hereby revoking any and all former wills and testamentary dispositions heretofore at any time made by me.

FIRST: I direct my Executrix hereinafter named to pay all my just debts and obligations including the expenses of my last illness as soon after my death as is practicable.

SECOND: To my children and step-children, ROBERT GLENN ST. CLAIR, ELIZABETH INGRAM, WILLIAM J. O'CONNELL, GEORGE WILLETT GREEN, and SHERRI LOU BROOKS, daughter of MARY ALICE BROOKS, deceased, I leave nothing.

THIRD: In the event that my death and the death of my said wife should occur simultaneously, or approximately so, or in the same common accident or calamity, or under any circumstances causing doubt as to which of us survived the other, or in the event that my said wife should predecease me, then and in such event I give, bequeath, and devise the sum of One Dollar ($1.00) to Sherri Lou Brooks, daughter of Mary Alice Brooks, deceased, and all the rest and residue of my estate of every kind and description whether real, personal, or mixed, wherever located, to my children and step-children, ROBERT GLENN ST. CLAIR, ELIZABETH INGRAM, WILLIAM J. O'CONNELL, and GEORGE WILLETT GREEN, share and share alike.

[signature: James S. Green]

Figure 23: Green Family Collection, James Samuel Green, Last Will in Testament, 10 January 1964, p.1 of 2

FOURTH: I hereby nominate and appoint my wife, ABBIE L. GREEN, to be Executrix of this my Last Will and Testament and direct that she not be required to give any bond as such Executrix. In the event of the inability of my wife, ABBIE L. GREEN, to serve as such Executrix, I hereby nominate and appoint ELIZABETH INGRAM to be Executrix of this my Last Will and Testament and direct that she not be required to give any bond or undertaking as such Executrix.

IN WITNESS WHEREOF, in the presence of the undersigned persons whom I have requested to act as attesting witnesses, I have hereunto and at the foot of the one preceding page hereof, set my hand and seal this 10th day of January, A. D. 1964, at Socorro, New Mexico.

James S. Green (SEAL)

The foregoing instrument consisting of two pages, this attestation clause being on the second page thereof, was subscribed, published, and declared by James S. Green as and for his Last Will and Testament, in our presence and in the presence of each of us, and we at the same time, at his request, in his presence and in the presence of each other hereunto subscribed our names as attesting witnesses, together with our respective places of residence, this 10th day of January, 1964.

Mrs Raymond Olivas
residing at Box 337
Socorro N.M.

Mary B. Aguilar
residing at 367 Terry Ave
Socorro, New Mexico

Figure 24: Green Family Collection, James Samuel Green, Last Will in Testament, 10 January 1964, p.2 of 2

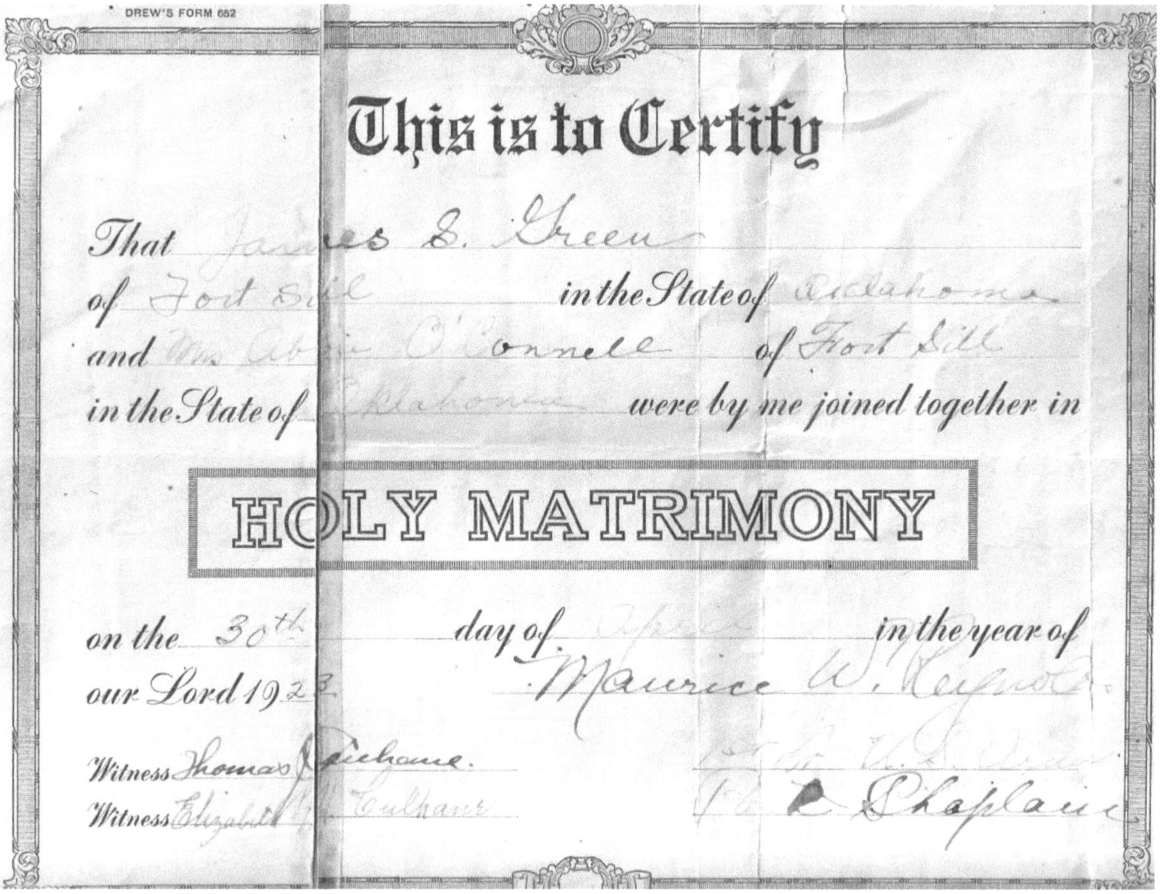

DREW'S FORM 652

This is to Certify

That James S. Green

of Fort Sill in the State of Oklahoma

and Mrs. Abbie O'Connell of Fort Sill

in the State of Oklahoma were by me joined together in

HOLY MATRIMONY

on the 30th day of April in the year of

our Lord 1923 Maurice W. Re...

Witness Thomas J. Culhane. 1st Lt. U.S. Army

Witness Elizabeth M. Culhane Chaplain

Figure 25: Green Family Collection. James Samuel Green and Abbie Glenn Marriage Record, 30 April 1923.

Appendix H
Other Select Personal Records

J. S. GREEN

OUR NOBLE SIRE

Whose heart is it that fills with pride
When we in our first trousers stride,
And when we fly a little higher,
Rejoices? 'Tis our noble sire!

Who sees we kids grow into boys,
Puts up with our infernal noise,
Tells us stories, each a whopper
Full of genii? 'Tis our popper!

Who buys us firecrackers and toys
And stuffs our paunch with sugared joys,
The circus shows us filled with awe?
Why, sure! It is our genial pa!

Who thrills when we athletes become
And "break the record", jump or run,
Or sighs if fortune proves a traitor?
It is our omnipresent pater!

Who, when we come to man's estate
Is anxious till we strike our gait,
And frets himself into a lather
If things go wrong? It is our father!

Who shoves his snout into the trough
To root the other porkers off,
And swipes the stuff that makes us glad?
It is our philanthropic dad!

Who gained the prize we value most,
Our truest friend and fondest boast;
Who annexed mother to the clan,
And got her for us? The old man.

Figure 26: Green Family Collection, James Samuel Green. Personal poem written by James S. Green to show his children and step-children that all roads lead back to dad (date of being written is unknown)

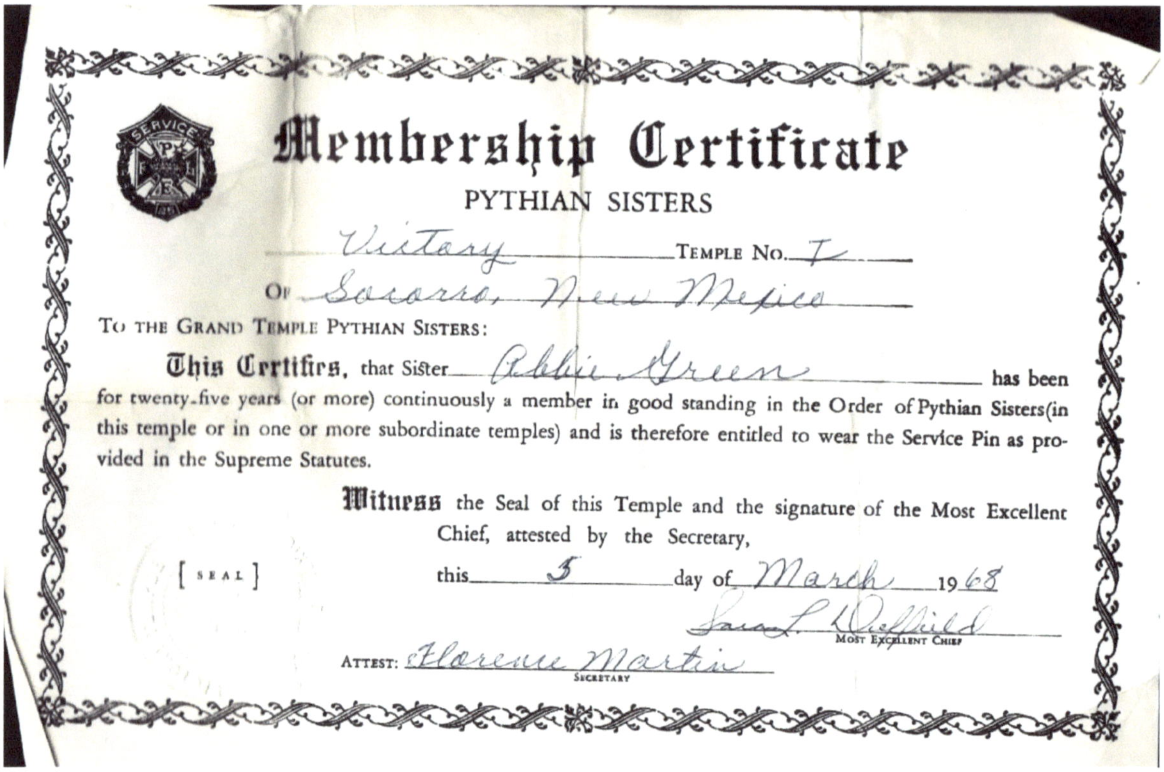

Membership Certificate

PYTHIAN SISTERS

Victory TEMPLE No. 1

OF Socorro, New Mexico

TO THE GRAND TEMPLE PYTHIAN SISTERS:

This Certifies, that Sister Abbie Green has been for twenty-five years (or more) continuously a member in good standing in the Order of Pythian Sisters (in this temple or in one or more subordinate temples) and is therefore entitled to wear the Service Pin as provided in the Supreme Statutes.

Witness the Seal of this Temple and the signature of the Most Excellent Chief, attested by the Secretary,

[SEAL] this 5 day of March 1968

MOST EXCELLENT CHIEF

ATTEST: Florence Martin
SECRETARY

Figure 27: Green Family Collection, Abbie Glenn, Certificate Membership to Pythian Sisters, 05 March 1968.

Jan 22 1960

Dear Mrs Green:

I am writing this for your daughter Mary. She has been very ill with a rare blood decease It's a desease that the dr's around here haven't heard of for 12 yrs She became very enemic and was in bed for about 2 months off and on befor going to the Dr. she got so weak her legs wouldn't hold her up and they finally had to take her to the hospital, it took them a wk of taking tests to find out what she has. She does not have Leucemia and will get well though she will need care for some time as far as I have found out she has Pur-puro which the membrains of the tissues break & bleed.

Figure 28: Green Family Collection. Personal Letter to Abbie (Glenn) Green from a caretaker to her daughter Mary Alice, 22 January 1960, p. 1 of 2.

and caused the ends of her fingers & toes and end of her nose to look like they had been smashed. They were deep purple and she had splotches all over her. These have cleared up pretty well on the outside but she has them internally too. She is feeling quite a bit better and is leaving the Sanatarium where I work Sunday she told me today. One of the head nurses told me she is likely to be in and out of the hospital for some time, though she doesn't know this so don't mention it when you write.

Soon as she feels well enough I understand she is going to Arizona for a visit and rest up time. I understand she will have to take medicine for quite a while.

Sherrie is fine and growing up.

I am Mary's Aunt by marriage and think a lot of her. God Bless You
Mrs Earl Brooks

Figure 29: Green Family Collection. Personal Letter to Abbie (Glenn) Green from a caretaker to her daughter Mary Alice, 22 January 1960, p. 2 of 2.

BUDDY GREEN HONORED IN SCOUT MEETING

Buddy Green was awarded the Eagle Scout Badge in a District meeting Tuesday night at the Socorro Cafe, refreshments and eats were served.

We congratulate Buddy Green for being one of the few to earn the eagle scout badge in the Socorro District—an award given after many outstanding services, there has only four such awards in the "Socorro Boy Scouts History". Last Eagle Scout possesor prior to this was about thirteen years ago.

Mrs. J. S. Green was honored by Dr. C. C. Clarke when she received the badge for her son Buddy.

The following were present: Field Executive, Edward Ball; Socorro District Scout Committee: Dr. C. C. Clark, Dan Barry, Percy Sickles; Scout Masters: Ed. Eiland, Troop 36 and Vincent Pino Troop 173; Julius Fraissinet, Mr. and Mrs. J. S. Green and Mr. and Mrs. Thomas Hazelrigg.

Figure 30: Green Family Collection, George W. Green, Newspaper Clipping announcing his award of being an Eagle Scout.

Honorable Discharge

FROM THE NATIONAL GUARD OF

NEW MEXICO

AND THE NATIONAL GUARD OF THE UNITED STATES

To all whom it may concern:

This is to Certify, That GEORGE W. GREEN, 25 635 288, PRIVATE FIRST CLASS, BATTERY "C", 120TH AAA GUN BN (90MM), NATIONAL GUARD, SOCORRO, NEW MEXICO as a testimonial of honest and faithful service, is hereby Honorably Discharged from the National Guard of NEW MEXICO and the National Guard of the United States.

CHARLES G. SAGE, Brigadier General
The Adjutant General
COMMANDING.

WD NGB FORM 55
18 JUL 1946

Figure 31: Green Family Collection, George Willett Green, Military Records. Letter of Honorable discharge from the U.S. National Guard, p. 1 of 2.

ENLISTED RECORD

1. NAME (Last, first, middle initial) GREEN, GEORGE W.	2. SERIAL NO. 25 635 288	3. GRADE PFC	4. ARM OR SERVICE CAC
5. ORGANIZATION BTRY "C", 120TH AAA GUN BN (90MM)	6. SEPARATION DATE 14 Feb 1950	7. PLACE OF SEPARATION SOCORRO, NEW MEXICO	
8. PERMANENT MAILING ADDRESS P.O. BOX 936, SOCORRO, NEW MEXICO	9. DATE OF BIRTH 3 Apr 1931	10. PLACE OF BIRTH FORT SILL, OKLAHOMA	
11. CIVILIAN OCCUPATION SERVICE STATION ATTENDANT		12. NUMBER OF DEPENDENTS NONE	
13. COLOR EYES BROWN	14. COLOR HAIR BRUN	15. HEIGHT 5 FT. 9 IN.	16. WEIGHT 196 LB.	17. CITIZEN YES	18. RACE ☒ WHITE ☐ NEGRO OTHER	19. MARITAL STATUS ☒ SINGLE ☐ MARRIED

MILITARY HISTORY

20. ENLISTMENT DATE	21. MILITARY OCCUPATION
24 JUNE 1948	COOK (060)

22. MILITARY QUALIFICATIONS AND DATES (Expert infantryman, marksmanship, etc.)

23. LATEST IMMUNIZATION DATES				24. HIGHEST GRADE HELD IN SERVICE	25. CHARACTER
SMALLPOX 5/25/49	TYPHOID 5/15/49	TETANUS 8/31/49	OTHER (Specify)	PFC	Excellent

26. EDUCATION (Circle highest grade completed)
GRAMMAR SCHOOL 1 2 3 4 5 6 7 (8) HIGH SCHOOL 1 2 3 (4) COLLEGE 1 2 3 4

27. SERVICE SCHOOLS ATTENDED: NONE

28. PRIOR SERVICE: NONE

29. REASON AND AUTHORITY FOR SEPARATION: Incompatible Occupation per par 11, SO #13, AGONM, eff 14 Feb 50, dtd 2 Feb 50.

30. LONGEVITY (For pay purposes): 1 YR 7 MO 20 DA

31. REMARKS:
Retirement credits earned this period of service: 1 July 1948 to 30 June 1949, incl., 65 points; 1 July 1949 to 14 Feb 1950, incl., 47 points; total retirement credits this period of service 112 points.

32. SIGNATURE OF SOLDIER

33. SIGNATURE OF OFFICER: *Raymond L. Senn*

34. TYPED NAME AND GRADE OF OFFICER: RAYMOND L. SENN, Captain

35. ORGANIZATION: CAC

36. RIGHT THUMB PRINT

Figure 32: Green Family Collection, George Willett Green, Military Records. Letter of Honorable discharge from the U.S. National Guard, p. 2 of 2.

Socorro, N. M. July 12, 1969

Mrs. Elizabeth Ingram

109 6th St.

Socorro NM

IN ACCOUNT WITH

STEADMAN FUNERAL HOME

"Memorial Chapel"

Telephone 835-1530 P. O. Box 693 Garfield at Grant Street

SERVICES RENDERED FOR Abbie L. Green

Casket and to include use of facilities, equipment and Professional Services	$ 982.00
Pine Box Grave Liner	35.00
Sales Taxes	40.68
ACCOMODATION ADVANCES	
3 Certified Copies of Death Certificate	3.00
Family Flowers	31.20
Opening and Closing Grave and Cemetery Eqpt.	50.00
TOTAL DUE	$1141.88

Pd 7/13/69 Leo Lujan 641.88

Due from Ins. 500.00

Thank You

Leo Lujan

Leo Lujan.

Figure 33: Green Family Collection. Copy of the Steadman Funeral Home for the burial of Grandmother Abbie (Glenn) Green, 12 July 1969.

REAL ESTATE CONTRACT—FORM 103 (REVISED 3-61)

BOOK 302 PAGE 463

THIS CONTRACT, made in triplicate, this 28th day of August, 1971,

by and between AURELIA GALLEGOS, a/k/a HELEN GALLEGOS, a/k/a HELEN GOMEZ, a single person

of the first part hereinafter called the Owner, and GEO. W. "BUD" GREEN, a/k/a GEORGE WILLETT GREEN and PHYLLIS G. GREEN, his wife of the second part hereinafter called the Purchaser.

WITNESSETH:

1. That the said Owner, in consideration of the covenants and agreements on the part of the said Purchaser, hereinafter contained, agrees to sell and convey unto the said Purchaser the following real estate situate, lying and being in the County of SOCORRO and State of New Mexico, to-wit:

That certain real estate, together with improvements, in the City of Socorro, County of Socorro and State of New Mexico, described as follows, to-wit:

Beginning at Corner No. 1 of the tract of land herein conveyed, which is the N.E. Corner of land originally of Raymond G. Gallegos, situate south of City Survey 508, as Corner No. 1 of the tract of land herein conveyed;
thence in a Southwesterly direction 185.0 feet to Cor. No. 2;
thence Westerly 102 feet to Corner No. 3 of the tract herein conveyed;
thence North 185.0 feet, more or less to Corner No. 4 of the tract herein conveyed;
thence Easterly 141 feet to Corner No. 1, the place of beginning;
Bounded on the North by City Survey 508, on the South by Lucero Avenue, on the East by City Survey 549 and on the West by the remaining portion of original tract of land.

2. The Owner undertakes and agrees, upon full performance of the conditions, covenants and agreements to be performed by the said Purchaser, to make, execute and deliver to said Purchaser, a good and sufficient warranty deed for the above real estate.

3. In consideration of the premises, the said Purchaser agrees to buy said real estate and to pay said Owner therefor the sum of SEVEN THOUSAND FIVE HUNDRED AND NO/100ths**************Dollars ($ 7,500.00) lawful money of the United States of America, which sum is to be paid as follows, to-wit:
SEVEN HUNDRED FIFTY AND NO/100ths*********Dollars ($ 750.00), cash in hand paid, the receipt of which is hereby acknowledged, and the balance of $ 6,750.00 shall be payable as follows, to-wit:

Beginning on the 20th., day of September, 1971, the sum of SIXTY FIVE ($65.00), DOLLARS, and a like sum each and every month thereafter, on the 20th., day of such month, until the entire sum, hereinbefore named, is paid in full.
Such monthly payments of $65.00 to be applied first to the interest, at the rate of FIVE (5%) PERCENT per annum on the unpaid balance, and the remainder, if any, to be applied on the principal.

STATE OF NEW MEXICO } ss.
SOCORRO COUNTY
THIS INSTRUMENT OF WRITING WAS FILED FOR RECORD AT 1:25 O'CLOCK P. M. ON
SEP 9 - 1971
AND DULY RECORDED IN VOL. 302
of _____ PAGE 463-465
County Clerk
By _____ Deputy

If not otherwise specified the above-mentioned payments shall continue until the full purchase price and interest on deferred payments shall have been fully paid. All of said unpaid balance of the purchase price shall bear interest at the rate of Five per centum (5 %) per annum from date, payable Annually

Further, it is agreed that if this Real Estate Contract is placed by the Owner, in the hands of an attorney upon default by the Purchaser in the payment of any monies due hereunder for the purpose of mailing of written demand, pursuant to the termination provision of Paragraph 8 hereof, the Purchaser shall pay, in addition to the payment of all other sums required hereunder, the sum of $25.00 to cover the costs, expenses, and fees involved in such action.

4. Said Purchaser agrees to keep the buildings upon said real estate insured against the hazards covered by fire and extended coverage insurance in an insurance company satisfactory to said Owner in the sum of $ 7,000.00, for the benefit of said Owner as his interest may appear, and deliver said insurance policy to said Owner.

5. Said Owner undertakes and agrees to pay all taxes up to and including First half of 19 71 together with all other liens and charges now against said real estate, except as herein stated, and said Purchaser agrees to assess said real estate for taxation to himself for the year 1972, and, thereafter, pay all taxes and assessments and make all street improvements of every kind and nature whatsoever that may hereafter be levied or ordered by lawful authority and which would in the event of failure so to do create a charge against the said real estate. All taxes, assessments, liens, and other charges against said real estate have been prorated to the date hereof and the Purchaser has assumed the payment of the same for the current year.

Figure 34: Green Family Collection. Real Estate Record of Home Purchase on 28 August 1971, p.1 of 4.

Jesus Said,

"Let the little children

come to me,

and do not

hinder them, for the

kingdom of heaven

belongs to such

as these."

Mathew 19:14

IN LOVING MEMORY OF
OUR INFANT DAUGHTER

Georgie Verla Green

May 24, 2004 - May 24, 2004
Martin Army Community Hospital
Fort Benning, Georgia

GRAVESIDE SERVICES
4:00 P.M., Saturday, May 29, 2004
Newtown Cemetery
Newtown, Missouri

OFFICIATING
Bro. Denny Daum

Services Conducted By
Payne Funeral Home
Galt, Missouri

Figure 35: Green Family Collection, Death Announcement of Georgie Verla Green, grand-daughter to the author, and daughter to the author's youngest son, 2004.

Appendix I

Map Graphic that include a Narrative

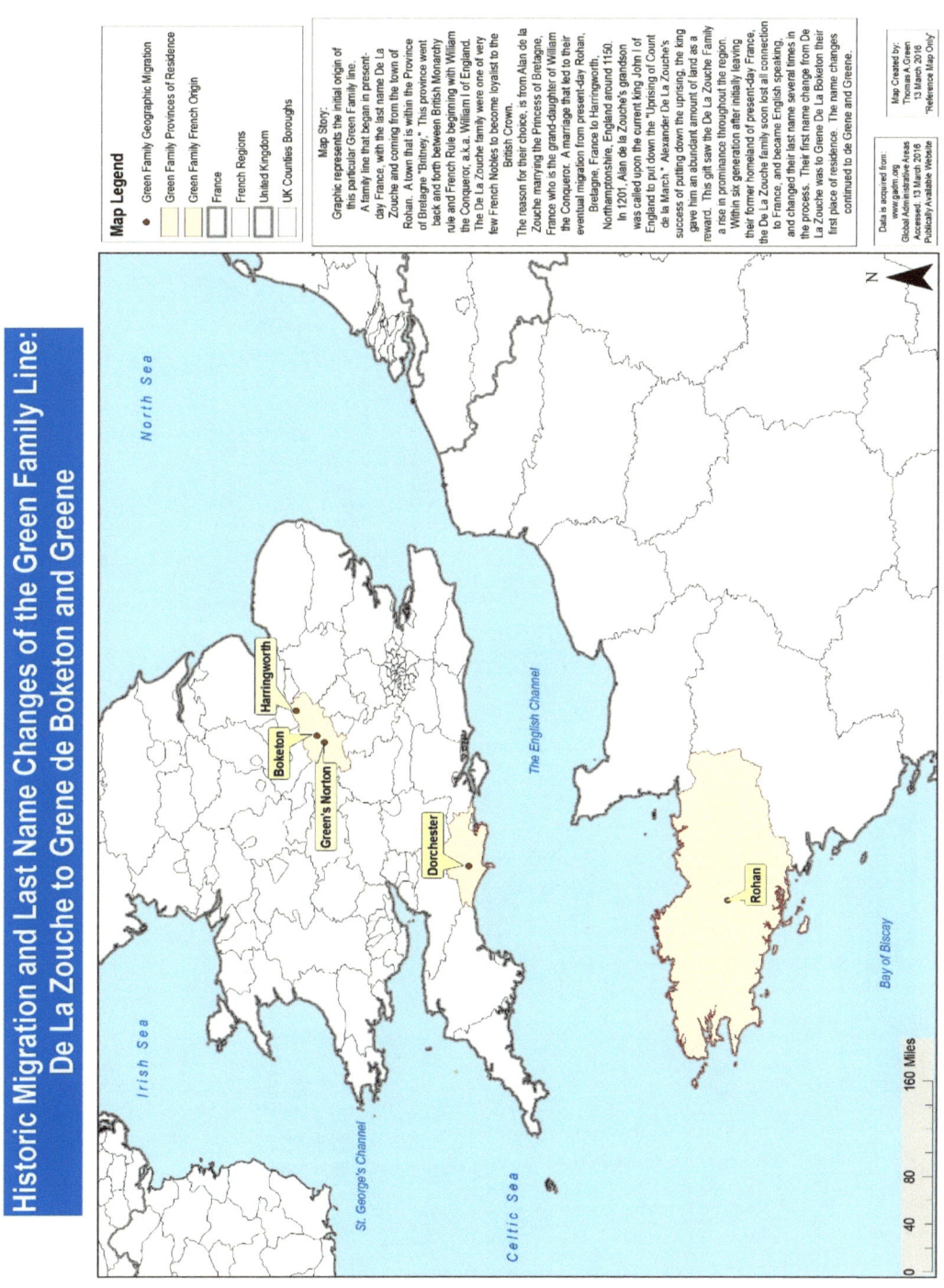

Figure 36: Green, Thomas A. 2016. Data collection acquired from www.gadm.org; accessed 13 March 2016. Refer to map narrative on the right hand side of the map graphic for further information.

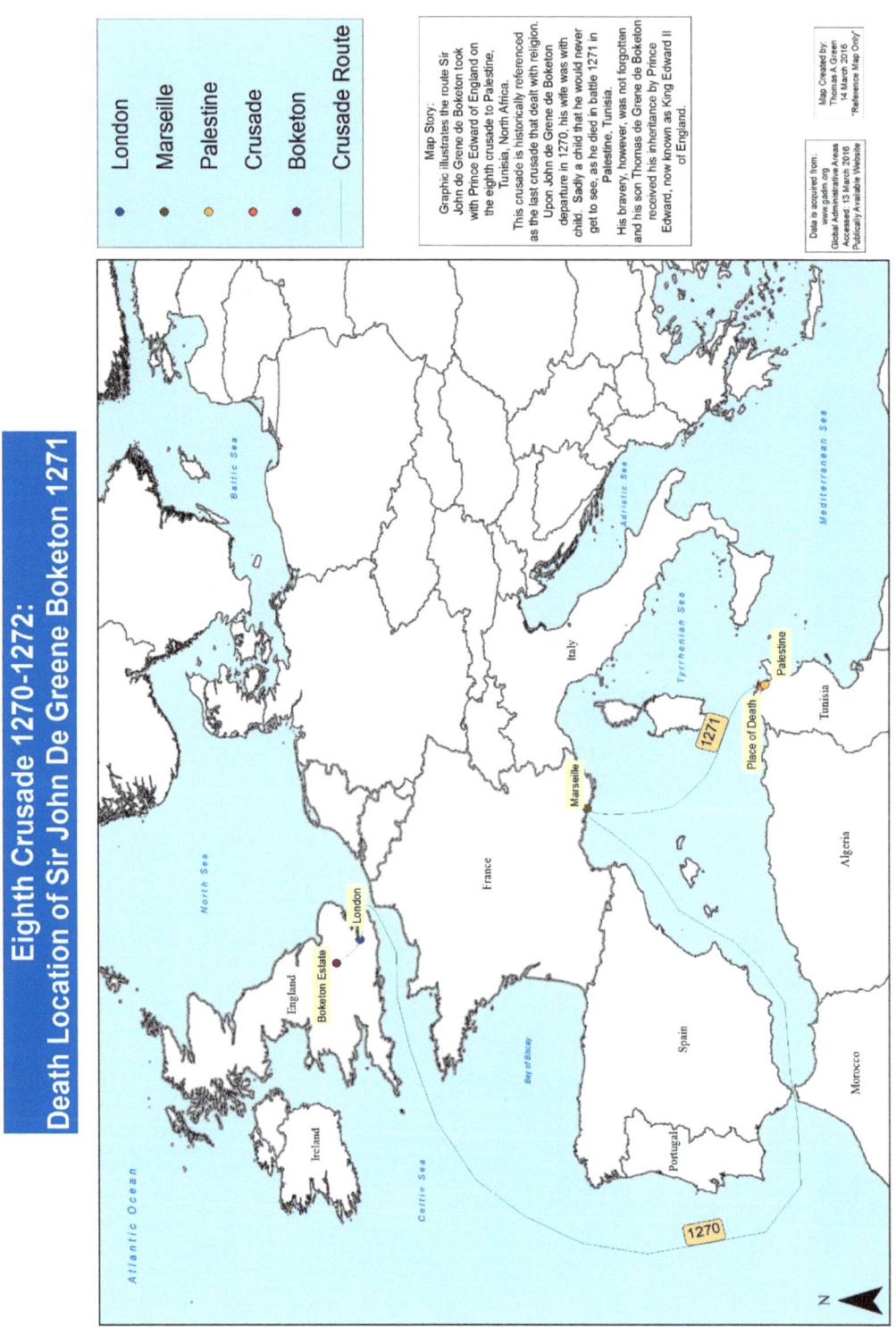

Figure 37: Green, Thomas A. 2016. Data collection acquired from www.gadm.org; accessed 13 March 2016. Refer to map narrative on the right hand side of the map graphic for further information.

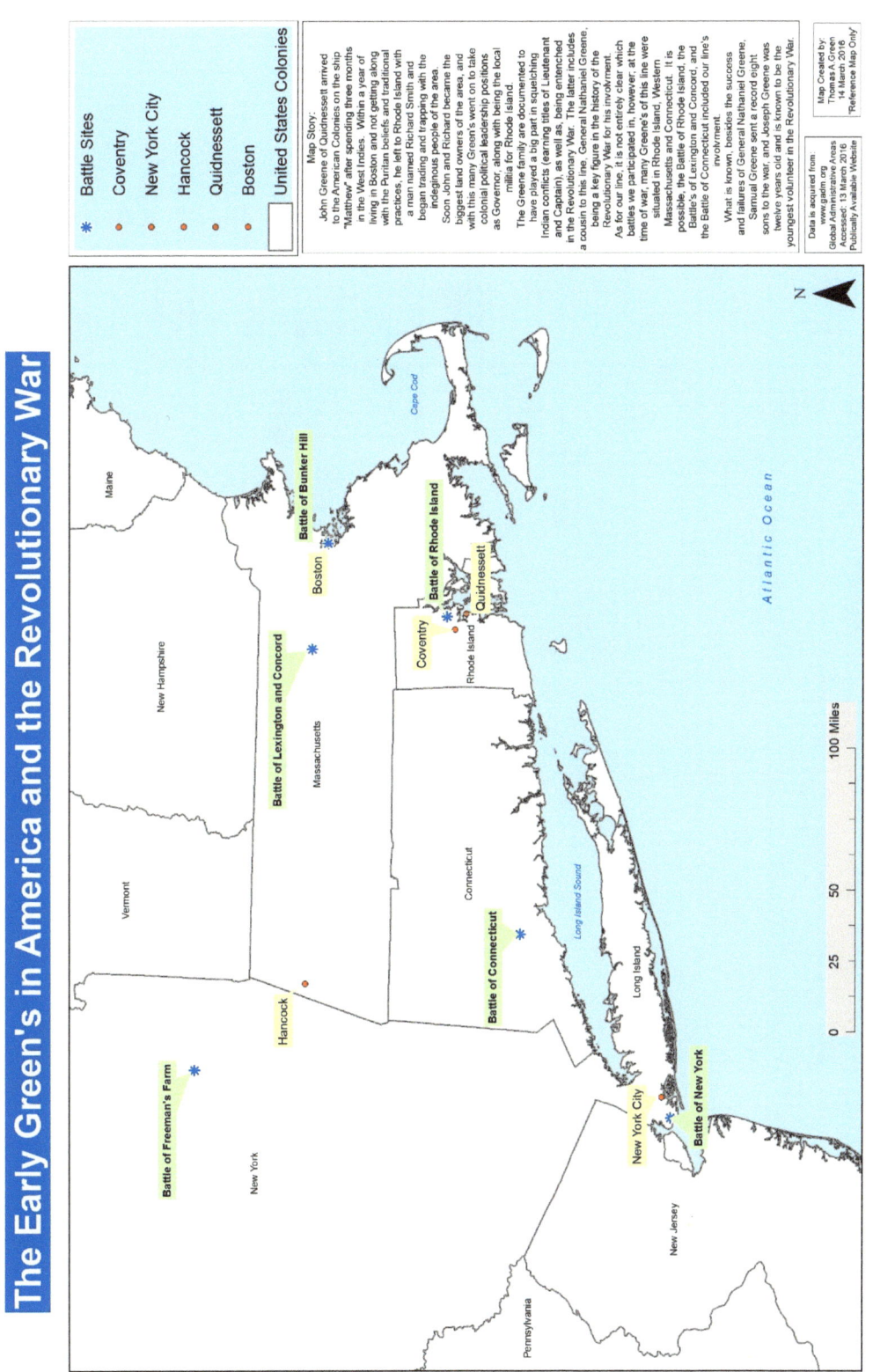

Figure 38: Green, Thomas A. 2016. Data collection acquired from www.gadm.org; accessed 13 March 2016. Refer to map narrative on the right hand side of the map graphic for further information.

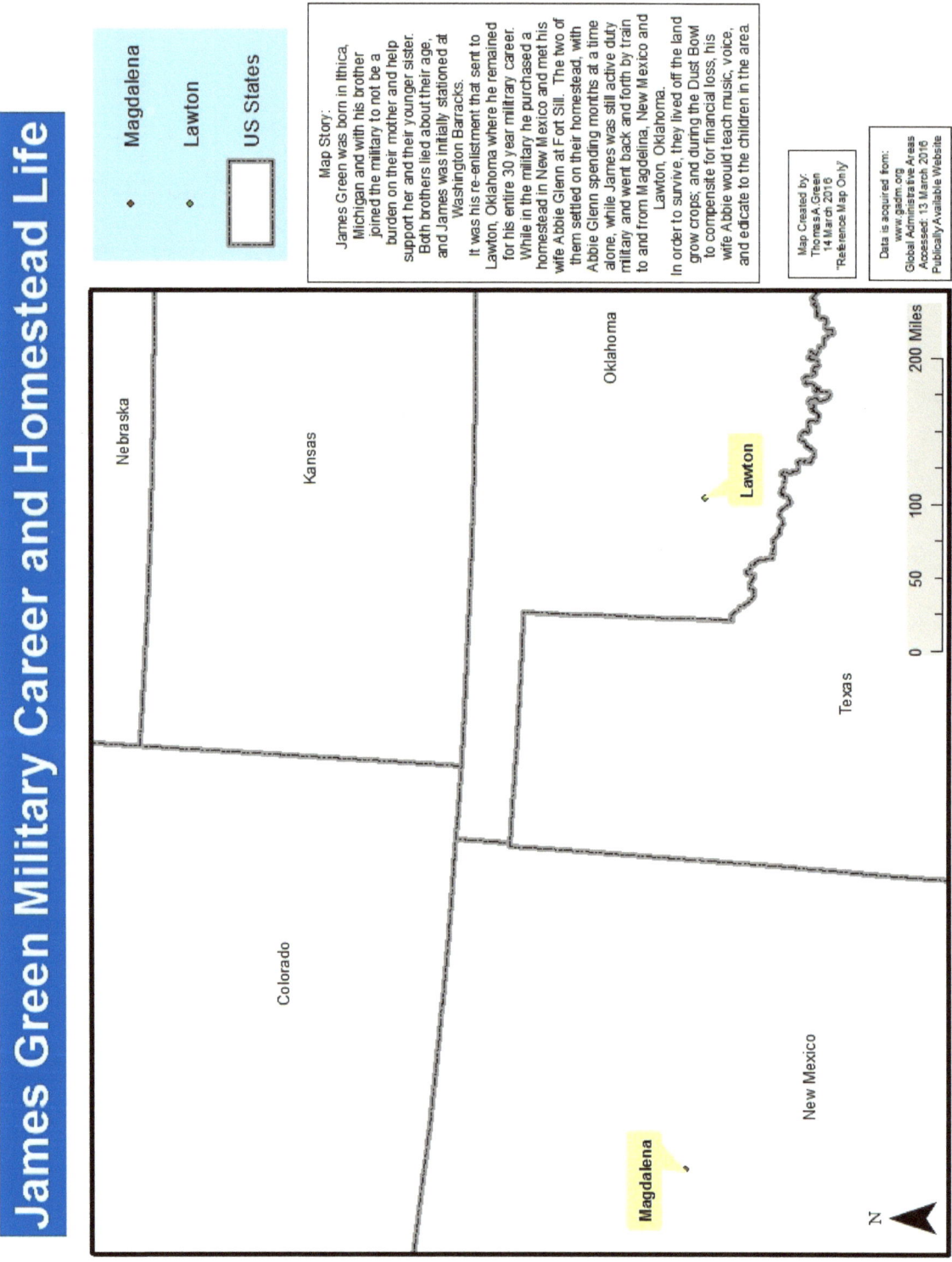

Figure 39: Green, Thomas A. 2016. Data collection acquired from www.gadm.org; accessed 13 March 2016. Refer to map narrative on the right hand side of the map graphic for further information.

Appendix J

Green Family Select Photo Collection

George Willet Green

Image 3: George Willet Green and Lena Harter, the parents of James Samuel Green, who is the father to George W. "Bud" Green

Image 4: James Samuel Green with his mother Lena

Image 5: James Samuel Green with his sister Cordelia and brother Virgil

Image 6: James Samuel Green with her brother Virgil in the military

Image 7: Virgil, James Samuel Green's younger brother, with his wife Stella

Image 8: James Samuel Green and Abbie (Glenn) Green's children with cousins

Image 9: Virgil Green, younger brother of James Samuel Green

Fort Sill, Oklahoma

Image 10: Grandfather James Samuel Green clowning around at Fort Sill, Oklahoma

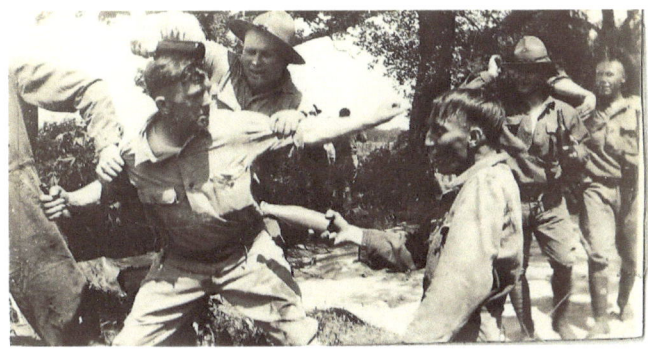

Image 11: Grandfather James Samuel Green clowning around at Fort Sill, Oklahoma

Image 12: James Samuel Green at Fort Sill, Oklahoma

Image 13: A U.S. soldier poses for a picture at Fort Sill, Oklahoma

Image 14: Grandfather James Samuel Green, showing his children how to fish with only a knife

Image 15: Grandfather James Samuel Green standing outside his quarters in the making of an army base

Image 16: Soldier posing with Fort Sill artillery

Image 17: Grandfather James Samuel Green clowning around with army buddies, Fort Sill, Oklahoma

Image 18: Grandfather James Samuel Green sitting on top of the world

Image 19: Grandfather James Samuel Green posing with the artillery, Fort Sill, Oklahoma

Image 20: Grandfather James Samuel Green posing with the artillery, Fort Sill, Oklahoma

Image 21: Grandfather James Samuel Green, is third from the left in making of an Army Base

Image 22: The men of Fort Sill, Oklahoma in 1902

Image 23: Troops relaxing on base, Fort Sill, Oklahoma

Image 24: Vehicle stuck on Fort Sill, Oklahoma

Image 25: Grandfather James Samuel Green, receiving an award for the local veteran's post (1940's)

Image 26: Georgia, William "Bill" and Elizabeth, siblings of George W. "Bud" Green, whose mother is Abbie (Glenn) Green, the wife of James Samuel Green.

Image 27: Father of the author, George W. "Bud" Green and older half-brother William "Bill" outside of their Fort Sill, Oklahoma base housing.

Image 28: Grandfather James Samuel Green with his children Georgia, and the author's father, George W. "Bud" Green, outside of their Fort Sill, Oklahoma base housing.

Image 29: Children of Abbie (Glenn) Green and step-children of James Samuel Green, Mary Alice, Glenn, Elizabeth and William "Bill".

Image 30: William "Bill" with his younger half-sister, Georgia

New Mexico Homestead

Image 31: Georgia playing her ukulele, older sister of George W. "Bud" Green

Image 32: George W. "Bud" Green, father of the author

Image 33: George W. "Bud" Green on the New Mexico homestead with older sister Georgia

Image 34: George W. "Bud" Green playing Guitar

Image 35: Grandfather James Samuel Green with his son George W. "Bud" Green

Image 36: Grandfather James Samuel Green in his military uniform on the New Mexico homestead

Image 37: George W. "Bud" Green with his sister Georgia on the New Mexico homestead

Image 38: George W. "Bud" Green with Georgia at the New Mexico homestead

Image 39: Grandfather James Samuel Green with his children George and George W. "Bud"

Image 40: George W. "Bud" Green, father of the author, hiding from what he called "the meanest pig"

Image 41: half-brother William "Bill" kneeling next to wagon that George W. "Bud" is sitting in, with Bud's full sister (Georgia) sitting on the opposite side of wagon and Bud's oldest half-brother Glenn standing.

Image 42: Abbie (Glenn) Green at homestead with her two youngest children Georgia and George W. "Bud" Green

Image 43: half-brother William "Bill" in the background looking away from camera with Georgia and George W. Bud Green posing at the New Mexico Homestead.

Image 44: Main Street in Magdalena, New Mexico 1932, now a part of U.S. Highway 60

Image 45: Magdalena, New Mexico 1932 Railroad Station

Image 46: Georgia, George W. "Bud" and Glenn getting a visit from an aunt at the New Mexico Homestead

Image 47: Standing on the running board are George W. "Bud" Green's half-sister Elizabeth and half-brother William "Bill." Abbie (Glenn) Green is holding George W. "Bud" Green. In front from left to right, Georgia, half-brother Glenn, cousin Vivian and half-sister Mary Alice. Photo taken on the New Mexico Homestead.

Image 48: George W. "Bud" Green, age three, on the New Mexico homestead (1934)

Image 49: George W. "Bud" and Georgia playing their musical instruments

Image 50: Picture of the New Mexico homestead, taken about 1932

Image 51: Glenn oldest child of Abbie (Glenn) Green posing in military uniform with youngest half-brother George W. "Bud" Green

Image 52: James Samuel Green posing on his horse at the New Mexico homestead

Image 53: Grandfather James Samuel Green and Grandmother Abbie Lusina (Glenn) Green

Image 54: George W "Bud" Green with the farm animals on the New Mexico Homestead

Image 55: Glenn and Georgia, playing their musical instruments

James Green, Abbie (Glenn) Green and Family

Image 56: Abbie Lusina (Glenn) Green

Image 57: Pictured left to right, Grandmother Abbie (Glenn), Georgia, Grandfather James Samuel Green and George W. "Bud" standing in front of his father.

George W. "Bud" Green

Image 58: George W. "Bud" Green, estimated year of photo is 1937, age six

Phyllis (Crockett) Green

Image 59: Phyllis Florine (Crockett) Green, wife of George W. "Bud" Green, estimated year of photo is 1942, age eight.

George Green and Phyllis Crockett

Image 60: George W. "Bud" Green and wife Phyllis (Crockett) Green, 1952

Image 61: George W. "Bud" Green and wife Phyllis (Crockett) Green, 1953 after wedding day

Image 62: George W. "Bud" Green and wife Phyllis (Crockett) Green, 1953

Siblings of George W. "Bud" Green, son of James and Abbie Green

Image 63: Georgia, full sister of George W. "Bud" Green

Image 64: William "Bill", half-brother of George W. "Bud" Green

Image 65: Musical play at the old opera house. Picture includes all characters and musicians including Georgia and half-brother William "Bill" standing in the far back holding his guitar and wearing tan hat.

Image 66: Georgia posing with her Accordion

Image 67: Georgia sitting on a hay bale with her accordion with half-brother William "Bill" behind her with his guitar.

Image 68: Georgia, about age four, older sister of George W. "Bud" Green, picture taken about 1929

Image 69: Georgia (13), George W. "Bud" (8) and their niece Betty Gale, 1939

Image 70: Elizabeth, older half-sister to George W. "Bud" Green, with her daughter Betty Gale, picture taken about 1942.

Image 71: Father George W. "Bud" Green, standing in far back of picture with his oldest half-brother Glenn and oldest half-sister Mary Alice standing to his left; and full-sister Georgia, half-sister Elizabeth and their mother Abbie (Glenn) Green up front. Not pictured was the other half-brother William "Bill" who was on deployment at Fort Sill, Oklahoma, at time of photo.

Image 72: Georgia, full sister of George W. "Bud" Green

Relatives to Author on mother and father's side

Image 73: From left to right, Uncle Richard (half-brother to Grandmother Abbie (Glenn) Green), Great Grandfather Robert Glenn, Great Grandfather's second wife Sophia, and other half-brother to Abbie, Robert.

Image 74: Great Grandfather Robert Glenn standing in front with his daughters behind him, from left to right, Esther, Lela, Abbie (Grandmother to author), and Roberta; and to the far right is his second wife Sophia. Sophia being the mother of the two half-brothers seen above in image 73.

Image 75: Iva (Powell) Crockett, grandmother to the author, and mother to Phyllis (Crockett) Green

Image 76: Elzia Isaac Crockett, grandfather to the author, and father to Phyllis (Crockett) Green

The Author

Image 77: The Author

Image 78: The Author

Image 79: The Author

Author's Children

Image 80: Private

Image 81: Private

Image 82: Private

Image 83: Private

Image 84: Private

Image 85: Private

Image 86: Private

Image 87: Private

Image 88: Private

Image 89: Private

Figure 40: Private

Figure 41: Private

Figure 42: Private

Figure 43: Private

Figure 44: Private

Full Bibliography

Adams, Michael C.C. *The Best War Ever: America and World War II*. 1st ed. Baltimore: John Hopkins University Press, 1994.

Bailyn, Bernard. *Face of Revolution: Personalities and Themes in the Struggle for American Independence*. New York: First Vintage Books Edition, 1992.

Baker, Charlotte and Dick Baker. "Greene Family Being a Record of the Ancestry and Descendants of Maxson Alvaro Greene, The." PHGS Members.

Balkoski, Joseph. *Utah Beach: The Amphibious Landing and Airborne Operations on D-Day*. Mechanicsburg: Stackpole Books, 2005.

Beck, William Henry., A Family Genealogy: Harkness, Carmichael, Lester, Greene, Andrews, Brown, White, Polhill, Beck families. Lettercraft Shop, Inc., East Point, Georgia. Universal Standard Encyclopedia, Vol. 12, 1958.

Beevor, Antony. *Ardennes 1944: The Battle of the Bulge*. New York: Penguin Random House, 2015.

Boulyon, D'Arcy Johnson Dacre. *The Knights of the Crown: The Monarchial Orders of Knighthood in Later Medieval Europe, 1325-1520*. 2nd revised ed. Woodbridges, UK: Boydell Press, 2000.

Brownell Clarke, Louis. *Greenes of Rhode Island with Historical Records of England Ancestors, The*. New York, NY: Knickerbocker Press, 1903.

Caddick-Adams, Peter. *Snow & Steel: The Battle of the Bulge 1944-1945*. 1st ed. London: Oxford University Press, 2015.

Carnine, Douglas et al. *World History: Medieval and Early Modern Times*: McDougal Littell, 2006.

Casteland.com, http://www.casteland.com/puk/castle/bretagne/morbihan/josselin/josselin.htm, Last Modified: 02 July 2013, Accessed 16 April 2016.

Church of Jesus Christ of Latter Day Saints, FamilySearch.org, United States Census Records, 1860, https://familysearch.org/pal:MM9.1.1/MCHJ-W8T, Accessed 23 July 2012, Records of Samuel W Green, Oswego, New York.

Church of Jesus Christ of Latter Day Saints, FamilySearch.org, Michigan, Deaths and Burials, 1800-1995, Index, https://familysearch.org/pal:/MM9.1.1/FHN2-H89, Accessed 20 July 2012, Samuel Green in entry for George Green, 1860.

Church of Jesus Christ of Latter Day Saints, FamilySearch.org, Michigan, Marriages, 1868-1925, index and images, https://familysearch.org/pal:/MM9.1.1/NQ7B-JV6, Accessed 20 July 2012, George W. Green, 1889.

Church of Jesus Christ of Latter Day Saints, FamilySearch.org, United States Census Records, 1900, index and images, https://familysearch.org/pal:/MM9.1.1/M911-TPT, Accessed 20 July 2012, George W Green, ED 18 Victor Township, Clinton, Michigan, United States.

Church of Jesus Christ of Latter Day Saints, FamilySearch.org, Michigan, Marriages, 1868-1925, index and images, https://familysearch.org/pal:/MM9.1.1/NQ7B-JVF, Accessed 20 July 2012, Julia A. Dutton in entry for George W. Green and Lena A. Harter, 1889.

Church of Jesus Christ of Latter Day Saints, FamilySearch.org, Michigan, Marriages, 1868-1925, index and images, https://familysearch.org/pal:/MM9.1.1/NQ7B-JVX, Accessed 20 July 2012, Sam W. Green in entry for George W. Green and Lena A. Harter, 1889.

Church of Jesus Christ of Latter Day Saints, FamilySearch.org, United States Census Records, 1880, index, https://familysearch.org/pal:/MM9.1.1/MWS9-2RQ, Accessed 20 July 2012, Samuel Green, Dallas, Clinton, Michigan.

Church of Jesus Christ of Latter Day Saints, FamilySearch.org, United States Census Records, 1870, index and images, https://familysearch.org/pal:/MM9.1.1/MHHF-W22, Accessed 20 July 2012, Samuel Green in household of Samuel Green, Michigan, United States.

Church of Jesus Christ of Latter Day Saints, United States City Directories, 1821-1989, Provo, Utah, USA: Ancestry.com Operations, Inc., 2011, Accessed 22 July 2012.

Church of Jesus Christ of Latter Day Saints, FamilySearch.org, Michigan, Deaths and Burials, 1800-1995, index, https://familysearch.org/pal:/MM9.1.1/FHWC-1VN, Accessed 20 July 2012, Samuel Green in entry for George Green, 1859.

Church of Jesus Christ of Latter Day Saints, FamilySearch.org, Michigan, Births and Christenings, 1775-1995, index, https://familysearch.org/pal:/MM9.1.1/F4R5-9QV, Accessed 20 July 2012, George W. Green in entry for James S. Green, 1889.

Church of Jesus Christ of Latter Day Saints, FamilySearch.org, Michigan, Births, 1867-1902, index and images, https://familysearch.org/pal:/MM9.1.1/NQVW-4QD, Accessed 20 July 2012, George W. Green in entry for James S. Green, 1889.

Church of Jesus Christ of Latter Day Saints, FamilySearch.org, Michigan, Marriages, 1822-1995, index, https://familysearch.org/pal:/MM9.1.1/FC22-F9Q, Accessed 20 July 2012, Samuel Watson Green, 1854.

Church of Jesus Christ of Latter Day Saints, FamilySearch.org, Michigan, Marriages, 1822-1995, index, https://familysearch.org/pal:/MM9.1.1/FCN9-7QN, Accessed 20 July 2012, Samuel Watson Green, 1854.

Church of Jesus Christ of Latter Day Saints, FamilySearch.org, Rhode Island, Births and Christenings, 1600-1914, https://familysearch.org/pal:/MM9.1.1/F8M4-LPP, Accessed 28 March 2013, James Green, 18 August 1685.

Church of Jesus Christ of Latter Day Saints, FamilySearch.org, Rhode Island, Births and Christenings, 1600-1914, index, https://familysearch.org/pal:/MM9.1.1/F87Q-T94, Accessed 28 March 2013, John Greene, 30 September 1685.

Church of Jesus Christ of Latter Day Saints, FamilySearch.org, Rhode Island, Births and Christenings, 1600-1914, index, https://familysearch.org/pal:/MM9.1.1/F87Q-T97, Accessed 28 March 2013, James Greene in the entry for John Greene, 01 February 1670.

Church of Jesus Christ of Latter Day Saints, FamilySearch.org, Rhode Island, Births and Christenings, 1600-1914, index, https://familysearch.org/pal:/MM9.1.1/F83X-SX5, Accessed 28 March 2013, James Greene in entry for Jeremiah Greene, 01 June 1736.

Church of Jesus Christ of Latter Day Saints, FamilySearch.org, Michigan, Marriages, 1822-1995, index, https://familysearch.org/pal:/MM9.1.1/FC6P-QFL, Accessed 28 March 2013, Samuel W. Green in entry for George W. Green and Lena A. Harter, 09 March 1889.

Church of Jesus Christ of Latter Day Saints, FamilySearch.org, index and images, https://familysearch.org/pal:/MM9.1.1/NQ7B-JV6, Accessed 28 March 2013, George W. Green and Lena A. Harter, 09 March 1889.

Church of Jesus Christ of Latter Day Saints, FamilySearch.org, Rhode Island, Births and Christenings, 1600-1914, index, https://familysearch.org/pal:/MM9.1.1/F83X-WRP, Accessed 28 March 2013, Russel Greene, 24 December 1760.

Church of Jesus Christ of Latter Day Saints, FamilySearch.org, Rhode Island, Births and Christenings, 1600-1914, index, https://familysearch.org/pal:/MM9.1.1/F83X-WR5, Accessed 28 March 2013, Jeremiah Greene in the entry for Russel Greene, 24 December 1760.

Church of Jesus Christ of Latter Day Saints, FamilySearch.org, Rhode Island, Births and Christenings, 1600-1914, index, https://familysearch.org/pal:/MM9.1.1/F8M4-LP5, Accessed 28 March 2013, John Green in the entry of James Green, 18 August 1685.

Church of Jesus Christ of Latter Day Saints, "United States Civil War Soldiers Index, 1861-1865," database, *FamilySearch* (https://familysearch.org/ark:/61903/1:1:F9T8-F2R: accessed 24 April 2016), Willet G. Green, Private, Company B, 8th Regiment, Michigan

Infantry, Union; citing NARA microfilm publication M545 (Washington D.C.: National Archives and Records Administration, n.d.), roll 16; FHL microfilm 881,929.

Church of Jesus Christ of Latter Day Saints, "United States Civil War Soldiers Index, 1861-1865," database, *FamilySearch* (https://familysearch.org/ark:/61903/1:1:F9T8-FTL: accessed 24 April 2016), Willett P. Green (alias: Willet G. Green), Private, Company B, 8th Regiment, Michigan Infantry, Union; citing NARA microfilm publication M545 (Washington D.C.: National Archives and Records Administration, n.d.), roll 16; FHL microfilm 881,929.

Church of Jesus Christ of Latter Day Saints, "United States Civil War Soldiers Index, 1861-1865," database, *FamilySearch* (https://familysearch.org/ark:/61903/1:1:FSHG-LPF: accessed 24 April 2016), Willet C. Green (alias: Willet G. Green), Private, Company B, 8th Regiment, Michigan Infantry, Union; citing NARA microfilm publication M545 (Washington D.C.: National Archives and Records Administration, n.d.), roll 16; FHL microfilm 881,929.

Church of Jesus Christ of Latter Day Saints, United States Pensioners, 1818-1872. Name: Russell Green, Widow's Name: Patience Green, Pension City: Albany, State: New York' year range 1836-1848.

Church of Jesus Christ of Latter Day Saints, "United States General Index to Pension Files, 1861-1934", database with images, *FamilySearch* (https://familysearch.org/ark:/61903/1:1:KDYP-ZRN: accessed 24 April 2016), Willett G Green, 1863.

Church of Jesus Christ of Latter Day Saints, "United States Census, 1800", database with images, *FamilySearch* (https://familysearch.org/ark:/61903/1:1:XH55-Y9L: accessed 24 April 2016), Russell Greene, 1800.

Church of Jesus Christ of Latter Day Saints, "United States Census, 1830," database with images, *FamilySearch* (https://familysearch.org/ark:/61903/1:1:XHP6-FG8: accessed 24 April 2016), Russell Greene, Providence West Side of River, Providence, Rhode Island, United States; citing 86, NARA microfilm publication M19, (Washington D.C.: National Archives and Records Administration, n.d.), roll 168; FHL microfilm 22,267.

Church of Jesus Christ of Latter Day Saints, "United States Census, 1810", database with images, *FamilySearch* (https://familysearch.org/ark:/61903/1:1:XH2G-R78: accessed 24 April 2016), Russell Green, 1810.

Church of Jesus Christ of Latter Day Saints, "United States Census, 1790", database with images, *FamilySearch* (https://familysearch.org/ark:/61903/1:1:XHKT-SGT: accessed 24 April 2016), Russell Green, 1790.

Church of Jesus Christ of Latter Day Saints, "United States Census, 1790", database with images, *FamilySearch* (https://familysearch.org/ark:/61903/1:1:XHKT-3HG: accessed 24 April 2016), Russell Green, 1790.

Church of Jesus Christ of Latter Day Saints, Rhode Island Births and Christenings, 1600-1914," database, *FamilySearch* (https://familysearch.org/ark:/61903/1:1:F83X-SXP: accessed 24 April 2016), Jeremiah Greene, 01 Jun 1736; citing Rhode Island, USA, reference v 1 p 17; FHL microfilm 925,978.

Church of Jesus Christ of Latter Day Saints, "Rhode Island Marriages, 1724-1916," database, *FamilySearch* (https://familysearch.org/ark:/61903/1:1:F8K1-PTB: accessed 24 April 2016), Jeremiah Greene and Freelove Hopkins, 20 Feb 1803; citing West Greenwich, Kent, Rhode Island, reference; FHL microfilm 908,269.

Church of Jesus Christ of Latter Day Saints, "Rhode Island Marriages, 1724-1916," database, *FamilySearch* (https://familysearch.org/ark:/61903/1:1:VK1V-93X: accessed 24 April 2016), Jeremiah Greene and Freelove Hopkins, Oct 1760; citing West Greenwich, Kent, Rhode Island, reference; FHL microfilm 908,269.

Church of Jesus Christ of Latter Day Saints, "Rhode Island Deaths and Burials, 1802-1950," database, *FamilySearch* (https://familysearch.org/ark:/61903/1:1:F8X9-TX8: accessed 24 April 2016), Jeremiah Greene in entry for Sally Warner, 29 Jun 1880; citing Cranston, Providence, Rhode Island, reference p 16; FHL microfilm 2,384,565.

Church of Jesus Christ of Latter Day Saints, "Rhode Island Births and Christenings, 1600-1914," database, *FamilySearch* (https://familysearch.org/ark:/61903/1:1:F83X-4MJ: accessed 24 April 2016), Jeremiah Greene in entry for Anne Greene, 04 Oct 1773; citing Rhode Island, USA, reference v 1 p 141; FHL microfilm 925,978.

Church of Jesus Christ of Latter Day Saints, "Rhode Island Births and Christenings, 1600-1914," database, *FamilySearch* (https://familysearch.org/ark:/61903/1:1:F83X-4MS: accessed 24 April 2016), Jeremiah Greene in entry for Barbery Greene, 08 Jul 1762; citing Rhode Island, USA, reference v 1 p 141; FHL microfilm 925,978.

Church of Jesus Christ of Latter Day Saints, "Rhode Island Births and Christenings, 1600-1914," database, *FamilySearch* (https://familysearch.org/ark:/61903/1:1:F83X-4M7: accessed 24 April 2016), Jeremiah Greene in entry for Gardner Greene, 15 Dec 1763; citing Rhode Island, USA, reference v 1 p 141; FHL microfilm 925,978.

Church of Jesus Christ of Latter Day Saints, "Rhode Island Births and Christenings, 1600-1914," database, *FamilySearch* (https://familysearch.org/ark:/61903/1:1:F83X-4MH: accessed 24 April 2016), Jeremiah Greene in entry for Waite Greene, 25 May 1766; citing Rhode Island, USA, reference v 1 p 141; FHL microfilm 925,978.

Church of Jesus Christ of Latter Day Saints, "Rhode Island Births and Christenings, 1600-1914," database, *FamilySearch* (https://familysearch.org/ark:/61903/1:1:F83X-4M8: accessed 24 April 2016), Jeremiah Greene in entry for Jeremiah Greene, 14 Dec 1768; citing Rhode Island, USA, reference v 1 p 141; FHL microfilm 925,978.

Church of Jesus Christ of Latter Day Saints, "Rhode Island Births and Christenings, 1600-1914," database, *FamilySearch* (https://familysearch.org/ark:/61903/1:1:F83X-4MX: accessed 24 April 2016), Jeremiah Greene in entry for Abiale Greene, 09 Jun 1771; citing Rhode Island, USA, reference v 1 p 141; FHL microfilm 925,978.

Church of Jesus Christ of Latter Day Saints, "United States Census, 1830," database with images, *FamilySearch* (https://familysearch.org/ark:/61903/1:1:XH5V-RPS: accessed 24 April 2016), Jeremiah Green, South Reading, Middlesex, Massachusetts, United States; citing 144, NARA microfilm publication M19, (Washington D.C.: National Archives and Records Administration, n.d.), roll 66; FHL microfilm 337,924.

Church of Jesus Christ of Latter Day Saints, "United States Census, 1830," database with images, *FamilySearch* (https://familysearch.org/ark:/61903/1:1:FC6P-QF2: accessed 24 April 2016), George W. Green, indexing batch number M73660-5, film number 985694, reference id: BK 1866-1903 V. A-C.

Church of Jesus Christ of Latter Day Saints, "United States Census, 1870," database with images, *FamilySearch* (https://familysearch.org/ark:/61903/1:1:MHCL-N4M: accessed 24 April 2016), George Green in household of Ashley Samphear, Michigan, United States; citing p. 11, family 100, NARA microfilm publication M593 (Washington D.C.: National Archives and Records Administration, n.d.); FHL microfilm 552,207.

Church of Jesus Christ of Latter Day Saints, "United States Census, 1870," database with images, *FamilySearch* (https://familysearch.org/ark:/61903/1:1:MHCH-HDQ: accessed 24 April 2016), George Green in household of Lucinda Green, Michigan, United States; citing p. 35, family 250, NARA microfilm publication M593 (Washington D.C.: National Archives and Records Administration, n.d.); FHL microfilm 552,190.

Church of Jesus Christ of Latter Day Saints, "United States Census, 1910," database with images, *FamilySearch* (https://familysearch.org/ark:/61903/1:1:ML5H-S7Q: accessed 24 April 2016), George Green in household of Fredrick H Paepke, Ithaca, Gratiot, Michigan, United States; citing enumeration district (ED) ED 70, sheet 24B, NARA microfilm publication T624 (Washington, D.C.: National Archives and Records Administration, n.d.); FHL microfilm 1,374,661.

Church of Jesus Christ of Latter Day Saints, "United States Civil War Soldiers Index, 1861-1865," database, *FamilySearch* (https://familysearch.org/ark:/61903/1:1:F9T8-F4W: accessed 24 April 2016), George Green, Private First Class, Company H, 1st Regiment, Engineers and Mechanics, Michigan, Union; citing NARA microfilm publication M545 (Washington D.C.: National Archives and Records Administration, n.d.), roll 16; FHL microfilm 881,929.

Church, Steven (1995) Papers from the sixth Strewberry Hill Conference 1994. Woodbridge, England: Boydell & Brewer, 1995, pgs. 41-100.

Clark, Hugh. A concise History of Knighthood: Containing the Religious and Military Order Which Have Been Instituted in Europe. London, 1784.

Cunningham, Sean. *Richard III: A Royal Enigma*. Kew, Richmond, Surrey TW9 4DU, United Kingdom: National Archives, The, 2003.

Cunningham, Sean. Documents, The. "Evidence of the King's Fate." 46-47. Kew, Richmond, Surrey TW9 4DU, United Kingdom: National Archives, The, 1483.

Dempsey, Jack. *Michigan and the Civil War: A Great and Bloody Sacrifice*: The History Press, 2011.

Dolan, Robert Emmett. White Christmas. Curtiz, Michael. Los Angeles: Paramount Pictures, 1954.

Duiker, William J. & Jackson J. Spielvogel. *World History*. Fourth Edition Ed. Vol. Volume 1. Belmont: Wadsworth, A Division of Thomson Learning Incorporated, 2004.

Egan, Timothy. *The Worst Hard Time: The Untold Story of Those Who Survived the Great American Dust Bowl*. New York: Houghton Mifflin Company, 2006.

Fast, Howard. *The Crossing*. New York: Open Road, 1971.

Fraser, Antonia. *Wives of Henry VIII, The*: Vintage Publishing, 1993.

Gale Research, Provo, Utah. "Passenger and Immigration Lists Index, 1500s-1900s." Ancestory.com Operations, Inc.

Golway, Terry. *Washington's General: Nathanael Greene and the Triumph of the American Revolution*. New York: Henry Holt and Company, 2005.

Green, Iva. Personal Green Family Archive Collection. 1800's-2016.

Greene, Major General George Sears, Louis Brownell and F.V. Greene. *The Greene's of Rhode Island: with Historical Records of English Ancestry, 1534-1902*. Albany: Knickerbocker Press, 1903. Information sent via Campus serve by Dwight Beman, 54 Main St., Nantucket, MA 02554

Harris, Gerald. *Shaping the Nation: England, 1360–1461*. Oxford: Oxford University Press, 2005, 486-487

Ingall, David & Karin Risko. *Michigan Civil War Landmarks*: The History Press, 2015.

Josselin Society of England, http://web.archive.org/web/20070823124010/http://www.peterjoslin.btinternet.co.uk/chateau_josselin.htm, Last Modified 14 October 2006, Accessed 16 April 2016.

Kershaw, Alex. *The Longest Winter: The Battle of the Bulge and the Epic Story of World War II's Most Decorated Platoon*. Cambridge: First De Capo Press, 2004.

La Mance, Lora S., *The Greene Family and Its Branches; From A.D. 861 to A.D. 1904*. Mayflower Publishing Company, Floral Park, New York 1904; Beck, William III, A Family Genealogy.

Leckie, Robert. *George Washington's War: The Saga of the American Revolution*. New York: HarperCollins Publisher Incorporated 1992.

Lixey L.C., Kevin. *Sport and Christianity: A Sign of the Times in the Light of Faith*. The Catholic University of America Press, 2012.

McElvaine, Robert S. *The Great Depression: America 1929-1941*. New York: Radom House, 1984.

Middlekauff, Robert. *Glorious Cause: The American Revolution, The*. London: Oxford University Press, 1982.

More, Thomas & Simon Webb. *The History of King Richard III*. Durham: Langley Press, 2015.

Morton Szasz, Ferenc. *Day the Sun Rose Twice, The*. Albuquerque: University of New Mexico Press, 1984.

Nash, Gerald D. *The Crucial Era: The Great Depression and World War II 1929-1945*. 2nd ed. Prospect Heights: Waveland Press Incorporated, 1992.

Porter, Linda. *Katherine, the Queen: The Remarkable Life of Katherine Parr, the Last Wife of Henry VIII*: Macmillan, 2010.

Rothbard, Murray N. *America's Great Depression*, Fifth Edition. Auburn: The Ludwig von Mises Institute, 2000.

Saul, Nigel. *Richard II*. New Haven: Yale University Press, 1997, 406-417

Shaara, Jeff. *The Glorious Cause: A Novel of the American Revolution*. New York: The Random House Ballantine Publishing Group, 2002.

Secretary of the Commonwealth. Massachusetts Soldiers and Sailors of the Revolutionary War, A Compilation from the Archives, In Accordance with Chapter 100, Resolves of 1891. Boston: Wright and Potter Printing Company, 1900.

Shakespeare, William. Richard II, Acts I & II, the Quarto Edition, 1597.

Stokesbury, James L. *A Short History of the American Revolution*. New York: HarperCollins Publisher, Incorporated, 1991.

Sterns, Peter N., General Editor, 6th edition. Encyclopedia 195 and World History Vol. 1 to 1800 325, Copyright 2001 Houghton Mifflin Company 215 Park Avenue South, New York, New York.

Turner, Ralph V. *King John: England's Evil King?* Stroud, Gloucestershire, GL5 2QG: The History Press, 1994.

Weir, Allison. *Princes in the Tower, The*: Random House Incorporated, 1992.

Whellan, Francis. "History, Topography and Dictionary of Northamptonshire." In *Archaeologia Cantiana*, 516-17. London: Whittaker and Company, 1874.

Wiltsee, Jerome. *A Genealogical and Psychological Memoir of Philippe Maton Wiltsee and Descendants*. Atchison: G.W. Myers, 1908.

Wood, Gordon S. *Revolutionary Characters: What Made the Founders Different*. New York: The Penguin Press, 2006.

Worster, Donald. *Dust Bowl: The Southern Plains in the 1930's*. Oxford: Oxford University Press Incorporated, 2004.

Yates Publishing. "U.S. And International Marriage Records, 1560-1900." Ancestry.com Operations, Inc., 2004.

Notes

In regards to dates before January 25, 1752, there is a 12-day difference in "Old Style" versus "New Style," so to convert to "New Style adds 12 days. In addition, the number next to each family member denotes the number of generations from Sir Alexander, the first Lord de Grene. Once the transition to America was complete, the numbers start with the first immigrant to those countries.

In order to better future searches I first give credit to The Church of Latter Day Saints for such impeccable record keeping. This is always a great place to start. While my researching my family lines of Green, Crockett, Glenn and Powell, it is important to note the types of records I searched. The following were reviewed, on line or in person: birth records, death records, marriages records, church records, military records, divorce records, burial records, city indexes, census records, voter's registrations, Dawes Rolls, land records, Last Will and Testaments, Social Security Indexes, family Bibles, old letters, old diaries, and family documents.

It is imperative to point out that conflicting information is out there. Many times a person's name can be initials or completely misspelled. So sometimes we need to remember many documents on line are transcribed by someone attempting to read someone from another time periods handwriting. In addition, there are times those who were sent out were spelling the names and may not have spelled them correctly. A good example of this is the first wife of Samuel Watson Greene, my great-great grandfather. Julia. Her first name has been spelled, Julia, Jula, Jelia, and Julliea. Her last name has been spelled Dayton, Datton and Daton. But with deeper investigations, and cross references of family members this can be clarified as the correct person in the line. When it comes to censes records they did not always contain names and instead had a number next to age ranges of male/female household members and free/slave members in households.

For future researchers of this line. Do not be discouraged, when you find the information on my own parents is incorrect on many sites on line. In addition, both death certificates on my parents are in accurate. Not only is there incorrect death indexes that show my father died before his last three children were conceived, I have found on line family trees that show my father married to a totally different woman. A special needs woman, I have met in my youth, who claimed to be a half-sister, when she was born in Socorro County, in the early 1920's before the homestead was purchased by my grandfather. Clearly, there are many erroneous documentations available, and people are using them instead of digging deeper and cross referencing. My father's death certificate has errors as well. While I held his hand at the time of death, then was escorted to a room and asked questions and completed the required paperwork, including regarding his parents, giving the correct information, a family member who was very distraught was then asked the questions and my answers were changed. The biggest error to point out is his mother's name. She is Abbie Lusina Glenn, Not Abbigail Glenn. Knowing how angry my grandmother would get when she was called Abbigail and corrected everyone who made the error, stating her name was Abbie L. not Gail, if possible she would have come back from the grave to shake her fist one last time and correct this injustice.

On my mother, current online sources, if they have her at all, list her as being born in a foreign country a good hundred years before her birth. Her death certificate lists her name as Phyllis C. Green. While it is customary in some cultures to lose the middle initial and replace it with the initial of a woman's maiden name this is not always practical in present times. The C is for Crockett. So when researching, this is another trick of the trade so to speak.

www.ingramcontent.com/pod-product-compliance
Lightning Source LLC
Chambersburg PA
CBHW041151290426
44108CB00002B/36